MUCH OF JACKSON POLLOCK IS VIVID WALLPAPER:

An essay in the epistemology of aesthetic judgements

Graham McFee

University Press of America™

Much of Jackson Pollock is vivid wallpaper.

Steiner "The Retreat from the Word"
in his <u>Language and Silence</u>
Penguin (1969)

We know that nature isn't always neat.
We need to recognise that logic isn't either.

Wisdom "Critical Notice: Sears"
<u>Mind</u> 1946 (omitted when reprinted
<u>in his Philosophy and Psycho-Analysis</u>
Blackwell (1953))

He continues quick and dull in his clear images;
I continue slow and sharp in my broken images.

He in a new confusion of his understanding
I in a new understanding of my confusion.

Robert Graves "In Broken Images"
from <u>Collected Poems (1975) of</u>
<u>Robert Graves</u>.   Cassell 1975.

Acknowledgements.

Grateful acknowledgement is made to the following for permission
to use copyright material in this book:

To Dr. George Steiner, for the quotation which forms a part of
the title of this work.

To Basil Blackwell and Mott Ltd. for quotations from the works of
Wittgenstein and Wisdom.

To Alfred A. Knopf Inc. and Faber and Faber for quotations from
The Collected Poems of Wallace Stevens.

To Robert Graves and Cassell and Co. Ltd. for quotations from
The Collected Poems of Robert Graves.

To Laurence Pollinger and the Liveright Publishing Corp., New York,
for quotations from The Collected Poems and Selected Letters and
Prose of Hart Crane.

To Penguin Books Ltd. for quotations from works of Wollheim and
Stebbing.

"MUCH OF JACKSON POLLOCK IS VIVID WALLPAPER":

an essay in the epistemology of aesthetic judgements.

Contents

(a) Preface

    Aesthetic judgements, which are a part of the subject matter
of philosophical aesthetics, are a motley crew. And the example
which provides the title for this work is more motley than most.
It combines admirable vigour with a certain indifference to the
reader's own judgements. It is calculated to shock, and has an
appropriately subjective 'feel' about it. And so it raises,
with suitable vividness, philosphical problems about just how such
statements are to be taken. (But more of that later.)

    Discussion of problems in philosophical aesthetics may no
longer be considered "dreary" (1), but it must be admitted that
they are all too often far from satisfying. Not merely because
no conclusions are arrived at (who wants conclusions anyway?); but
because one is left with the feeling that so little has actually
been said. One can understand (and sympathise with) Richard
Wollheim's acid conclusion to Art and Its Objects (2):-

> § 65: It will be observed that in this essay next to
> nothing has been said about the subject that
> dominates much of contemporary aesthetics : that
> of the evaluation of art, and its logical character.
> This omission is deliberate.
>
>   (p.169)

Too much attention has certainly been given to these kinds of
problem, and perhaps not enough attention paid to the questions
Wollheim discusses. So yet another essay which it seems at first
sight must be about the evaluation of art might strike a reader as
superfluous. And particularly one by yet another professional
'discusser' of aesthetics. To explain is to confess.

    Both as a student and as a teacher of aesthetics I had
accepted (fairly uncritically, I must admit) the kind of lines on
aesthetic problems which might be expected to appeal to a follower
of Wittgenstein : but with this feeling that something important
remained unsaid. If, as argued, a grasp of philosophical
aesthetics really could produce an 'improved' kind of criticism in
the arts, why were there (virtually) no critics who had bothered
about gaining this grasp? And if I consoled myself with

---

(1) c.f. Passmore "The Dreariness of Aesthetics", reprinted in
    Elton ed. Aesthetics and Language. Blackwell (1954).

(2) Wollheim Art and Its Objects Penguin (1968)

arithmetic on the time for study required to become a good critic, and the time required to gain the appropriate grasp of philosophy, this was scant consolation. Almost simultaneously I became aware of writers on aesthetics doing the kind of things I'd hoped for, and a way of looking at reasoning in general (and at reasoning in aesthetics in particular) which made sense of it.

The second of my "revelations" came from those "features of Wittgenstein's technique" (3) which Wisdom was to draw out and make particularly his own: what he called "the case-by-case procedure" (4). Here was a way in which aesthetic problems could be shown to be rooted in more general philosophical concerns: and a way to attack such problems. The other "revelation" came from Stanley Cavell's interpretive essays in Must We Mean What We Say? (5), his book The Senses of Walden (6) (also his The World Viewed (7), to some extent) and from Peter Jones' Philosophy and the novel (8). Here was 'genuine' criticism being done by first-rate philosophers.

Emboldened by these discoveries, I felt that philosophical criticism could at last be justified. This work, which took rapid shape in my attempts at such justification, suggests why informed criticism, such as that of Cavell and Jones, is an essential and not merely a permissible part of the doing of philosophical aesthetics. And if the consequences of the arguments in this work are that philosophical aesthetics as such disappears, that should not 'feel' so unfamiliar to Wittgensteinians. There is a weaker sense (to be made clear) in which we can echo the Tractatus (9) :

> 6.54 My propositions serve as elucidations in the
> following way : anyone who understands me
> eventually recognises them as nonsensical, when
> he has used them - as steps - to climb beyond
> them. (He must, so to speak, throw away the
> ladder after he has climbed up it.)

---

(3) See Wisdom "A Feature of Wittgenstein's Technique" reprinted in Paradox and Discovery. Blackwell (1965) pp. 90 - 103.

(4) c.f. Lectures on "Proof and Explanation" given at the University of Virginia in 1957 (unpublished, and cited as V.L.)

(5) Cavell Must We Mean What We Say? Scribners (1969) esp. Ch.V, Ch.X.

(6) Cavell The Senses of Walden Viking (1972).

(7) Cavell The World Viewed : reflections on the ontology of film Viking (1971).

(8) Jones Philosophy and the novel O.U.P. (1975).

(9) Wittgenstein Tractatus Logico-Philosophicus RKP trans. Pears and McGuinness (1961).

The arguments in this essay are not so much <u>nonsense</u> (I hope!) as
reasons for taking but little note of most of what has gone under
the same title, aesthetics : and, possibly, a <u>great deal</u> of note
of other areas of philosophical enquiry.

This point touches on what must surely be an oddity of this
essay : its previously mentioned dependence on Wisdom's work, and
on his lectures on "Proof and Explanation" (<u>V.L.</u>) in particular.
That most of this work of his is not published is no explanation
(10). I would be happy to merely be <u>presenting</u> these views, as I
understand them, and some of their consequences : but I actually
think I am doing a little more than that. (The reader must
decide for himself.) The consequences of the case-by-case
procedure for aesthetics seem to me to be far-reaching, and
methodological as well as other things. Also it is pleasant to
tie-in work in aesthetics with what can (self-consciously) be
called an account of the Nature of Reasoning. For philosophy is
one subject (11), despite its diverse faces. There can be no
"isolated forays". To work in one area is to assume results in
other areas, and across the board.

It may no doubt be true that this work will rest, in the last
analysis, on a Constructivist logic and semantics (12). (Indeed
merely to talk of the epistemology, rather than the logic, of
aesthetic judgements is perhaps to acknowledge this fact.)
However these logical (et al) foundations are not our concern
here. We are not aiming to present those issues in philosophical
logic on which what we <u>do</u> present must ultimately depend. This
point actually becomes a part of our argument; for if it is a
consequence of acceptance of the contentions of this work that
philosophical aesthetics <u>as such</u> disappears - falling into a theory-
conscious or theory-aware philosophical criticism, and 'straight'
philosophy : that is, metaphysics, epistemology and philosophical
logic (in so far as one can draw these distinctions) - then any
writer on 'aesthetics' must choose to concentrate on one or other
of these areas. By training and inclination, I have made my
choice.

---

(10) A clear and helpful exposition of Wisdom's ideas in these
     lectures is to be found in R.W.Newell <u>The Concept of
     Philosophy</u> Methuen (1967) esp. Ch.4, Ch.8.

(11) c.f. D.Best <u>Expression in Movement and the Arts</u> Lepus (1974)
     p.xi, where both these war-cries occur.

(12) c.f. Baker "Criteria : a new foundation for semantics"
     <u>Ratio</u> 1975, also Hacker <u>Insight and Illusion</u> Oxford (1972)
     p.302 ff.

However, both inclination and choice owe the following specific debts, which I here acknowledge:

To my wife Kay, who kept me working on this book when I had (almost) given up, and to whom this and all my work is dedicated.

To John Wisdom for his encouragement and permission to draw so extensively on his unpublished works.

To Terry Diffey (University of Sussex) who read and commented on the whole book in manuscript, and still encouraged me.

To Brian Smart (University of Keele) for teaching me what philosophy can be, and for careful reading of some parts of this book.

To David Best (University of Swansea) whose aid and example I much value.

To Roy Holland (University of Leeds) for making helpful comments on the whole book in manuscript.

To Michael Finnissy for showing me most of what I know about music and bearing with my foibles.

To those friends and students who had a hand in this; especially Sue Jones and Joe Holly.

To those participants at the 10th National Conference of the British Society of Aesthetics, September 1975, whose comments on my paper "**Art : Definition and Appreciation**" made me see that <u>one</u> book would not be enough to defend this thesis.

(b) <u>Introduction</u>

Since the reader usually begins works at the title, it behoves the author to do the same. Since my title isn't quite self-explanatory that seems an especially good idea. Shouldn't I, after all, be talking about 'the <u>logic</u> of aesthetics' or 'the <u>language</u> of aesthetics'? Why the 'epistemology of aesthetics'? Well, the phrase itself comes from Wisdom, and it must be admitted that the contrast between the logic of . . . . and the epistemology of . . . . is just a matter of emphasis. But such emphasis is important. To talk of "the logic of . . . .", or even "the language of . . . .", is all too often to be bound (in a variety of ways) to classical logic, and to just those kinds of rigid distinction which a work such as this might question. And in particular to be bound to a rigid separation of questions about such-and-such <u>being</u> a so-and-so from questions about our <u>knowing</u> that it is, questions of <u>truth</u> from questions of knowledge. (13).

The following story puts the first of these points, if in a self-indulgently ego-centric way. When I was a boy, I made model aeroplanes - both in plastic and in balsa wood. And I had a wood glue and a plastic glue. (And never the twain shall meet!) Except that the wood glue wasn't much good. So one day I tried the plastic glue on the balsa wood. It worked beautifully. And I've given up categories, ever since. While this claim isn't <u>literally</u> true, which I shall argue would be an unintelligible position, it exposes my profound disbelief in the <u>university</u> of most categories. (Plastic glue <u>does</u> glue wood). Conceptual 'boundaries' in any or all areas may or may not be clear. That is a matter for investigation, not assumption. And the arguments in this work certainly point away from any hope of clear maps of "logical geography". (Indeed these arguments point to the limitations of that expression.)

As to the rest of the title, the quotation from Steiner is, of course, merely there to tantalise and as an example of an aesthetic judgement. Since George Steiner is a respected, and so presumably a respectable, critic we aren't out to challenge his claim that much of Jackson Pollock's work is no more than vivid wallpaper. At best we are trying to understand what it is to make such claims. And this involves considering the kinds of thing which could be reasons for such a claim, how the critic could know whatever he does know, and what exactly that could be.

And more than that : we aren't even out to <u>solve</u> the philosophical problems up for discussion - although one or two may just get dissolved in the process - but to <u>locate</u> them precisely. This will involve feeling the temptations they embody, as well as trying to see our way clear of these 'cramps'. If the argument tends to be diffuse, this perhaps reflects features of the subject matter.

But it also reflects a (polemical) point of this work; that the <u>style</u> of most philosophy does not sufficiently display its logic. Wittgenstein's later work is often difficult to understand <u>just because</u> it is so stylistically different from most of what had gone before as philosophy (14). It doesn't look like the logico-analytic work which (historically) preceded it. But that is a part of the point, Wittgenstein

---

(13) This is, of course, a characteristic of Realism. See Baker "Criteria : a new foundation for semantics." <u>Ratio</u> 1975.

(14) c.f. Bouwsma "The Blue Book" in his <u>Philosophical Essays</u> University of Nebraska (1965) p.181 on this point.

can be seen as trying to expose features of the subject-matter in this way. His image (15) of a landscape traversed in various directions is revealing. If we do go over the same ground in a variety of ways, we will inevitably repeat ourselves and our positions, but we will stand a better chance of understanding such bumpy terrain if we consider it from a number of perspectives.

And while I cannot claim anything like the same kind of scope or importance for this work, it seems to me important to place it in the tradition of Wittgenstein, Wisdom and Cavell _stylistically_ as well as (what should be obvious from the references to their work) in terms of philosophical position.

To return to the title, it seems likely that, if we had Steiner here to question, many of us (those who were Jackson Pollock fans at least) would want to know _why_ Steiner had made this extraordinary claim. That is, we'd be asking for his _reasons_. It is by no means clear that such a judgement does indeed rest on reasons at all. (Here the contrast might be with something like **preferences**.) Yet surely John Casey is right when, in _The Language of Criticism_ (16), he claims:-

> Criticism is not, and does not seek to be, a science.
> It is, however, a rational procedure rather than the
> expression of a set of more or less arbitrary preferences.
> (p.xi)

What remains at issue will be how the term "rational" is to be taken here. Is Steiner's claim rational? And if it is not, does that mean it is not criticism? It is towards such questions that this work is directed.

(c) The Argument

1. The unsatisfactoriness of much philosophical aesthetics is recorded : and the impetus and theme of the work is outlined.

2. The emphasis on a consideration of reasoning, justification and proof in this work makes us talk in terms of criticism. And criticism is often seen as 'chronically speculative', or as subjective, or as turning merely on matters of words. Replies such as these give rise to, or seem to give rise to, problems about what art _is_ (problems of definitions) and about the place of reasoning in aesthetics and in criticism of the

(15) Wittgenstein _Philosophical Investigations_ Blackwell (1953) p.ix.

(16) Casey _The Language of Criticism_ Methuen (1966)

arts (problems of appreciation or evaluation). It is argued that these difficulties in turn spring from a cramped notion of what reasoning is.

3. Reasoning examined. The case-by-case procedure introduced in more detail, and its relationship to recognition and to reflection in general pointed out. It is claimed that all reasoning in the end comes down to the case-by-case procedure : and hence that reasoning is not bad just because it is of a case-by-case, "direct", type.

4. The oddity of grounding aesthetic judgements or aesthetic reasoning on paradigms, one interpretation of the argument in Ch.2, is demonstrated by a consideration of George Dickie's views on artifactuality and an elaboration of the status of the 'particular cases' mentioned in Ch.2, Ch.3. In this context some of the problems raised by borderline cases are discussed.

5. Since this work focuses on art, such a focus is explained by a discussion of the notion of an "object of aesthetic appraisal". General lines are suggested for the drawing of distinctions within the class of "objects of aesthetic appraisal", but with the general qualification that these general lines must in the end rest on the case-by-case procedure.

6. Consideration of the place of reasoning in aesthetics will focus our attention on the critic. His role in 'getting us to see' is considered. The variety of possible interpretations might seem to cast doubt on the critic's value. His abilities to provide us with vivid comparisons, and a variety of these, establish his credentials : and ground his work in the case-by-case procedure. The critic's position as agent of Dickie's "art-world" is considered, and refined.

7. The evaluability of art is an old aesthetician's 'chestnut' : but a recognition of the viability of the case-by-case procedure as genuine reasoning and of the critic's job as presenter of cases suggests ways in which evaluation of the arts is to be explained as rational. The essential uniqueness of works of art, as stressed and explained by the so-called Heresy of Paraphrase argument, is considered : and shown to be entirely compatible with case-by-case procedures.

8. Since the critic's job in 'getting us to see...' in many ways resembles the philosopher's, the similarities between the methods of criticism and of philosophy are considered : and in particular the way criticism can focus on epistemological issues.

9. To establish the author's credentials as critic, the work closes with a discussion and interpretation of (some of) the poetry of Wallace Stevens.

To present philosophical aesthetics as though its scope or limits were obvious is likely to mislead.   For, in general, a part of the subject matter of any area of philosophical enquiry is certain to be the boundaries of that area.   Hence we can ask just what the subject matter of aesthetics is to be : and this is to ask upon what, or whom, the aesthetician focuses.   On the artist? On the work he produces? On what the artist says about his work? On what critics say about it? On the audience it acquires, or their reaction to it?

In the title, and in the introduction, discussion of the scope of this work has been presented in terms of "criticism" : and the inclusion of an example of an aesthetic judgement in the title of this work might be seen as reinforcing such a stance.   Yet it is not obvious that we can completely account for aesthetics in this way.   Even were we to restrict our attention in philosophical aesthetics to art, and ignore, say, natural beauty (which, as argued in Ch.5, is a mistake), it might <u>seem</u> as though a concentration on <u>criticism</u> is unnecessarily narrow.   But the term "criticism" is meant in a rather wide sense here : for if I claim that so-and-so is art, I can presumably be asked why I make this claim.   And my reply will amount to art-criticism in the intended sense.   What I am really dealing with is <u>reasoning</u> in aesthetics – but it is assumed that the natural home of such reasoning is criticism.   The explanations, justifications and the like associated with all the possible answers to questions about the proper object of philosophical aesthetics, as well as the questions themselves will be criticism in the appropriate sense.

Of course, there are a variety of issues raised by such an attitude to the scope of this work.   The most obvious must relate to the so-called "evaluative" and "classificatory" senses of the term "art".   Since there is <u>some</u> difference between describing Jones' flute sonata and judging it good or bad, yet since in doing both of these we might employ the **claim that** Jones' flute sonata is art, the term "art" is assumed to have two senses (1).   Or again, it is no doubt possible to distinguish between describing Jenkins' performance of the flute sonata and evaluating that performance.   The point here is surely the claim that evaluation is in some way not <u>reducible</u> to description, and that descriptions need not <u>commit</u> us to a particular evaluation.

---

(1) See, for example, Weitz "The Role of Theory in Aesthetics" reprinted in Margolis <u>ed Philosophy Looks at the Arts</u>. Scribners (1962).

For, it is claimed, even two people who agree about the "facts" (that is, offer the same description) may still disagree in their judgements. For example, consider the following (2):-

> The larger . . . . , _Prairie_, consists of four long poles of aluminium tubing suspended parallel to one another about eleven inches above a sheet of corrugated metal - more exactly, a flat sheet with four channel-like depressions in it - which runs north-south to the poles' east-west and is itself suspended about twenty-one inches above the ground.
> (p.97)

The kind of description would, it seems, be _neutral_ with respect to particular evaluations (3). Hence, it is thought, we can describe an object as a work of art without evaluating it, or we _can_ evaluate. Hence, two senses of the term "art".

This relationship between describing and evaluating will be touched on later (ch.6, ch.7) where we consider the connections between the critic's "descriptions" and his judgements. But if we concentrate on criticism, even in a wide sense of involving _reasons_, are we not limiting ourselves to a consideration of the evaluative sense of the term "art"? We might even take Morris Weitz's (4) point that the scope of criticism is wider than merely evaluation, and includes describing and other things. Still wouldn't we be, at the very least, limiting ourselves to questions about aesthetic _judgements_, the kinds of thing for which _reasons_ might be offered, and ignoring the claim that such-and-such is art?

Clearly this need not be so. As was said before, reasons can still be offered for my accepting such-and-such as a work of art, even in some classificatory sense. For example, to say that such-and-such is another work in stone by Michelangelo would be at least _some_ reason for calling it "art". Even in less specific cases, _rational_ considerations can be seen to be operative. Perhaps what is meant here is better termed reflection, rather than reasoning, although that too can be a misleading way of putting it. And if, as is claimed in Ch.3, all judgements involve reflection in this sense it does not seem silly to focus attention on this kind of reasoning or of reflection. So one reply, the concessive one, would be that a consideration of criticism in my sense can involve

---

(2) from Michael Fried "Two sculptures by Anthony Caro" in R. Whelan ed _Anthony Caro_ Penguin (1974).

(3) I have removed the word "sculpture" from the quotation, as it might be argued that this term is at least _minimally_ evaluative.

(4) from Weitz _Hamlet and the Philosophy of Literary Criticism_ Faber (1965) p. 269.

us in dealings with both classificatory and evaluative senses of "art".

The pugnacious reply would claim that, in so far as the line of enquiry genuinely was incompatible with this distinction of senses of the term "art", the distinction should be the one to give way : that, in effect, the line of enquiry involved a consideration of the <u>foundations</u> of such a distinction and hence should not rely on it.

Now, I would choose another time and place to fight the <u>general</u> battle against this "two senses" view, or even expanded versions of it, like a "three senses" view. But one brief observation is pertinent. If I claim that such-and-such is art and yet assure you that I am using the term in <u>neither</u> of your "two senses", or in <u>none</u> of your "three senses", what is to be your reaction? For you cannot really claim that I <u>must</u> be using one of your senses. <u>Why</u> must I? (Here the reply cannot be "because there <u>are</u> only two" : for I am offering a third). The difficulty seems to be that we rapidly get as many "senses" of the term "art" as we have uses of it. And then it is hardly helpful to talk of different senses at all.

At this impasse, some philosophers flourish a dogma about there being a limited number of uses of language : evaluative, emotive, descriptive, performative, prescriptive ... Take your pick. (Although the fact that there is so little agreement as to what are or are not <u>the</u> uses of language must do something to undermine the doctrine.) But even when you have taken your pick, the situation is no better. I can still claim to be using the term in a different sense, or language in a different way. And all they can offer then is stipulation.

Again, my point here should not be misconstrued. There is <u>of course</u> some value in talking about these senses of the term "art". As a pedagogic device, for example, it can be extremely useful. And, as we'll see when we discuss borderline cases (in Ch.4), it is useful to be able to say that such-and-such is art without this entailing some plus-evaluation of it. Yet do we really need separate <u>senses</u> to account for this difference? It is all a question of their <u>separateness</u>. After all the evaluative sense will entail the classificatory sense (I think), so could we not merely say that some cases where the term "art" is used are cases of evaluation, to greater and lesser extents?

There are connections between questions of the type under discussion and the claim that the expression "bad work of art" is some kind of alienans. We will need to consider that question too, at a later date (see Ch.7). For the present, we can come to learn a little more about evaluating and classifying indirectly, from a consideration of two kinds of problem : which we can call

the problem of definition and the problem of appreciation.   The
first asks what kind of thing works of art are - material object,
idea, intentional or presentational object, etc. - and hence about
the possibilities of giving necessary and sufficient conditions for
a things being art : and about the status of works as works of art.
The second problem deals with the logic of criticism and of
evaluation of the arts; how, and in what ways, this is a rational
procedure, as Casey suggested.   (Quoted in Ch.1). And how, and
to what extent, it is "objective" etc.   To see the contours of our
argument more clearly we must take these issues one at a time.
But we will hope to see how they interpenetrate; and how to place
the claim that much of Jackson Pollock's work is merely vivid wallpaper within an account of reasoning in aesthetics.

Specifically, I want to consider these two "dilemmas" (if that
is the word), often advanced in parallel, and show how each fails
to take account of the "solution" to the other.   My diagnosis,
like Wittgenstein's (5), is a craving for generality, for general
problems and general answers.   Examples, for polemical purposes,
are provided by some ideas in a recent paper on Wittgenstein by
Roger Shiner (6).

The problem of appreciation, or of criticism, is one about
the "objectivity" of certain judgements, etc. : that is, the
extent to which they are based on reasons. But reasons (that is,
genuine reasons) are often seen as coercive per se : so that someone might say:-

> The concepts of reason and rationality, at least as they
> are normally used in philosophy, are intended to represent
> something which is coercive per se and not coercive only
> to those who accept a certain set of assumptions.
> (Shiner p.262)

And of, for instance, the claim that (7) :-

> One wouldn't talk of appreciating the tremendous things in Art.

They might go on to comment:-

> There is a non-cognitivist sound to this passage, the
> judgements about the Good, etc., are primarily
> interjections, that aesthetics in the end simply rests

---

(5) c.f. Wittgenstein Blue and Brown Books. Blackwell (1958) p.17.

(6) Shiner "Wittgenstein on the Beautiful, the Good and the
    Tremendous" B.J.A. vol. 14. 1974.

(7) from Wittgenstein Lectures and Conversations on Aesthetics,
    Psychology and Religious Belief. Blackwell (1970) p.8.
       I.23

on the individual liking or not liking certain things,
that at the highest level one can't talk of reasons
or of appreciation.   The tremendous things either impress
us or they don't; but one cannot discuss the matter as
one can a particular...........musical passage.
(c.f. Shiner p.260).

Judgements in aesthetics, then, are to be "objective" in the
sense of being based on these very general reasons ("genuine
reasons"); and the right position in aesthetics will be that which:-

.... seeks to emphasise the analogies rather than
the disanalogies between aesthetics and other recognisably
objective or cognitive enquiries. (Shiner p.261).

Well, what kind of objectivity can we expect, or hope for, in
aesthetics? (Putting aside the "other recognisably . . . .
cognitive enquiries".   Shiner p.261).   The answer to that question
which goes along with the position we've been outlining would
certainly equate objectivity (and being based on reasons) with at
least a certain amount of generality.   Claims lacking this
generality will be dismissed as subjective, as mere opinion.   And
this will amount to something like the position (prevalent in
other areas of philosophy) that, for every justified critical claim,
the justification must consist in deriving a conclusion from
premises which are logically sufficient to establish it, in the
sense that to assert the premises and yet deny the conclusion
would be to contradict oneself.   Yet this is clearly not the
situation at work in current criticism, or in aesthetics.   (Or, as
is argued in Ch.3, elsewhere.   But that's a larger issue.)
Consider the following story (8):-

At the end of my first term's work I attended the usual
college board to give an account of myself.   The
spokesman coughed and said a little stiffly : "I
understand, Mr. Graves, that the essays you write for
your English tutor are, shall I say, a trifle
temperamental.   It appears, indeed, that you prefer
some authors to others." (p.240)

If criticism really were a matter of hunting down the
coercive per se "genuine" reasons, no doubt there would be
substance to the spokesman's point.   For whatever Robert Graves
wrote in those essays, we can safely assume that it was not
coercive per se.

---

(8) from R. Graves Goodbye to all that. Penguin (1957).

-13-

Or, to be more accurate, all that follows is that Graves'
views are not universally convincing. Despite an account being
coercive per se, someone might still refuse to accept it. He
might, for example, still claim that he was being poisoned from
his water supply even when chemical analysis and rational argument
provide 'conclusive' reasons for denying such a claim. Here we
would accuse him of unreasonableness, of failing to see. If we
had any reason to do so, we might dismiss his conduct as based on
delusion or misunderstanding, or a different conceptual scheme.
Such a move is not open to us in the case of Graves' inquisitors.
They understand what they have read, and share the conceptual back-
grounds. So they should be swayed by any coercive per se
'rational' arguments. Of course, they might be refusing to make
judgements of the works of art in question. But to refuse in such
a situation, that is, to refuse in the face of Graves' argument, is
either to abdicate responsibilities or to be unreasonable (see Ch.6).
To produce judgements of a different persuasion is another matter.
So let us give the inquisitors the benefit of the doubt. Let us
assume they are making judgements which differ from Graves' own.
In this way let us gloss over the difficulty. The situation then
is one where the tutors remain unconvinced even after reading Graves'
essay (9).

Here we are recording a feature of our reaction to critics and
writers on the arts : that readers might well not be persuaded by
Graves' "reasons", and might judge the work differently. That is,
they might arrive at radically different conclusions. Graves
asserts one thing : they assert another. So we have disagreement.
It seems that (on the position offered thus far) we must dismiss
these contrary remarks as mere expressions of preference (and not
bits of reasoning), if we are looking for "genuine reasons" in
aesthetics. The chain of reasons has come to an end. For all we
are offered as reasons here depend on our prior position or
initial assumptions. Our difficulty is to see how this can be
avoided, and aesthetics made "rational".

That, then, is one "horn" of our first problem. The alternative usually proffered, the other "horn" of the first dilemma, is
to take the Wittgenstein quotation about "the tremendous things
in Art" being above appreciation all too seriously. Given that
chains of reasoning do seem to come to an end (10), some writers
conclude that reasoning cannot be of any importance, or have any
place, in aesthetics (11). The problem is how we can both find

(9) The need for this qualifying paragraphy was made clear to me
    by Terry Diffey.

(10) c.f. Wittgenstein Philosophical Investigations. Blackwell
    (1953) § 211, § 217.

(11) I believe some remarks of Schopenhauer may be taken this way,
    c.f. P. Gardiner Schopenhauer Penguin (1967) p.192 ff.

-14-

a place for reasons in aesthetics <u>and</u> accept that chains of reasons must come to an end.

Here the difficulty might be that we have accurately outlined the kind of "reasoning", or of argument, which does go on in criticism and in philosophical aesthetics. But does it deserve the title "reasoning" at all? (We will consider this question in Ch.3, Ch.4). What have we said so far about the place of this "reasoning" in criticism of the arts? When we have, for example, studied a literary text, it seems as though empirical confirmation, empirical data, etc. has been exhausted; and yet one feels it <u>can't</u> have been, since no conclusions, no "answers", follow from what has gone before. With art, and with other things, we might say that it is as though all the facts can be <u>in</u>, and yet disagreements remain. It isn't that there is room for any further empirical investigation, no further "facts" can come to light, and yet we have no "answer". So the claim is made that either (a) the situation is just too complex, and hence that the logical connections ("what can be deduced") are too complex, although later civilisations might be able to sort them out; or (b) that art is (to use Ilham Dilman's phrase)(12) "chronically speculative" : and hence that the problems of appreciation are insoluble.

The third possibility seems to involve dismissing the problem as "merely verbal", merely a dispute about words. (And philosophers' prediliction for the remarks "it depends what you mean by ...." hardly helps matters here.) One group, it is claimed, want to use the term "art" in one way, another group in another way. This view of the problem of appreciation is interestingly connected with the view just referred to, on which what we have outlined as reasoning in aesthetics isn't genuine reasoning at all. And it has more direct connections with what we have called the problem of definition. For it is tempting to think that, if we had sorted out just what was meant by, say, the term "art" and other such terms, we would have dissolved the problem of appreciation.

We can put the point in a way which parallels our discussion of the problem of appreciation. Then our second "dilemma", or whatever, turns on what we've called the problem of definition. Yet our problem isn't quite that suggested by Clive Bell (13):-

Either all works of art have some common quality or when we speak of a work of art we gibber. (p.7)

---

(12) Dilman "Paradoxes and Discoveries" in Bambrough <u>ed</u>. <u>Wisdom</u> : <u>Twelve Essays</u> Blackwell (1974) p.91.

(13) Clive Bell <u>Art</u> Arrow Books (1961).

(although I suspect this may be the source of some of our secret fears). We post-Wittgensteinians are well aware <u>firstly</u>, that sets of necessary and sufficient conditions (or definitions) are not <u>required</u> in order that we understand a concept, and that they cannot possibly be provided for all concepts (14). And <u>secondly</u>, that an essentialist view such as Bell's presupposes these necessary and sufficient conditions (15).

But these recognitions do not entirely help, since "art" is a more "open" concept than most. We'd like a relatively "closed" concept : that is, one where the family resemblances, or whatever we are going to cash our "similarities" in term of, were fairly easily picked out. But with a concept which has application to so many diverse forms - painting, sculpture, poetry, drama, etc. - and in so many places, it is hard to see that this could be done. So that when Harold Osborne (16) claims that:-

.... the very notion of a "family" group implies that we have brought together just this set of things and not others because, we assume, they are linked by significant and coherent, not just arbitrary, relations of resemblance. (p.6).

we should feel inclined to reply that such "relations of resemblance" are not to be easily sorted out, <u>even if</u> we were to assume their existence. Thus it seems we do not have the relatively "closed" concept. Whatever "significant and coherent .... relations of resemblance" we think we have discovered, our apple cart can always be upset. Artists can always spring surprises on us : and that point is well put (17) by talking about the variability of the denotation of "art".

Yet sets of necessary and sufficient conditions, or something like them based on a relatively "closed" concept, would solve some of our problems. If we could give, say, necessary and sufficient conditions of a thing's being art, (18) we could pick out, at least roughly, the denotation of "art" (everything inside

---

(14) c.f. Wittgenstein's (famous) discussion of "game" <u>Philosophical Investigations</u> Blackwell (1953) § 66.

(15) c.f. Diffey "Essentialism and the definition of 'art'" <u>B.J.A.</u> 1973, also Kennick "Does traditional aesthetics rest on a mistake?" in Barrett <u>ed</u> <u>Collected Papers on Aesthetics</u> Blackwell (1965).

(16) in "Introduction to Osborne <u>ed</u> <u>Aesthetics</u> O.U.P. (1972).

(17) following Diffey "The Republic of Art" <u>B.J.A.</u> 1969 pp.148-149.

(18) In this context, see current attempts to give "institutional" necessary and sufficient conditions in, for example, Dickie <u>Art and the Aesthetic</u> Cornell U.P. (1974).

would be art, and the rest would not), which would make criticism a lot easier, for example. We'd at least be clear where to begin looking for criticism of the arts : and we would not be far from "general aesthetic criteria", for we would know what were only borderline cases of art and what were central cases.

But the denotation of art is not fixed. Putting aside the difficult question of works losing their art-status, works can certainly gain it (19). If it were fixed, the practice of many contemporary artists would be unintelligible, since they aim to extend the boundaries of the concept "art". Yet if what is and is not art can come and go like this, how can we mean anything very clear by the term "art"? On the one hand, we want something fairly definite to ground our use of the term "art" (in order that we mean something by it) and on the other hand, we want or perhaps require the variability of the denotation of "art". (N.B. If what counted as a reason for so-and-so being art were fixed, we could sort out the denotation of "art", since we'd then know if X was or was not art, by looking at the reasons : and this would solve the problem of definition.)

We are engaged in this search for some "definition" because no further empirical data will help us. So it seems (or is claimed) that if a problem is not amenable to further empirical observation and if reasoning (on a deductive model) is of no avail, as seems to be the situation here, the question at issue must be just a matter of words. If only we had precise definitions, or precise specifications of what words mean, it is claimed, we would be able to settle this issue.

In the first place (as will be argued in a moment), such an attitude betrays a misunderstanding of the character of definition, a mistaken longing for generality. In the second place, it is difficult to see in this context how what is at issue is indeed a matter of words, for both the revolutionary and the conservative artist are attempting to make art : that is, they see their work under the same concept. They would, for example, agree that certain works (say, some Old Masters) clearly were art, and that others (say, my brief case) clearly were not. They would be in a position to argue for their views on disputed works, and against their opponents views. The possibility of such argument shows that there is much that is shared in their understanding of the concept "art".

---

(19) c.f. the way Bell championed the works of Cezanne and persuaded (forced?) others to recognise them as (great) art. Story from Kennick "Does traditional aesthetics rest on a mistake?" in Barrett Collected Papers on Aesthetics Blackwell (1965) p.10.

We have breifly considerd how both the problem of definition and the problem of appreciation might be "solved" by some definition or stipulation, and related this answer to the view that the dispute was just one about words. We have seen that the assumption is made throughout that any reasoning which accompanies appreciation must be explained in terms of deductions, or it will not be "genuine" reasoning : and how this seems to rule out reasoning all together, in the absence of any absolute standards. The time has come to begin criticism of these views.

These views all rest on what Wisdom could doubtlessly call a "cramped"notion of what it is to reason or to prove. That is, it will be the contention of this work that positions such as that ascribed to Shiner involved radical misunderstandings of rationality and understanding generally, and hence manage to see (in Wittgenstein's work) what are two importantly connected aspects of one position as:-

> . . . . two pots on the stove at once, with very different and seemingly incompatible things bubbling away in them.
> (Shiner p.261)

The claim that reasons should be coercive per se is to be contrasted with what I take to be, for example, Wittgenstein's view (and which is certainly mine) : that within a form of life reasons will be coercive per se but that, from outside that form of life, what was a reason will no longer be a reason. We will be returning to this point (in Ch.3) but let us consider an example (20), by way of clarification. Consider the justification for returning home from a battle without your shield in Greek history. At one point, nothing except cowardice was a reason for coming home without your shield : but at a later time the need to be alive to fight another day did justify returning shieldless. If a Greek of the earlier time (call him A) met his later counter-part (B), and found him shieldless, he would not have accepted the "justification" that shields were cheap, men not so. A might even have accused B of cowardice : but B had a reason for his action - a reason which (for him) was coercive per se. It settled the dispute as far as he was concerned. Can we not accept this diversity of what is and what is not a reason without calling B's reason a "quasi-reason", as Shiner does? But there is more to it than this. For not merely does what is and what is not a reason allow of such diversity, but what it is to reason is not always to be cashed in terms of deductive models.

---

(20) Further, and possibly better, examples can be found in Phillips and Mounce Moral Practices R.K.P. (1969).

Earlier we hinted at a picture of what "reasoning" in criticism is like, which an example would clarify. We suggested, to put it bluntly, that the critic's assertions or the critic's "premises" only guarantee his conclusion when, or because, they include it, either secretly or openly.   Hence, of course, _if_ we accept those premises in the way the critic does, his conslusions will follow for us - but only because we've already tacitly accepted them.   So it seems _highly_ probable that if we begin where Leavis begins (21), believing his to be :

> . . . . an age in which there were no serious standards current, no live tradition of poetry, and no public capable of informed interest . . . . (p.11)

we will recognise those features in Ezra Pound's work which Leavis points out; and we _will_ conclude that "Hugh Selwyn Mauberley" (1925) is a great poem, "at once traditional and original" (Leavis p.113) and 'see' that "... the earlier poems have a minor kind of interest..." (Leavis p.113).   Now I wouldn't want to deny "Mauberley" its greatness.   It is a matter of these other poems. The "Homage to Sextus Propertius" (1917), for example, which Alfred Alvarez links with "Mauberley" as ".... two accepted master-pieces" (Alvarez (22) p.66).   It is far from clear that such disagreement could ever be satisfactorily resolved.   Yet both Alvarez and Leavis reach their positions by what we'd _normally_ call reasoning, or reflection, from (as it were) where they start to where or what they conclude.   So, I suggest, we know very well what reasoning in aesthetics is like.   Our picture here is an accurate one - but we may be loath to call _that_ reasoning at all. That we should do so is the point at issue in the next chapter.

Further spelling-out of the suggested situation current in aesthetics, together with some thoughts on the correctness of calling what we do in aesthetics "reasoning", can come from a recognition of familiar lines of argument when we look again at the definition problem.   For the difficulty here is that what are and what are not works of art comes, in a sense, _prior_ to the definition, account, test or whatever.   As Renford Bambrough (23) puts it:-

> .... in spite of philosophers fine talk about laying the foundations first and answering the questions afterwards, we know that the test will have to fit our knowledge and not the knowledge be brow-beaten to agree with the results of the test. (p.42)

---

(21) In Leavis _New Bearings in English Poetry_ (1932) Penguin (1963)
(22) In Alvarez _The Shaping Spirit_ (1958)
(23) Bambrough "To reason is to generalise" _Listener_ (1973)

It is common knowledge that we are fairly good at picking out works of art without a definition (or whatever) such as Bell's, Croce's, Santayana's, or Tolstoi's. Indeed it is <u>because</u> we can produce clear counter-examples, and recognise them as such, that we can show definitions or accounts such as these to be inadequate (either false or vacuous). So that, for example, aesthetics simply <u>can't</u> be:-

... of, or pertaining to, the appreciation or criticism of the beautiful. (O.E.D.)

since aesthetics will involve the study of works such as Picasso's "Guernica", Goya's "Saturn eating his Children", Shakespear's <u>King Lear</u> - which are clearly <u>not</u> beautiful in any ordinary sense of the word. And this falsifies the definition. Of course, its defenders may claim that some special sense of the term "beautiful" is involved here; say, an <u>aesthetic</u> sort of beauty. But that claim welds together the two ideas in such a way that I can only locate this kind of beauty by first locating objects of aesthetic appreciation, and (if the position is taken seriously) I can only locate objects of aesthetic appreciation by first locating bearers of this special kind of beauty.

This very familiar point should lead us, as it led Wittgenstein, to be suspicious of the <u>general</u> answer. For what is suggested by the "what is the so-and-so?" form of question is (often) that a substantive general answer which provides a characteristion of so-and-so which is both concise and yet comprehensive could (in principle) be given. That is, the very form of question imposes limits on the <u>sort of thing</u> which could count as an answer - it should be both general and succint (24). And no such answer could be forthcoming, as was argued earlier.

It follows that our grasp of particular cases as instances of art, or whatever, does not and cannot wait for definitions. Such definitions could not be provided. And yet we do genuinely understand these terms. Recognition of this fact places these <u>particular cases</u>, which can be used as counter-examples to definitions, in the centre of the stage, as it were. It will be the contention of this work that a clear realisation of the place of particular cases in reasoning in aesthetics will allow us to "solve" our problems, and others besides.

---

(24) c.f. Wittgenstein <u>Philosophical Investigations</u>
Blackwell (1953) § 203 on this point.

Wittgenstein (25) states this point clearly:-

> The idea that in order to get clear about the
> meaning of a general term one had to find the
> common element in all its applications, has
> shackled philosophical investigations; for it
> has not only led to no result, but has also made
> the philosopher dismiss as irrelevant the concrete
> cases, which alone could help him to understand
> the usage of the general term. (p.19)

This is a plea of Wittegenstein's against the tyranny of the
general and for the place of the particular. I wish to take up
this plea. But thus far this work is extremely thin in an
elaboration of just those cases which are claimed to be of such
importance. So here is a spelling-out of one way in which I
could attempt to persuade you to acknowledge a particular work of
John Cage, "4 minutes 33 seconds", as an example of a particular
art-form, music. (This is not intended to be anything like a full
case-by-case procedure (26).)

David Ewen (27) says of "4 minutes 33 seconds":-

> . . . . all the performer is required to do is to
> sit at the key-board and play nothing four minutes
> thirty-three seconds. (p.154)

Now there is a clear sense in which this description is simply
false on two counts. Firstly, and perhaps less importantly, Cage
explicityly states in the first score for this piece that its
duration is not fixed, the title coming from the length of the
first performance. And secondly the performer is required by this
score to mark the three "movements" of the piece. At the first
performance I understand that this was done by a raising and
lowering of the piano lid, which seems to me all too extravagant
a gesture. But perhaps the performer in question, David Tudor,
would usually lower and raise the lid between the movements of any
piece he were playing.

However, Ewen's description should make it clear why I have
selected this piece for consideration: that there is a sense in
which it is the most extreme departure in one direction. There

---

(25) Wittgenstein The Blue and Brown Books Blackwell (1958)

(26) c.f. Ch.3 for a discussion of the case-by-case procedure.

(27) D. Ewen Composers of Tomorrow's Music Dodd Mead (1971)

is a strong temptation, to which I once succumbed (28), to consider the piece as however long of silence. And you might well find it difficult to accept that as music. We'll go on to consider the inadequacies of such an account of "4 minutes 33 seconds", indeed that is a part of our point here : but let us assume that at the very least, if you accept it as music, you have accepted it as art (although not necessarily art of a very high quality).

There seem to be a variety of steps required for the kind of persuasion I have in mind, although no doubt not everyone would every step. And, of course, the method is merely one from among many that might be selected. But it seems that you must be led into accepting as music a variety of sounds other than those of classical harmony and the like. This might be done by a "consideration" of Schoenberg's 12-tone technique, for this is one way in which Cage's work might be understood. One possible objection can be prevented by introducing immediately the idea of sound-producers for music other than those "formal" instruments usually presented in a child's guide to the orchestra, although this might seem so obvious to those versed in trends in music as to be not ever worth saying. For what, after all, is or is not a musical instrument?

Our argument will consist in the importance of silence in music, and composers' growing interest in it, being brought to the forefront. But what must be stressed immediately is that this argument for "4 minutes 33 seconds" as music, this "proof" or "justification" of it as music, takes place at the level of listening and hearing. Any descriptions offered of works are not important features of the argument but are merely there to aid my presentation of the outline of the procedure which is up for consideration.

Having said that, we can begin by relating Cage's work to the 12-tone technique originated by Schoenberg. In advance of attempting to make the connection at the level of hearing, a theoretical statement may help in establishing "4 minutes 33 seconds" as music for you. Cage (29) actually claimed:-

Curiously enough, the twelve-tone system has no zero in it.

---

(28) In my "Art : Definition and Appreciation" : unpublished paper presented to 10th National Conference of British Society of Aesthetics in September 1975.

(29) In "Erik Satie" 1958. For this information, and for much of the information about music, I am indebted to Michael Finnissy. In particular his detailed analysis of the Webern "Symphonie" Opus 21 and the time he gave to explaining it to me were most helpful. He is, of course, in no way responsible for what I have done with my information, or for my conclusions.

Now, given that you know at least enough about the 12-tone technique (30) to know that all the twelve tones are given <u>equal</u> weighting, it may not seem at all far-fetched that the zero-value too should be given this same weighting. But since this had not happened in the past, Cage could be seen as trying to make the point by writing a piece using <u>only</u> this zero-value.

Here two things must be said immediately. The first relates to the <u>idea</u> of silence, for what Cage actually instructs the performer to do during the three movements of "4 minutes 33 seconds" is "tacet", an instruction which might ordinarily be given to a performer during a section in a piece where his instrument played nothing. It really amounts to a command to listen to what the <u>rest</u> of the orchestra is doing. And in "4 minutes 33 seconds", the "rest of the orchestra" will be the sounds coming from outside and those made inside the concert hall (or whatever). That is, we are being made to question the <u>nature</u> of silence in music, and the <u>context</u> in which music is played.

The second point is about the <u>kind</u> of acceptance of "4 minutes 33 seconds" to which such an explanation might lead. By relating it to (other) 12-tone compositions, we aren't assuring it any position as <u>valuable</u> music - but at least we are offering it a position <u>as</u> music. That is, the recipient of such an explanation would have been given guidelines on how to listen to the piece. And these guidelines would relate it to other <u>pieces</u> : that is, to other 12-tone pieces (say, Schoenberg's "Variations for Orchestra" Opus 31). Now it is insufficient to merely <u>explain</u> to someone that "4 minutes 33 seconds" is music. They must <u>hear</u> it as music.

Hence all that discussion is, in a sense, a prelude to the actual argument, the actual process of attempting to "get someone to hear" in a certain way. So my "justification" of "4 minutes 33 seconds" as music might begin with something you (31) probably will accept as music : Mahler's "Song of the Earth". For all its "progressive tonality" (32) this work can be seen as part of a tradition leading from Beethoven (33). And we could

---

(30) A work such as this is not the place to give exposition of the 12-tone technique, especially as it is simply written up in a number of places. See, for example, Machlis <u>Introduction to Contemporary Music</u> Dent (1961) or Mitchell <u>The Language of Modern Music</u> Faber (1966).

(31) It is important that this is "you" and not "one", for the point of departure of such an argument willbe related to the person(s) involved.

(32) The expression comes from Boyden <u>An Introduction to Music</u> Faber (1959) p.312, from where explanation may be sought.

(33) c.f. Davies <u>Paths to Modern Music</u> Barrie and Jenkins (1971) ch.6.

certainly have chosen to go historically further back to find an
appropriate starting point for our "argument".

A reason for taking this piece as a starting point is that
the 12-tone technique itself must be introduced gradually, and
who better to do this than a great friend of Schoenberg's?
In addition, of course, the musical texture of the piece is
important.   Now to the method of argument : having played "Song
of the Earth" to you, I play Schoenberg's "Gurrelieder", which
was basically completed in 1901, and is very Mahlerian.   I say :
"Listen to this (Song of the Earth), now listen to this
(Gurrelieder)", and you come to hear "Gurrelieder" as music.
Perhaps one listening wouldn't suffice; and perhaps you never
hear "Gurrelieder" as music, although if you are familiar with
"Song of the Earth" this seems unlikely.   However, this possibility is an important consideration later on.   For it must be
recognised that not everyone will come to hear all the pieces in
the "argument" as music, and hence will not follow or accept the
"argument" or "justification".   The implications of this
recognition will be discussed later.   (In this chapter, in Ch.3,
Ch.4.)

To return to our discussion, I now play for you "Gurrelieder"
and Schoenberg's "Three Piano Pieces" Opus 11 (1908), his first
work which is atonal from beginning to end.   Again I say :
"Listen to this, now listen to this".   (Are you getting the idea?)
This step may be important because music with no tonal centre at
all is not easily "swallowed" as music even by a number of those
who admire Mahler.   And one way of seeing the whole 12-tone
technique would be as an attempt to provide a principle of
unification in the absence of diatonic norms.   (Perhaps I even
give you this idea, as an aside).   Now I play "Three Piano
Pieces" Opus 11 and Schoenberg's "Variations for Orchestra" Opus
31, a fairly good example of his 12-tone technique pieces.

I go on to play some of the music of Webern, one of
Schoenberg's pupils.   First I play his "Five movements for
String quartet" Opus 5, asking you to listen to it with
Schoenberg's "Variations for Orchestra" Opus 31.   And, perhaps by
way of explanation, I read a statement of Webern's (34):-

Once an idea has been stated it has expressed everything
it has to say.   A composer has to go on to his
next thought.

---

(34)   Quoted in Ewen Composers of Tomorrow's Music Dodd Mead
(1971) p.70.

Perhaps this notion partly explains the brevity of Webern's works.
Next I play Webern's "Symphonie" Opus 21 (1928), comparing it with
his "Five movements . . . "   (This is a particularly appropriate
piece to become part of our process of comparison since Webern himself wrote that he intended the "Symphonie" to be "in the tradition
of Mozart - Beethoven - Mahler" (35).)   While there are dramatic
pauses in the Webern "Symphonie", perhaps the most noticable after
the very first horn note, there is also an emphasis on silence in
his concern with the production of a different normality : that is
most discernable in its use as standard of diminished intervals,
for example replacing octave which represents "normality" with
seventh, and fifth with tritone, but one feature of this "different"
normality would be that it focuses our attention on the "gaps"
between tones.   (In the Coda of the 2nd movement, bars 91, 94 and
97 are totally "silent".)   We are being asked, I suggest, to hear
"silences" in music as important.   Detailed treatment of Webern's
"Symphonie" Opus 21, therefore, gives us some insight into the
status of silence in music.

Since clear cases would be more important than chronology, I
might now compare that piece with Cage's "Piano Concert" (1958),
which is aurally very close to the Webern "Symphonie" (36).
Of course, to do so leaves out a great deal of importance, and
suggests kinds of connection which are (at best) highly
contentious.   Still, some of the complexity could be overcome by
the addition of more pieces into the "argument" - say, pieces of
Messiaen, Boulez and Stockhausen - and additional theoretical
discussion (of, for example, changes in attitude to composition

---

(35) Information from M. Finnissy in correspondence.

(36) In conversation on this point, Michael Finnissy felt bound to
add : "if orchestras could be persuaded to play it
correctly".   He explained the point in correspondence, with
reference to the Webern "Symphonie", as follows:-

The score is not "technically" difficult for any of the
individual instrumental parts, although it demands (as
with all Webern's music) extreme refinement and sensitivy
in performance.   Making two notes "speak" in a way that
is going to be meaningful to the listener is very much
more difficult than playing an entire melody.   The problem
of performing Webern well is the problem of "ensemble", of
sounding "together", of making your two notes blend with
two notes of someone else before and after you, and of
sublimating individual virtuosity in an essential unifying
approach.

41425

from the situation where a basic theme was orchestrated towards ideas of integrated composition for orchestras.) This work is not, however, intended to present all the complexities of this example, but merely to use it as an example to illustrate the complexity of the direct comparison of cases.

To get on with that, I can now play Cage's "Piano Concert" and "4 minutes 33 seconds, at each stage saying : "Listen to this, now listen to this". And perhaps you hear it as music.

As was said, no doubt one listening would not suffice, and we'd need more cases : but the principles of "justification" (we might even call it "proof") seems fairly clear. I get you to hear the piece in a certain way, by comparing it with other cases.

As an aside, it is worth noting how a kind of comparative procedure is used even in some outlandish examples of our discussion of works of art. When, for example, Ruskin (37) says the following:-

Beethoven always sounds to me like the upsetting of bags of nails, with here and there an also dropped hammer.

he is drawing comparisons between the music and familiar sounds. And his attitude to these sounds is clear enough. But can we assume that to accept the value of the comparison is to accept the judgement? Clearly not. One listener might think it the height of acceptability to sound like the upsetting of bags of nails.

We have looked at one way of (perhaps) getting someone to hear "4 minutes 33 seconds" as music. Another way, not unrelated, might be by stressing its similarities with trends in other art-forms. For example, the norms of theatre are shaken by Beckett (in, for example, his Endgame) when he presents the lives of characters in a way which emphasises their ordinariness (38), the similarity of their lives to our own day-to-day lives, as a way of making us see our lives more clearly. The idea, is roughly, that theatre differs only from life in as much as we look at theatre. If we look closely, and in a certain way, at life it becomes theatre. In a similar way, the sounds "4 minutes 33 seconds" admits may be some distance from the norms of what is ordinarily taken to be music, but it can be seen as making the point that music differs from sounds only in as much as our perception of

---

(37) In a letter to John Brown dated 6 February 1881, quoted in Slonimsky Lexicon of Musical Invective Coleman-Ross (1965) p.52.

(38) c.f. Cavell "Ending the Waiting Game" in his Must We Mean What we say? Scribners (1969) p.119

music takes place within certain contexts. It does not seem so far from the truth to say that it is a particular _kind_ of perception; and "4 minutes 33 seconds" asks us to attend to usual or familiar sounds in this way.

This method of "justifying" "4 minutes 33 seconds" would also be by the direct comparison of cases, although I've actually mentioned only one case. Of course, _mentioning_ as such is no good. We would need to consider the play in detail, and this would probably be best accomplished by reading the play, and seeing it, and the like. In that way you might "come to see" those features of the play that I am attempting to pick-out : and hence see those features in the Cage piece.

Of course, I need not use either of these procedures exactly in order to get you to hear the piece as music, as art. There are lots of others : but it _won't_ do just to say : "Well, listen to it", or "Listen to this". For _how_ should you listen to it? With what "ears"? What kind of thing would you be listening for? (For there are no "innocent ears", just as there are no "innocent eyes". (39))

This point, and its importance, will be discussed later (Ch.4) but here it is worth mentioning that it is impossible for us to approach works of art without any preconceptions. We are who we are, and we have the concepts we have, acquired through _our_ experiences. Nothing can change that. If I acquire new concepts, _I_ acquire them. And since perception can only be rendered intelligible by a recognition that it takes place under concepts (c.f. Ch.3), _what_ I see, what discriminations I am able to make, depends on what concepts I can employ. And this amounts to the number and kind of comparisons of cases which I can see and draw (c.f. Ch.6). I cannot "strip" myself of my concepts when I approach works. To do so would be to allow nothing the status of a _reason_ for any judgement, even a perceptual one.

Since I bring _myself_, as we might say, to works of art when I confront them, it will be obvious that any particular procedure, like those outlined above, _may not_ have the desired result. You may not come to hear "4 minutes 33 seconds" as music. Case-by-case procedures cannot _guarantee_ the successful outcome. You may not be able to see, or hear, the similarities between two of the pieces. The differences may hold your attention. (Or, if case-by case procedures were currently being used currently being used to mark disaffinities, the similarities might hold you captive.)

---

(39) c.f. Gombrich _Art and Illusion_ Phaidon (1960) p.246 ff.

You may not be able to make the leap from the attitude to silence in Cage's "Piano Concert" and the attitude to it in "4 minutes 33 seconds". Here other cases _might_ help. Or they might not. At each stage, a _grasping_ of similarities or dissimilarities is required (c.f. Ch.3), and such "grasping" cannot be guaranteed. It is not, after all, a causal mechanism.

What has been done, then, is to present an outline case-by-case procedure as an example of this model for our understanding procedures : and to see how grasping what has gone before (and this could certainly include the _rejection_ of past attitudes) allows us to understand the new, because it allows us to compare the new with the known. This may be "the New Music" but seeing it justified in this way brings home to us a new version of a familiar moral (particularly familiar in recent moral philosophy) (40) : that we cannot make _all_ things new. Aiming to make _all_ things new will involve us in incoherence, since the _only_ way in which a reason could be offered for any change would be by appeal or reference to something that we not itself at the same time being questioned (c.f. Ch.5). And what could this "something" be? Only some particular case or group of cases.

There may be no limit to the extent to which we can reasonably be called upon (for example, by Bell when championing Cezanne) to change our ideas or whatever, but any such call, however extensive the change called for, must rest on an appeal to what is left unchanged. As Wittgenstein said (41):-

Doubt itself rests only on what is beyond doubt. (p.68)

If this view were accepted, we can see _one_ way in which a certain corpus works of art could be _beyond_ appreciation. Perhaps we can draw the moral with another quotation from Wittgenstein (42) (one of which he admits to being "suspicious", by virtue of its generality.) :

. . . . any empirical proposition can be transformed into a postulate - and then becomes a norm of description . . . . (p.41)

And the suggestion is that this corpus of works of art together form the standards etc. by which we render intelligible the notion of a work of art. They become, to use Wittgenstein's

---

(40) See, for example, **Phillips and Mounce** Moral Practices R.K.P. (1969)

(41) Wittgenstein On Certainty Blackwell (1969) § 519

(42) Wittgenstein On Certainty Blackwell (1969) § 321

word, _postulates_ : they become part of the background or framework against with aesthetic claims are understood or misunderstood. This portion _does_ have the effect of placing particular cases beyond the scope of appreciation, in a sense to be made clear later. (Ch.4) To see why, consider Rush Rhees (43) asking that we :

> . . . . compare saying that it must be possible to decide which of two standards of accuracy was the right one. We do not even know what a person who asks this question is after. (p.100)

How could **you** begin assessing or deciding between standards? What **considerations** could you appeal to? So how could you be said to _appreciate_ or _judge_ standards, except by reference to _other_ standards?

But there is a danger here (the one Wittgenstein noted) that what we are saying _seems_ like a wholly general answer. And in a way it is, but we must realise to what extent it rests on particular cases. We are claiming that this or that is art : and this is surely the right sort of picture. We cannot (philosophers' cries to the contrary not withstanding) know everything in general without knowing at least _something_ in particular. If we can never know that this or that is right, we can never know what in general is right. Likewise, if we can never know that this or that is art, if we cannot be sure of some particular cases, we cannot know what in general is art : and we cannot begin to appraise art-objects.

And this realisation should also allow us to see how the problem of appreciation is to be "solved" : for now I have a corpus of particular cases in which to ground the reasoning in my criticism. The chain of reasons will stop when I get to one of the works of art within this corpus. That is to say that it is against the background provided by this corpus of works that our comments and justifications of other works are intelligible. And this seems the only possible picture, for how else could, for example, a new work be accepted as art? What considerations could be appealed to, by those who saw it as art? Only the

_____

(43) Rhees "Wittgenstein's view of ethics" in his Discussions of Wittgenstein R.K.P. (1970) and c.f. also Malcolm Knowledge and Certainty Prentice-Hall (1963)

> But what would be the standard of comparison in relation to which it would have _meaning_ to say those judgements were false?(p.196 fn.)

previous practices of artists, against which this new practice
could be rendered intelligible (44). That is, this corpus could
provide what Wittgenstein (45) described as:

> . . . the inherited background against which I distinguish
> between true and false. (p.15)

And we could even claim that it was from this corpus that we learn
the meaning of the term "art", although this form of words isn't
to be taken too seriously. (It is logical rather than a
psychological model).

Now suppose that it is a logical requirement that our notion
of work of art be grounded in a corpus of works of art, so what?
And especially, how does this help with, for example, Picasso's
"Guernica" : for if the status of "Guernica" as a great work of
art is open to dispute (as it clearly is) how can it be a part of
such a corpus? And if it is not, how can anything else be? Again
we can look for guidance to Wittgenstein (46) :

> It is not single axioms that strike me as obvious,
> it is a system in which consequences and promises
> give one another mutual support. (p.21)

Explication of this idea must wait (until Ch.4), but the point can
be roughly put with another quotation from Wittgenstein (47) :

> "We are sure of it" does not mean that every single
> person is certain of it, but that we belong to a
> community which is bound together by science and
> education. (p.38).

We agree in large measure as to what counts as a work of art,
what counts for and against a painting or a piece of poetry, and
the like. And it is this large measure of agreement, rooted in
similarities of ways of living and acting, which Wittgensteinians
claim is grounded in a form of life (c.f. Ch.3). Within a form
of life, I can be sure of certain judgements, if only because I
know what counts as a proof, and can agree with and accept the
methods of proof employed by others. This is one of the things
Wittgenstein meant by being "bound together by science and
education".

---

(44) On this point, c.f. Ch.5.

(45) Wittgenstein On Certainty Blackwell (1969) § 94.

(46) Wittgenstein On Certainty Blackwell (1969) § 142.

(47) Wittgenstein On Certainty Blackwell (1969) § 298.

Of course, an account such as has been offered here, which is merely the bones of an account (48), is at best a first approximation to a position. For what counts as a "large measure" of agreement? And who are the "we" in question? Resolutions of these difficulties might be extracted from what follows, although the problems will not be faced head-on. But any account must allow room for conceptual modification and change. Indeed the case-by-case procedure as outlined (see also Ch.3) is offered as a logical model for such change. Yet it may seem that a picture of understanding such as that offered here does not have this room. For won't the "large measure" of agreement militate against such changes? Doesn't it then become something rather like a tautology that whatever there is a "large measure" of agreement about is therefore indeed the case. This idea will be discussed later (Ch.4). For now, it is sufficient to recall that our claims about this prerequisite of understanding are not to be interpreted as statistical ones, based on observed correlations. This in itself provides some insight into the role of particular cases, or examples, of such-and-such in the face of pressure for conceptual change.

We can imagine a concerted attack on all that we've called works of art : but some of these works will surely stand firm for us. They will become the "postulates" : and any group of artworks, even mediocre ones, could stand firm to ground our judgements. But does it seem likely that all would have the same status, in practice? Doesn't it seem more likely that works of which we think highly will be those which can't be dislodged? So I don't think it so far from the truth to refer to the core of the corpus of works of art which "stands firm for me" as "the tremendous things in Art".

To those who claim that the kind of reasons offered in aesthetics are only reasons:-

. . . . in terms of some antecedently accepted set of standards . . . . (Shiner p.262)

the answer is simple. Of course they are right in thinking that

---

(48) c.f. Toulmin Human Understanding Oxford Vol. I (1972)
Vol. II, Vol. III forthcoming. Toulmin's analysis of collective 'rationality' and the evolution of concepts might perhaps fill in this kind of gap. To be sure, we must await the publication of the rest of that work.

our reasoning is to be grounded in certain "standards" based on a corpus of particular cases. But their explanation of this is mistaken since we don't _accept_ these standards, if this is thought of in terms of some decision on our parts. Instead, to put it crudely, we grow up in them.

This notion of "growing up with ......" is one through which our investigations will pass many times. For it does not _seem_ like an answer to the question: "How do you know X?" to reply that I grew with with it true that X. We could put our point another way, by saying that we are inducted into various standards and the like. Then we don't so much see them as right as come to understand the term "right" by reference to them, which point is well made in a recent article by Richard Beardsmore (49). The whole process of this inducting will be extremely complex. Indeed it is this complexity to which Wittgenstein (50) alludes, when he says:-

It is not only difficult to describe what appreciation consists in, but impossible. To describe what it consists in, we would have to describe the whole environment. (p.7)

To completely, describe the process of "growing up with . . . . " these aesthetic standards, we would have to describe in minute detail _everything_ about growing up in our society. And that, as Wittgenstein asserts, would be impossible (51).

Having considered the line of argument which asserts that ante-cedently accepted or acquired standards are required in order that what pass for reasons in aesthetics should be genuine reasons, and rejected that view as involving a misunderstanding of reasoning, we are in a position to deal with another line : that which urges that no justification is required for some "self-evident" propositions or claims. Our reply would follow that offered by Wisdom (**V.L.** p.128) : that even "Not both P and not-P" is not something a person knows to be true just by looking at the symbols.

(49) Beardsmore "Consequences and Moral Worth" Analysis 29 (1969) c.f. Ch.4 where some more detail, and quotation from Beardsmore, are provided.

(50) Wittgenstein Lectures and Conversations on Aesthetics, Psychology and Religious Belief. Blackwell (1971) I.20

(51) On the evolution of concepts, see my "Conceptual Change and this History of Art" in Chelsea Papers in Human Movement Studies (Philosophy and Movement : collected lectures by Graham McFee) 1977.

We come to understand it by looking at cases : by my saying "A thing couldn't both be a tree and not be a tree, could it?". We teach instances, and then say "and so on . . . ." (That is the process of proving is seen as the process of learning in reverse. And this seems intuitively correct, for if the final appeal in our arguments, justifications, proofs, explanations, or whatever is to instances, we will be doing something not so radically different from what we "did" to acquire the concepts).

In both the cases of the lines of argument just considered, we attacked the account of reasoning, proving and explaining offered. Our own position, as so far articulated, seems vulnerable to attack from at least two directions. Firstly our account of reasoning may look extremely suspect : and Chapter Three aims to quieten those fears. Second, the diversity of critical opinions may make the claims of any corpus of works to be beyond critical assault seem eminently dubious. That objection will be met in Chapter Four.

It was claimed in the previous chapter that the picture often proffered of reasoning in aesthetics was an inadequate one, which tended to ignore the role of particular cases. Some mention of the case-by-case procedure (or "proof by parallels", to supply another of Wisdom's titles for it) was introduced to combat this picture. In general, a "cramped" notion of what it was to reason was diagnosed. As Wisdom (1) puts it:-

We are trying to get away from calling unprovable those cases which can only be proven by the case-by-case procedure. (V.L. p.93)

And this attempt can be seen as trying to "explode" a cramp. When we say of what a literary critic (for example) does, "this isn't genuine reasoning!" it is claimed that we are often subject to just this cramp.

Since I can only do less well than Wisdom at giving exposition of the case-by-case procedure, the chapter will contain a great many quotations from him, loosely strung together with comments of mine (2). Le us begin by asking just what this "cramp"is? More

_____

(1) Note on V.L. : The text of Wisdom's Virginia Lectures on "Proof and Explanation", from which I am quoting, is a version prepared from transcripts by S. Barker of the University of Virginia, and distributed to "a limited number of especially interested persons". In correspondence, Wisdom expressed the hope that he might publish these lectures in the near future (1976). I hope that readers will not be too infuriated by the references to and quotations from this unpublished work, until that time. The quotations speak for themselves, and are merely making points with a clarity I cannot attain. The references are there for those who have access to a copy of V.L.

I would like to thank John Wisdom for all his help and encouragement : and especially for giving me permission to quote so extensively from his unpublished writing. (V.L.)

(2) An alternative but related model for reasoning might be drawn from Stanley Cavell's as yet unpublished doctoral dissertation "The Claim to Rationality", Harvard University (1962); and suggested in his Must We Mean What We Say? Scribners (1969). I have only seen those parts of the dissertation quoted in Pitkin Wittgenstein and Justice University of California (1972). The work of Cavell, like that of Wisdom, derives from Wittgenstein.

can be made explicit : the first factor is diagnosed as:-

. . . . a cramped notion as to what it is to establish a
conclusion of fact, in that we don't recognise the part
of reflection in this process. (V.L. p.86).

As this idea will be under discussion throughout this chapter, we
can move on:-

The second factor is a cramped notion of what reflection
is; a tendency to think that all respectable reflection
is deductive . . . . (V.L. p.86)

Wisdom attempts to justify the case-by-case procedure by
"exploding" such cramps. The second cramp is to be "exploded"
by showing, or by recognising, that deduction itself (as
exemplified by the syllogism) must in the end come down to a
case-by-case procedure (3). We can begin with an example
(c.f. V.L. p.54) : "This is an argument in the 4th figure of the
syllogism which obeys the general rules of the syllogism and the
special rules of the 4th figure : all arguments which answer
these conditions are valid : therefore this argument is valid."

Now do you or don't you include this argument under the
general principle which is the major premises in this syllogism?
If you do, your argument is circular; for it only yields a true
conclusion if the major premises is true, and yet this argument
itself would produce a counter-example to the major premises if
the conclusion is false - for this argument would then be invalid.
And, of course, if you don't include this argument under your
principle, the major premises is false in its full generality and
so the "conclusion" isn't established "deductively".

This view parallels Mill's (4) attack on the syllogism.
What it is designed to show is that even the paradigm of
deduction doesn't establish its conclusions any better than a
direct (that is, a case-by-case) procedure. Another example of
Wisdom's (V.L. pp.51-2) may help to clarify this point. We are
asked to consider a child confronted with the following a priori
problem : six airlines fly from England to France, and for each

---

(3) c.f. Dilman Induction and Deduction Blackwell (1973)
pp.115-6, where similar arguements can be found. Indeed
Dilman quotes V.L. at this point.

(4) Mill System of Logic (1843) II iii 4. However Mill's own
account can be seen as attempting to reduce the syllogism to
real analogies (c.f. V.L. p.101). This point will be taken
up later in the chapter, but it will be obvious that the
scope of the case-by-case procedure is wider than that.

of these there are six ways of going to France by one airline and
coming back on that airline by a different plane. Now the
question is : how many ways are there of going to France by one
plane of any given line and coming back on a different plane of
that line? When the child is perplexed by this problem, its
parents give it two sorts of advice. The mother's method of
enlightening the child is to offer simple examples. For instance,
she asks : if you have two boxes and two beads in each box, how
many beads have you? (5) As these cases become more difficult,
the child is brought to see the similarities between these cases,
which it can deal with, and the one which perplexes it. (how
reminiscent of the extended music example in Ch. 2!) By being
able to deal with cases ever closer to that set up by the problem,
the child sees how to deal with the problem. It is brought to
see the "deductive" connection between, for example, P ("There
are six airlines") and Q ("There are six times six ways of ......
etc.") It will come to see, or be brought to see, by a
comparison of cases.

The father's method of explaining to the child involves
offering just such a principle : that, if there are N sorts of
thing X, and for each of these there are N sorts of thing Y, then
there are N times N sorts of thing Y. As Wisdom remarks
(V.L. p.52):-

> Short, conclusive, the father's procedure.
> That's more what one might call a proof.

Once the applicability of the principle to this case is
asserted, the answer is transparent. The difficulty comes when
the child attempts to see from where the father's principle comes.
It can see that, by fitting the data from the example into the
formula, we can answer the question. But why is the formula
acceptable? In particular, is the "instance" on which it sheds
this light one of the father's grounds for believing it? If it
is, then there will be a circularity, for the principle will be
acceptable only if the answer genuinely is N times N, and the only
reason offered for the answer "N times N" is the principle. And
if this instance isn't one of the father's grounds for believing
in the principle, how does he know that it is covered by the
principle? If he doesn't (and how could he?), his principle is
inconclusive. And to deduce that principle from one yet more
general will not help the situation. For the questions currently
asked of this principle can then be asked of that one.

---

(5) For "the mother's method and the father's method", see Wisdom
"The Metamorphosis of Metaphysics" reprinted in his Paradox
and Discovery. Blackwell (1965) p.69. Also Newell The
Concept of Philosophy Methuen (1967) p.70.

What is being claimed, then, is that syllogisms do not establish their conclusions any better than a case-by-case procedure like the mother's. And it is not hard to see why. Any statement C is deducible from P when and only when every investigative measure and every reflective measure, every comparative act for the justification C is also required for the justification of P. (V.L. p.125, also V.L. pp.53-4). If this were not so, we would be able to establish or justify P without at the same time establishing C, by leaving out just those investigative or reflective measures (or whatever) which were required to establish C but weren't required to establish P. Hence we could establish a premise without establishing what is deducible from it - which would surely make a nonsense of the notion of deduction. Of course, it may well be the case that P requires more justification that C but it cannot require less. To suggest that would be to allow just this attack on the notion of what deduction is. There is no wonder, that in a deductive proof we don't present better justification than we do when we use a case-by-case procedure to establish C.

The basis for our claims (what we might call "the real inference") is a move from the evidence on which our assertion P is based to our conclusion C : to take the familiar example, from the particular observations etc. that Smith is mortal, Brown is mortal . . . . to the claim that Socrates will also die. We can capture this point by saying that "All men are mortal" is not so much a premise from which we conclude that Socrates is mortal as a formula to remind us of the manner in which we have "inferred" in the past, and are in the future entitled to "infer". Now reasoning can proceed quite well without such a formula. In our ordinary life it generally does, and the foregoing arguments are designed to suggest that this is no criticism. But we can see why we should bother with deduction at all, for such formulae have their uses. Scientists, for example, prefer to make explicit the "formulae" of their inferences, as scientific "laws" or whatever. They argue from particular cases to the general rule, which becomes a scientific law or principle, and then from this rule to further particular cases. The rule allows us to bring a number of particulars to bear on the particulars in question in a simple fashion. Hence it has a generalising facility - but such generality must in the end be susceptible to disputes where individual differences are stressed.

For example, the over-famous premise "All swans are white" may well bring a number of cases to bear on the particular case in question. Your son has seen a brown bird and claims it was a swan. You assure him that all swans are white. And this clarifies the matter for him. But the generality of your assertion is false generality. Presented with a black swan, you can retreat in various ways : for example to "Some swans ...."

or to "All swans native to England ...." To say these in the
beginning might well confuse the lad.   And this retreat is
from the force of a particular case.   In the end, the scope of
your assertion would be all and only those situations (those
cases) where it was true :   that is, where you had ruled out all
falsifying cases.   And you go about ruling out these falsifying
cases, and ruling in the others, by an essentially case-by-case
procedure.

What is urged here is that formal deduction has its place,
and its own virtues.   But it does not exhaust the models for
sound reasoning.   Indeed it must rest, in the end, on one
other such model.   The example of the white and black swans
emphasises another point :   that we tend to use deduction, and
universal premises such as these, in clear-cut cases.   That is
not to say that the case-by-case procedure isn't in fact just
as clear-cut in principle.   The deductive process (or perhaps
better, the deductive model) is convenient and is never anything
but absolutely conclusive, given no misfires in its handling.
When we come to a borderline dispute, we will tend to use an
explicitly case-by-case process (that, is a case-by-case model),
and such disputes are often far from conclusive.   Indeed, it
is because they are far from conclusive that we call them
borderline disputes.   But the case-by-case type of argument
can be used to produce "conclusive" results :   and, as suggested
previously, deduction does not establish these results any more
conclusively.

Presumably, a full case-by-case procedure for establishing
"if a thing is a square then it is also a rectangle" (6) would
involve consideration of every actual and possible (conceivable) instance of a rectangle and noticing that all squares were
rectangles :   whereas to justify the "conclusion" about such and
such being a square, we need only consider every actual and
conceivable instance of a square.   (To put the point this way
reiterates our earlier contention that the premises may require
more justification than the conclusions, but they cannot require
less.)   That, then, is a picture of the case-by-case procedure.

Now this picture does support our contention that, in the
last analysis, deduction is no better than the case-by-case
procedure.   But it poses a problem : for we won't usually
present, or perform, this kind of case-by-case procedure.
We will select, as in the extended music example (C.2), a
number of cases and argue with them.   And if we are not

---

(6) Example drawn from Yalden-Thomson "The Virginia Lectures"
in Bambrough ed. Wisdom : Twelve Essays Blackwell (1974)

presenting a full case-by-case procedure, do we have anything better than an argument from analogy? Our reply has suggested that what we offer, when we offer parts of a case-by-case procedure, is still valuable : and that a grasp of the case-by-case procedure is an advantage in understanding the bases of reasoning, since all reasoning in the end comes down to it.

But the line of counter-argument might be extended by attempting to display that the case-by-case procedure is nothing but an argument from analogy. As an example of such a view, consider a discussion from Susan Stebbing's Thinking to some Purpose (7). She presents the logical form of the argument from analogy as :

$$X \text{ has properties } P, P_2, P_3 \ldots \ldots \text{ and } f$$
$$Y \text{ has properties } P, P_2^2, P_3^3 \ldots \ldots$$
$$\text{Therefore } Y \text{ also has property } f.$$

and comments :

> The force of the argument depends upon the resemblance between X and Y with regard to the P's.
> (Stebbing p.113)

Then she goes on to discuss a biblical example, the story of how Nathan brings home to David the wrongness of his actions with regard to Uriah the Hittite by employing the parable of the ewe-lamb (8). The story goes roughly like this. After taking a fancy to Uriah's wife, David has Uriah put in the front line in a battle, where he is duly killed. Then David takes the woman for himself. Nathan the prophet arrives the next day, and tells David a story:-

> There were two men in one city; one rich, and the other poor. The rich man had exceeding many flocks and herds: but the poor man had nothing save one little ewe lamb, which he had bought and nourished up : and it grew up together with him, and with his children : it did eat of his meat, and drank of his own cup, and lay in his bosom, and was unto him as a daughter. And there came a traveller unto the rich man, and he spared to take of

---

(7) Stebbing Thinking to Some Purpose Penguin (1939)

(8) This case, from the second book of Samuel, is mentioned by Wisdom (V.L. pp. 132-3) : and, in correspondence, Wisdom drew my attention both to the importance of the example and to Stebbing's treatment of it.

-40-

his own flock and of his own herd, to dress for the
wayfaring man that was come unto him; but took the
poor man's lamb, and dressed it for the man that was
come to him.

And David's anger was greatly kindled against
the man; and he said to Nathan, As the Lord liveth,
the man that hath done this thing shall surely die :
And he shall restore the lamb four fold, because he
did this thing, and because he had no pity.

And Nathan said to David, Thou art the man . . .
And David said unto Nathan, I have sinned against the
Lord.

With reference to this story, Stebbing remarks :-

. . . its use is confined to instruction; it is not
a form of argument. (Stebbing p.116)

Presumably, she would regard the change in David's attitude as
the only kind of thing such "parables" are good for. For her,
the genuine argument from analogy may be a _little_ better : but
that will depend on the force of the resemblances. With a
genuine argument from analogy, one of the logical forms
previously mentioned, the argument is seen as just as strong as
the resemblances. And here the resemblances are minimal.
Hence the position is that the _dissimilarities_ between the case
Nathan presents to David and David's own case make it virtually
worthless. It seems that we can only be entitled to draw
conclusions from analogy if the analogies drawn are strong.
Nor is this counter-intuitive. If A is like B in but one small
respect, it does seem foolish to attempt to predict the
behaviour of B on the basis of the behaviour of A. Water and
liquid helium are both fluids : and water will be contained by
a cooled beaker. But liquid helium is a super-fluid, and climbs
the sides of such vessels. The two fluids are so different as
to render useless any argument based on their points of
similarity.

Whatever analogies we draw must break down somewhere, for
whatever analogies are drawn must be drawn between things which
are different, which have differences. And when we have
acknowledged such differences have we not, the position might
run, pointed to an inadequacy in such arguments? If there are
bound to be these differences, and if differences can be
important, can we be sure that the examples between which we
draw the analogy are sufficiently similar? Clearly we cannot
be absolutely sure. Any difference may cause a breakdown, and
so even the most carefully drawn analogy may contain a fatal
flaw. The analogy may _not_ hold in the appropriate places.

-41-

It is surely for this reason that, later, Stebbing remarks:-

. . . although argument by analogy may be used to suggest
a conclusion, it is incapable of establishing any
conclusion at all.   (Stebbing p.126)

She would regard the conclusion of the argument from analogy,
even when these were the best that such argument could offer, as
inherently dubious, since the argument from analogy moves from
similarities we do know about towards similarities we do not
know about.   And such "similarities" simply may not exist.

Now one reply to Stebbing's actual claims would be to show
that arguments she thinks stronger or sounder than the case-by-
case type ultimately rest on such a type.   (Of course, Stebbing
is discussing the argument from analogy, not the case-by-case
procedure.   But one of the examples she gives, Nathan's story,
is an example Wisdom uses of case-by-case.)   We suggested, in
our discussion of deduction, that it was no better than a
"direct" case-by-case procedure, and that should suffice here.
However, it is worth considering the differences between the
genuine argument from analogy and the case-by-case procedure.

In ordinary cases of the argument from analogy, we may ask
whether what the analogy suggests is true, whether what the
analogy gives us reason to think is so is indeed so : and we may
then carry out a further process of investigation of some sort
to decide whether or not it is.   This was roughly what occurred
to find the water/liquid helium analogy wanting.   Similarities
the analogy suggested, for example staying in a beaker, were not
to be found.   But with the case-by-case procedure there is no
way of taking further measures to find out whether the parallel-
ism suggested is in fact the case.   (c.f. V.L. pp. 131-2).
With an argument from analogy which leads us to believe that A
resembles B it is still appropriate to ask, "And does it?" in a
way which is inappropriate when we have come down to an explicitly
case-by-case procedure.   To put it over-crudely, this is because
we have come to the lowest possible level of reasoning when we
are employing the direct comparison of cases.

An example may help here.   With an argument from analogy,
we are sometimes inclined to say, "But that pushes the analogy
too far!"   What is being protested is that the similarities do
not carry over into these dissimilar cases.   States, for
example, may resemble persons in some respects - giving perhaps
some value to talk of a "body politic" - but no states require
three meals a day, even if a number of people do.   To argue
from that conclusion about some people to a similar conclusion
about some states would be to stretch the analogy until it breaks.

A similar situation cannot occur for case-by-case procedures, for if all reasoning in the end comes down to a case-by-case procedure the reasoning in any investigation or whatever will itself be case-by-case. How can we begin to question the resemblance of cases A and B if to do so we must compare cases and note their resemblances? With genuine arguments from analogy, we can compare the results obtained with "how things are". We can _see_ that no states require three meals a day, and so we _know_ that the analogy has broken down. Or if we do not see this, we know how to go about investigating it. But how can we begin to question a case-by-case procedure in this way? If we attempt to show the **differences** between the case of Uriah and David and **the** case of the man with one ewe lamb and his rich neighbour, we must do so in terms of this case or of other particular cases. That is, we can show how David and the rich man **differ in** other respects : one is a king, father of so many sons, etc. and the other isn't. We can note that Uriah's wife isn't a sheep, but a person; and that she was coveted, not killed. Still, all these remarks seem beside the point. We recognised them when we began the comparison.

Or we can look at other cases : say, a case in which a man needs a particular sheep so much that he will die if he is not given it. We might fill in appropriate details here, if necessary. In this case, his doctors might take another man's sheep and give it to him. And a second Nathan might again say : "Thou art the man." But here too we are looking at a case which **resembles** the one in question, David's, but also differs from it. And in just the kinds of way that the original Nathan's case did. Now this second case might convince David, or us, that he did the right thing all along.

We cannot claim that **either** of these cases fits "how it is" exactly. For "how it is" will be David's actions with respect to Uriah the Hittite and his wife. Indeed the cases differ in similar ways. And in looking at them we have not escaped from the case-by-case procedure but merely re-employed it, for any case is bound to differ **in some respects** from the case under consideration, or it would not be a different case. If we ask whether or not David **in fact** resembles the rich neighbour, the answer is **bound** to be that in the last analysis he does not. That is, there are dissimilarities as well as any similarities between them. But how could such similarities be further **invest-igated**? We are not moving from the known to the unknown here but, we might say, from the clearly to the unclearly apprehended.

Another point surfaces here. Wisdom claims (**V.L.** p.131) that in analogy we can employ actual cases, while the case-by-case procedure encompasses the use of conceivable or imaginable cases as well. Taken at face value, it seems that Wisdom must

-43-

be offering a stipulation here, for we will employ imaginary cases in ordinary discussions from analogy. But we can catch the spirit of his remark when we recognise how vulnerable such a procedure as analogy with imaginary cases is. The crucial thing is that we should know the details of the case in advance of drawing the analogy. Unless we know the properties or features or whatever of those things from which we draw our analogy, the analogy will be useless. If we don't know appropriate things about the behaviour of monkeys, we cannot even begin drawing (questionable) analogies between their behaviour and human behaviour. When we use imaginary cases, we supply the details of these features or properties or whatever, so we can even specify that the analogy will hold. But in doing so we remove the point of the analogy.

Elaboration of the example brings this out clearly. We say that the so-and-so monkeys possess all the traits of humans. These so-and-so monkeys are an imaginary species, and we have imagined them with all the traits possessed by humans. Now we can come to ask questions about, for example, the innateness of greed in humans by "analogy" with the so-and-so monkeys. But are such monkeys greedy? They are (a) if we imagined them to be (which doesn't help us to answer the questions) or (b) if humans are, since we set up the case with them having all human traits. But are humans greedy? That we have to answer that question before attempting to discover, by using our analogy, whether or not humans are greedy exposes the inadequacy of the whole business. We imagined the monkeys to help us with the case of the humans : but the question of the humans must be answered before the monkeys can be of any use. Analogies are valuable in pointing towards just the kind of information which analogy from an imaginary case will usually need to have provided or stipulated.

This does not, of course, mean that all analogies have to be drawn with actual instances. However, the details of cases need to be specified in advance of the analogy. That is why cases from fiction, from novels and plays for example, are often most helpful. We know how such-and-such a character reacts in a given situation. That is in the work of art. So we do not have to invent his reaction. If we did, his case would not help us in predicting or commenting on the behaviour of others, for we would be depending on our guesses or whatever in just the same way with or without this man's case. And only when we have this kind of prior information about his behaviour, the kind of information a novelist might have given us, can we go on to find out if the results suggested by an analogy with this man's case do in fact hold. In the other situation, we are not finding that out but finding out whether or not we guessed correctly. If we said that in this second case we

were not able to <u>search</u> for our answer, we would not be so far
wrong. And this echoes a remark of Wittgenstein's (9):-

    . . . . "search" must always mean : search systematically.
Meandering about in infinite space on the lookout for a
gold ring is no kind of search.

You can only <u>search</u> within a system : And so there is
necessarily something you <u>can't</u> search for. (p.175)

Here we would say that we cannot <u>search</u> for evidence of
similarities between the cases in our comparative procedure.
There is no room for "finding out" here, no possible methods of
"making sure". We <u>specify</u> the similarity, not look for it.

Consider a claim that Wisdom quotes for discussion (<u>V.L.</u> p.50):

The proof lies in further observation.

Well, sometimes it does. But equally sometimes it does not. If
we return to the two Nathans, both telling their stories to David,
we can see this point very clearly. No further <u>observation</u> of
David's actions is necessary. They both know what he did. Yet
they disagree as to the rightness of what he did, or as to the
degree to which he was justified. And what do they do? In
correspondence, Wisdom recounted to me the following story:-

Broad on one occasion (I think he was talking to Blanshard
and myself) said something like : "It seems to me that when
one person differs from another over a moral question (and
it was clear from the context that Wisdom would have added
'or an aesthetic question') he can do no more than 'twit
the other with inconsistency'."

This seems to me to be <u>just</u> the sort of thing the two Nathans
would do. Each would point to the similarities between <u>his</u>
preferred story and the actual situation and emphasise the
dissimilarities he saw in his rival's story. What they would be
doing then would be an integral part of the case-by-case procedure.
Wisdom said that Broad did not consider this "twitting" to be any
sort of <u>reasoning</u> at all. But we can see clearly now that it is,
for it is the direct comparison of cases, pure and simple. More
needs to be said about this business of "twitting" the other with
inconsistency however. Notice even at this stage how, in our
extended music example (Ch.2), this "twitting" could take place.
The kind of thing I'll say if you don't hear "4 minutes 33 seconds"
as music is : "You mean you don't consider 'Song of the Earth'

---

(9) Wittgenstein <u>Philosophical Remarks</u> Blackwell (1975)

music?", that is, I'll suggest you are being inconsistent. And
if you disagree you'll be "twitting" me with inconsistency by
suggesting that I am treating what are obviously different cases
in the same fashion. Then we can get down to . . . . a discussion
of cases.

Our aim in this chapter so far (like Wisdom's aim in V.L.) has
been to suggest what that case-by-case procedure is like, and that
it is just as respectable as deductive reasoning. But we have
done rather more than that, for we have suggested that not merely
is the case-by-case procedure as respectable as deduction, but
that deduction or deductive reasoning in the last analysis comes
down to the case-by-case procedure. The major premises of
syllogisms have to be established, and understood — and this can
only be done by acquaintance with particulars. As suggested
before, the principles used as major premises are established by
the observation of particular cases. The evidence for the
assertion about the mortality, of all men must consist in our
experience of particular cases. To repeat, we know Smith is
mortal, Brown is mortal, etc. And on the basis of this we
conclude that Socrates is mortal. We could pause between these
positions to assert that all men are mortal. We could, but we
generally do not : and claiming (10) that we must employ some
such general premises does not help. As commonly occurs with
moral principles but could occur with any, we can always ask :
from whence comes this principle? In moral philosophy the reply
is often to present particular cases, to say of a story, "Well,
that was wrong, wasn't it?" Here we should recognise that this
method, closely akin to the kind of "twitting" with inconsistency
mentioned earlier, must be at the basis of any dispute, in moral
philosophy or elsewhere. What is done is to produce an instance

---

(10) The beliefs that such general premises are implied by
     reasoning, and even the claim that all reasoning is
     syllogistic, do exist. c.f. Joyce Principles of Logic
     Longmans 3rd ed. (1920)

         "It has already been pointed out that, though we
         think in syllogisms . . . . yet we do not
         ordinarily express each of the three constituent
         judgements." (p.252)

     Our reply would be with an attack on the syllogism's ability
     to establish its conclusions any better than direct
     procedures. And this may cast some doubt on our calling
     arguments enthymemes, if an enthymeme is ". . . . a syllogism
     abridged by the omission of one premise . . . ." (Joyce p.252)
     Our inclination would be to regard the kind of argument which
     looks like a syllogism without a major premises as (part of)
     a case-by-case argument.

recognisably similar to the instance under consideration, and to ask for consistent judgements. For example, we attempt to produce cases where consistent application of Utilitarian principles for right action leads to the espousal as good of actions which can be, and are, seen to be wrong. We aim to find instances of argument elsewhere which closely resembles "argument" in aesthetics or ethics, and then ask for consistency of those who urged that there is never argument in aesthetics or ethics.

But such consistency is not always possible : or rather, there may be too many similarities between A and a variety of things unlike B for me to mark the similarity between A and B, even though I do mark the similarities between B and C. Here I cannot have my consistency in all directions. Since I must search for the similarities and differences if I am to be as consistent as possible, it will probably be of help to me in you point out some of these. I may have missed them. And to do this pointing out is, in effect, to "twit" me with inconstiency. It is in this way that I come to recognise the similarities and differences between one thing and another.

Wisdom (11) came to recognise that:-

. . . . with every name we apply we compare one thing with another, with many others. (p.274)

Yet this point is far from easy to see. What exactly is Wisdom claiming? Crudely, that it is in such comparisons with other objects that we see what sort of thing it is, what kind of feature it has, and how they are related together. To keep with Wisdom's own examples, when we are wondering if the object before us is a spade, whether the right decision has been reached, whether the firm of Baker and Sons is bankrupt, what we do is to look for parallels, notice affinities and dissimilarities between the objects or cases before us and instances we can see or conceive. And this insight is behind Wisdom's insistence of recognition of the place of the case-by-case procedure, which seeks to make such comparisons explicit.

Of course, we will be variously misled in our searches to understand. Misleading analogies will suggest themselves. (Or, to put the point polemically, will be suggested by our language.) One such, an important one exposed by Wisdom, concerns the role of comparison in our placing of objects as of a kind K. As Wisdom says:-

---

(11) Wisdom "Philosophy, Metaphysics and Psycho-Analysis" in his Philosophy and Psycho-Analysis Blackwell (1953)

> We tend to lose sight of the role of comparison in the
> process of ascertaining whether a thing is of kind K
> (or has the property K) if we think of the process like
> that of looking for something to be detected in several
> things . . . . we do better to think of the process of
> ascertaining whether a thing is of a certain kind as that
> of ascertaining its place amongst what is conceivable.
> We may then if we like compare and contrast this process
> with that of one who ascertains where a thing is, or if
> you like at what point in space it is, by noting how far
> it is from other things in space. (V.L. p.45 (a))

He goes on to explain this point a little, by noting how well it
does agree with some of our actual practice in describing:-

> In saying that a thing is of a certain kind, I place it.
> This is a form of expression we do in fact use (I couldn't
> place him', 'I couldn't place it'. (V.L. p.63)

It is by comparing one thing with another, indeed with many others,
that we see what sort of thing it is. For, to repeat, what sort
of thing it is, what kind of features it has and how these features
are related to one another, is a matter of how that thing stands
with regard to other things. That is to say that to know 'the
nature' of a thing is to know how it resembles other things and
how it differs from other things. This is to know (and here we
can take this idiom literally) what the thing is like.

The very possibility of comparisons such as these requires
an immense "stage-setting", as Wittgenstein (12) called it.
For when a comparison brings out the respects in which one thing
resembles another thing or other things, it does so by virtue of
the surroundings within which the comparisons are made. Only
when two people share certain reactions, opinions, convictions
and the like, only when they can jointly take part in certain
activities or (to put it crudely) only when they share a common
understanding that one can show the other something he had not
seen before, by means of a 'new' comparison.

Such a shared or common understanding requires a shared
language, where this notion is taken in some wide way. For to
say "This is like that" or "This is like that in such-and-such
ways" (or to present the comparison in some other way), and to
expect to be understood, is to assume that such similarities
can be discriminated by those to whom you speak. And this means
rather more than just that both groups be speaking the English
language.

---

(12) Wittgenstein Philosophical Investigations Blackwell (1953)
§ 257.

To explain what more, and to argue in detail for this claim
would take us beyond the scope of this work. However, we must
outline the argument in its simplest form, and hope the reader
will clothe the bones with appropriate flesh. (And not be too
insulted by its simplicity.) If we consider an apparently
straightforward operation, like addition, it will be obvious that
a certain leap of understanding is required. I have presented
you with the following sum:-

$$9562 + 1467 = ?$$

If you are not up to performing this piece of addition, how can
I help you? How can I make it simpler for you? It is insufficient
to merely reduce the complex sum to a simpler one, for example:-

$$1 + 1 = ?$$

For you must _still_ understand the addition sign. That is, you
must make essentially the same leap of understanding in both cases.
You must see 'how to go on' (13). I cannot _tell_ you how to take
the addition sign, and if I show you, I am depending on you to
take what I am showing in roughly the way I intend it.

We can illustrate this by repeating an example of
Wittgenstein's (14). My pointing at objects and calling out
their names requires not only that you recognise this as some
kind of name-calling ceremony, but also that you take my pointing
to be from shoulder to fingertip and not vice versa. In either
of these examples, the naming or the adding, it might seem that
some simple instruction or rule could sort out the confusion, but
a moments reflection shows that this is not so. The rule itself
must be taken correctly - or a further rule would be needed, and
so on.

Hence the very possibility of our having a shared language
requires that we take things like pointing in the same way or
rather that we are able to be taught to take pointing in the same
way; which in turn requires that we take such teaching in the
right way. Or rather, the way in which we do all take it _becomes_
or _is_ "the right way". We are now far from our track, discussing
the anthropological roots of logical necessity which Wittgenstein
(15) captures when he says:-

---

(13) For another discussion of this issue, see Winch The Idea of
      a Social Science R.K.P. (1958) pp.55-7.

(14) c.f. Wittgenstein Zettel Blackwell (1967) § 355.

(15) Wittgenstein Philosophical Investigations Blackwell (1953)
      § 242.

If language is to be a means of communication there must be agreement not only in definitions but also (queer as this may sound) in judgements.

The group within which this "agreement in judgements" exists, Wittgenstein (16) calls a "form of life". To share the same form of life is, roughly, to have those similar reactions and convictions mentioned earlier : that is, to share the same "stage-setting". Within a form of life, we can begin to take for granted certain opinions as well as certain reactions, for we agreed in our concepts. We can begin to agree in judgements not only like "this is a spade" but also as to what would show that it wasn't a spade, how we expect it to behave under pressure or the cold, how long we expect it to last, and what sorts of thing would break it. These are not issue we'd expect to discuss with our neighbours. Our expectation would be that they would agree with us. But our shared expectations as to the recognition and behaviour of spades in fact rests on a vast complex of the bits of behaviour we have seen, or would individually expect, from spades.

We can see these things clearly in considering this example. But there is more to it. As Wisdom says:

"Its a spade" involves reflection as well as verification of enormous complexity, running over the whole of time and space. (V.L. p.90)

We have seen the sense of this claim, and this reference to the verification is one feature of studies of the epistemology of such-and-such. And also ties in with claims such as Peter Strawson's (17):-

. . . . Concepts of objects are . . . . necessarily compendia of causal laws . . . . (They) carry implications of causal power or dependence. (pp.145-6).

How would such "compendia of causal laws" be brought together? And how would we come to understand which causal laws were a part of the concept of object such-and-such? Clearly this would come about when we learnt that concept; which is (at least partly) to say, when I learnt language. And this would be part of the "stage-setting".

---

(16) Wittgenstein Philosophical Investigations Blackwell (1953) § 241.

(17) Strawson The Bounds of Sense Methuen (1966)

The conclusion required at this juncture is that no claims could stand entirely on their own, divorced from implicit or explicit comparisons. As Wisdom puts it:-

. . . . every statement calls for reflection. (V.L p.56)

And here he would include perceptual statements, as well as others. Let us take recognition as an example, in case the arguments thus far suggested do not seem appropriately conclusive.

Recognition would not normally be thought of an involving reflection and comparison; but some simple examples illustrate that, in some wide sense of the term "reflection", reflection is a pre-requisite of recognition. A common enough, and intuitively plausible, model for recognition is that I just see an object and recognise it as a spade. Of course, if its half-hidden by undergrowth, I may need to consider whether or not it really is a spade : but often I won't.

While it is certainly the case that no overt consideration will be involved in most cases of recognising a thing as of kind K, or of recognising a thing as a K, we must not be misled into viewing recognition (perception, even) as a passive process : that is, as the passive reception of sense-impressions. A sense-impression alone cannot tell me (say) that what I'm looking at is a table. At best, I might know I was having the impression of a brown patch. To be seeing a table is to subsume the impression under a concept. (If we talked of my knowing I was seeing a table, we'd be re-emphasising the connections with epistemological issues.)

The suggestion of a 'pure' unconceptualised sense-impression is an unintelligible one, on reflection, since even knowing that I was having the impression of a brown patch requires concepts such as shape and colour. Yet it might seem that some simpler perceptual claim could escape this "restriction" of being brought under concepts. But this is not so. Even a statement such as "This is equal in length to that" is not one where we can just say: "Open your eyes and you'll be able to use the word "equal"". What is required is not just looking and making a noise. We need to compare this case with other cases, for example where they are end to end here and not here. (c.f. V.L. p.89)

At this point we are again emphasising the similarities between proving and learning : that I can go about proving such-and-such to someone who understands about that kind of thing in a way not so very dissimilar to the way I'd teach someone about that kind of thing. And, as a conclusion, I suggested that even questions of equality of length will call for reflection. (c.f. V.L. p.91)

A creature that has the best eyesight (Wisdom's example is a parrot) and views the two sticks in the best sort of light may not know that they are of equal length. And even if it utters the words, or better the sounds, "These are of equal length" we may not accept that it genuinely knows. In situations where it doesn't even do that, or something like that, what can we mean by claiming that it sees or knows that the sticks are of equal length? (Here again is the tie-in with verification : that is, with epistemological questions.)

We are considering how we could come to know that the creature knew, and that surely has connections with how any creature could come to know that two sticks were of equal length. Now we might imagine it being trained to do this. (Some very elaborate training would no doubt be required, but that is a difficulty we can skip over.) But here the creature would be able to demonstrate that it knew. It might select objects of the same length in other contexts, and have a sign which it could give when it recognised objects as being of different lengths. And we can even imagine it making the odd mistake, which its handler would correct and explain in some way.

What I am attempting to do here is to suggest that there might indeed be situations were we would be justified in saying that (to keep with Wisdom's example) a parrot knew that two sticks were of equal length. But that these would be just those cases where the parrot could demonstrate this knowledge in a variety of circumstances. That is, where the parrot could compare the case before him with a variety of other cases. Here we would be quite justified in claiming such knowledge for the parrot. But this justification, or one very similar, would be required for claiming that a particular person had a group of such-and-such a concept. And both would allow for defence of our claims that such-and-such was of kind K, or that two sticks were of equal length, or whatever. To repeat, the only (possible) proof that a person recognised an object would depend on 'how he could go on' : whether, for example, he could produce the right word or action on the right occasion. (c.f.V.L. p.59, p.60)

But here we are pre-supposing some tie-up between how things are, and how we can find out that they are like that. That is, we are claiming some sort of relation between the logic of such claims and their epistemology. And this brings us back to the title of this work.

Even though it is a digression, something must be said on this point. Well, what arguments might be offered for some sort of connection here? In essence, the argument is that to deny any kind of tie-up is to leave yourself prey to various

mentalist legends.   Just how can we ever know anything about
what a person recognises as what, if in no case at all is his
behaviour including his verbal behaviour any sort of evidence
that he recognises this as of kind K - as, say, a parrot or of
the same length, or coloured brown?   If we acknowledge that in
some cases some bits of behaviour have a role not so very different
from evidence (18) here, we have acknowledged the basis for the
logic/epistemology tie-up.

This is far too complex an issue to be gone into here, but
it does seem odd to claim that such-and-such is in no way open to
perception, verification or any such, and yet is still present.
Strawson (19) has glorified that piece of common sense with the
title "Principle of Significance":-

> If we wish to employ a concept in a certain way, but are
> unable to specify the kind of experience - situation to
> which the concept, used in that way, would apply, then
> we are not really envisaging any legitimate use of that
> concept at all.   (p.16)

To specify the kind of experience-situation to which a concept
will apply is to allow that we have some kind of verificatory
access to that concept.

This familiar point can be put in terms of a particularly
appropriate example (20).   We can imagine someone becoming an
extremely famous and influential art-critic even though he in no
way appreciated the arts.   He does this by, for example, using
vis-a-vis one work terms and expressions he has heard employed in
relation to another work.   That is to say, he exhibits understanding-behaviour but does not genuinely understand.   (All
additional details can be supplied to this example.)   Yet clearly
the critic can only do this because, in some cases, people do
genuinely understand at times when they are exhibiting understanding-behaviour.   Otherwise, how could this behaviour be called
"understanding-behaviour" at all?   How could its connections with

---

(18) This hedging is to take into account the fact that my own
     (Wittgensteinian) solution to the problem of 'other minds'
     rests on denying that this is actually evidence at all, but
     instead insists that it has a criterial role.   On this
     contrast, see Best Expression in Movement and the Arts
     Lepus (1974) p.93.

(19) Strawson The Bounds of Sense Methuen (1966)

(20) c.f. Jones Philosophy and the Novel OUP (1975) pp. 201-3,
     where this example is treated in some more detail, although
     for a slightly different purpose.

understanding be seen or established? Hence it is impossible
('logically impossible') that all understanders or all critics
should be like this man. (Although the cynical might think that
all professional critics were.) And to accept such a position
is to acknowledge some tie-up between so-and-so's state of mind
and our knowledge of his state of mind.

Now this emphasis on the verification of claims to know, or
generally on how we could know that so-and-so knows such-and-
such, will doubtless be a red flag to much philosophical bull.
Does it really rest on the (discredited) verification principle?
An example may help to answer that question (21). In order
that we disagree about which witch put the spell on you, it is
clear that we must agree about what was done and roughly how it
was done. We have in fact to agree on what shows that there
are witches, and on what shows that the evil which befall you is
witch-caused. If we do not, it is hard to see that we can begin
to disagree as to which witch is the guilty party. But to agree
on what shows that there are witches, etc. is to agree, in some
way, as to the verification (or falsification) of statements like
"There are witches". What this case stresses is the insight on
which the verification principle was erected : that there are
situations where how a statement is known to be true, or how it
is falsified, is a useful piece of information.

But all this is a digression. We were discussing how our
perception and recognition of things as of kind K was grounded
in reflection, and hence in the case-by-case procedure. Part of
what we'd been saying was that recognition will involve the
bringing under concepts of one's 'impressions', to put the point
rather tendentiously. To talk of perceiving taking place under
concepts is to invoke some kind of manifold (to use Wisdom's
phrase) within which what is perceived is recognised : that is,
placed or located. And how could such concepts or manifolds be
acquired? A moments reflection should make it clear that these
concepts will chiefly be acquired in, or through, incidents :
that is, in particular cases. Thus to talk of perception as
"under concepts" is to pre-suppose implicit comparison with
other objects which fall under the same concept. Or, as Wisdom
might put the same point, with objects close by in the manifold.

In addition, there are connections with other problems
previously discussed. To talk in terms of perception under

---

(21) Example drawn from Bambrough Conflict and the Scope of
Reason University of Hull (1974) p.9. A more complete
answer would display the verificationist element in a
Constructivist account of meaning.

concept is, among other things, to emphasise what has so far merely been implied : that the justification of statements such as "This is of kind K" is not really helped by the provision of a definition of K. Suppose I say : "This is a chair". In answer to your question "How do you know?", I need to point out both that I am in a good position to see it clearly and that I know what chairs are like (22), if I am to deal adequately with your question. That is, I assert both my expertise and the clarity of my perceptual field : and to assert my expertise in this way is to assert that I can correctly apply those concepts under which I am perceiving.

Now suppose that you have a definition of the term "chair". To take an extreme example, let it be : "object for sitting on". (Its absurdity as a definition of "chair" is beside the point here.) So that when I've said that this is a chair, you check up by asking if its an object for sitting on. If I say that it is indeed an object for sitting on, it may appear that you have actually checked my claim. Or if I reply that it is an object for sitting on when you ask how I know it is a chair, it may appear to you that I have justified my claim that it is a chair. Not so. I am still predicating a general term, though now a more complex one, of a particular case. There is no reason to suppose that I am more or less likely to have made a mistake in the second than in the first of my judgements. I can only use such-and-such, here the definition, as a yardstick if my yardstick itself, which is my independent guarantee, is obvious. And clearly it will not be obvious in any case like this. Throughout this discussion my grasp of the concepts, for example "chair", must, in a fairly clear sense, antedate my application of those concepts.

Some thinkers find it difficult to accept that this must be so. And particularly since its mechanism seems very far from clear. It is at this point that we should realise (again) the importance of what Wittgenstein called "a form of life", for a part of what it means to say that so-and-so grows up within a particular form of life is that he 'learns' to grasp certain concepts and certain conceptual connections. We might say that he takes them in with his mother's milk. Within a form of life, people have just those shared reactions and convictions, beliefs and disbeliefs etc. required for understanding. This issue has been mentioned before (Ch.2, this ch.), and recurs throughout this work : but no closer specification of the scope of the expression "form of life" is offered.

---

(22) c.f. Austin "Other Minds" reprinted in his Philosophical Papers OUP (1961) on this point.

What is argued is that within a form of life a certain amount of shared understanding can be taken for granted. And our shared understanding amounts, we might say, to shared manifolds. But there are dangers even in this form of words. For instance, Wisdom says:-

> You might be tempted to say that a person's grasp of a manifold is complete when he's caught every affinity and every difference - but of course this doesn't happen.

This claim of Wisdom's has a Realist sound to it (23). It seems that just so many connections etc. make up a manifold, and to know that manifold completely is to mark them all. Yet this is claimed as impossible. Are there just <u>too many</u> connections, similarities etc. for anyone to know or mark them all? And if not, why is it that a complete grasp of a manifold is impossible?

The answer lies in the fact that anyone's grasp of a concept will, in principle, allow for additional richness. I may be an expert in such-and-such, and this will amount (crudely) to my being able to draw a vast number of revealing comparisons. Yet someone can always present me with <u>another</u> comparison, another way of looking at X, a way which exposes another aspect of X to my view. Bambrough (24) makes the point with the following example:-

> Air travel has reduced the size of the earth, but has also given us a sharper view of its vastness.
> (Bambrough p.284)

There was a time when deserts, etc. seemed infinite. Now we can <u>see</u> that they are not : but this makes us aware of just how big they are. The expert geographer of the last century could not have had <u>quite</u> this sense of both the vastness and the smallness of the desert, although he may have had another version of it. Even today many geographers of note will not have had this personal experience of the <u>size</u> of deserts. Perhaps it would alter their grasp or understanding of deserts if they were to experience it. Again, if they were compelled to cross the desert on a camel, this too might affect their understanding of deserts and their size.

---

(23) For a characterisation of Realism as an account of meaning, see Hacker <u>Insight and Illusion</u> OUP (1972).

(24) Bambrough "Literature and Philosophy" in Bambrough ed. <u>Wisdom : 12 Essays</u> Blackwell (1974).

And both these methods of transportation might suggest
additional comparisons to the geographers. As Bambrough
continues:-

> And yet somebody who crosses the great plain or the
> unlimited desert, whether in a comet or a train or a
> stage-coach, may know that he is also to be compared
> with the fly on the window pane, the microbe on the
> speck of dust. There is not here a choice of
> alternative aspects, but two slides in the same lantern-
> lecture, and if you miss one of them you have not seen
> the whole show or heard the whole story. Or rather ......
> there is not and could not be a whole story, but that means
> there is always more and more to learn and not that
> nothing can be known.   (Bambrough pp.284-5)

Once we accept that our concepts and our understanding are always
revisible in this way, that new comparisons and new similarities
may always come to our attention, we can see why the whole of a
manifold cannot possibly be known. Not, as might be suggested
by the form of words, because some features remain hidden; but
because, as Bambrough put it:-

> . . . . there is not and could not be a whole story.

And once we have recognised that fact we have banished the
apparent Realism from Wisdom's claim. No longer do we appear
to be offering a picture where there are N number of features
which could, in principle, be known although this may be
practically impossible. Now our picture is of an infinite
number of possible comparisons any of which might shed light on
the concept in question.

Since the aim of this chapter has been general discussion
of the case-by-case procedure, any summary would be inappropriate.
One point remains to be made, however. As Wisdom remarks (V.L.
p.78), an understanding that all reasoning in the end comes down
to the case-by-case procedure is not a proof that any case-by-
case procedure is a good procedure. All it shows is that a
piece of reasoning by the comparison of cases is not bad, or
defective, reasoning by virtue of being case-by-case. If we are
offered a new freedom in what counts as reasoning, we are also
given new responsibilities. No longer can we glibly offer case-
by-case procedures in the certain hope that they will be dismissed
from the pantheon of reasoning.

This point can be seen as stressing that the case-by-case procedure is not to be taken as a <u>method,</u> or as a recipe, for getting right answers, as for example the method of fluxions (the differential and integral calculi) is. With the method of fluxions, if the operations are performed correctly, correct results are yielded. The same cannot be said of the case-by-case procedure, for the comparison of cases can lead away from the crucial similarities, towards others. The reasoning which will, perhaps, lead us to recognise the asymmetrical logic of some psychological expressions is just the reasoning which leads <u>the sceptics</u> to an insoluable 'other minds' problem. Hence our claims for the values of the case-by-case procedure also emphasise its liabilities : that it does not infallibly produce answers, and that it must be carefully handled.

The arguments in Chapter Two led us to a logical model for reasoning on which some cases were <u>beyond</u> doubt, for us; and hence to the conclusion that we could ground our judgements of other works of art on our 'judgements' of those works.   And these would be central cases in a case-by-case procedure to establish that such-and-such was a work of art.   This appears to place such cases <u>above</u> comment : and one way in which it might seem that these cases acquire their 'indubitable' status would be as paradigms.   To see that this is <u>not</u> what is intended, it is useful to begin in a roundabout way, by a consideration of a modern 'definition' of "art" (1):-

A work of art in the classificatory sense is (1) an artifact (2) a set of the aspects of which has had conferred upon it the status of candidate for appreciation by some person or persons acting on behalf of a certain social institution (the art world).

George Dickie's definition of "art" will doubtless concern, amuse, infuriate and interest philosophers (to mention but <u>some</u> of my reactions) for some time to come.   It is relevant here to consider <u>one</u> of its features, namely artifactuality" (the requirement that works of art be artifacts, in some sense.) And this only as a way of introducing familiar methodological points.   (The other feature receives <u>some</u> discussion in Ch.6.)

In response to the apparent counter-example to his definition of a piece of driftwood taken as art, as offered by Weitz (2), Dickie has two lines of argument.   The first is to claim that Weitz has failed to show that this driftwood is art in a classificatory rather than an evaluative sense (3).   As Dickie amits, the very best verdict he can hope for from <u>this</u> argument is 'not proven'; so we need not concern ourselves with it directly (4).

---

(1) From Dickie <u>Art and the Aesthetic</u> Cornell U.P. (1974) p.34

(2) Weitz "The role of theory in aesthetics" reprinted in
    Margolis <u>ed</u>. <u>Philosophy Looks at the Arts</u> Scribners (1962)
    p.57.

(3) See Dickie p.24.

(4) However, if the methodological points hinted at here, and
    made more clearly elsewhere (See Ch.2, Ch.3, Ch.7) are
    right they should do something to cast doubt on the whole
    classificatory/evaluative distinction.

Dickie's other line derives from a paper by Richard
Sclafani (5), which he explains as follows:-

> He begins by comparing a paradigm work of art, Brancusi's
> <u>Bird in Space</u>, with a piece of driftwood which looks very
> much like it. Sclafani says that it seems natural to
> say of the driftwood that it is a work of art and that
> we do so because it has so many properties in common with
> the Brancusi piece. He then asks us to reflect on our
> characterisation of the driftwood and the <u>direction</u> it
> has taken. We say the driftwood is art because of its
> resemblance to some paradigm work of art or because the
> driftwood shares properties with the several paradigm
> works of art. The paradigm works of art are of course
> always artifacts; the direction of our move is from
> paradigmatic (artifactual) works of art to non-artifactual
> "art". Sclafani quite correctly takes this to indicate
> that there is a primary, paradigmatic sense of "work of
> art" (my classificatory sense) and a derivative or
> secondary sense into which the "driftwood cases" fall.
> Weitz is right in a way in saying that the driftwood is
> art, but wrong in concluding that artifactuality is
> unnecessary for (the primary sense of) art.
>
> There are then at least three distinct senses of
> "work of art" : the primary classificatory sense, the
> secondary or derivative, and the evaluative . . . .
> (Dickie p.25)

The direction of this 'direction' argument is (crudely) this :
that the <u>paradigm</u> works exemplify "art" in the primary sense and
works which are accepted by comparison with them exemplify "art"
in derivative senses of the term. It is important to recognise
here that Sclafani and Dickie do take these works as exemplars
of <u>new</u> senses of the term "art", rather than instantiations of
the <u>old</u> sense.

A problem with this argument is that it seems to cut both
ways, and with a vengeance. First let us imagine a society
where artists regularly 'exhibited' driftwood as art, and only
occasionally were pieces of a more traditional type of sculpture,
or of painting, seen within this community. Now the children
of such a society would be in a strange position vis-a-vis
Brancusi's <u>Bird in Space</u>. They'd see it <u>as art</u> by comparison
with what they'd grown up to accept as art : that is, the driftwood. So their primary sense of the term "art" <u>wouldn't</u> be an
artifactual one.

---

(5) Sclafani "'Art' and Artifactuality" <u>Southwestern Jnl. of
Philosophy</u> Fall 1970. We are considering Dickie's sketch of
Sclafani's argument.

One point must be made, rather as an aside. Dickie assumes that the driftwood is left in situ. He feels that if it is moved, artifactuality is 'conferred' upon it. (Dickie p.45). For the purpose of the argument here, we can concede this point, to take up a variant of it later (in Ch.6). However, with Blizek (6), I find it hard to accept this move of Dickie's as anything but an attempt to save the requirement for artifactuality at the expense of content : for now "artifactual" will be logically welded to the term "art", since the kind of artifactuality in question will (for Dickie) have become a special art type.

To continue, we recognise the example of the 'driftwood art' society just presented as highly fanciful : but it should be brought to earth by our recognition (in Ch.3) of the place of the case-by-case procedure at the roots of reasoning in aesthetics (and elsewhere). So how do we come to accept Brancusi's Bird in Space as art? The case for Brancusi cannot be open and shut, for it was (perhaps) another work of Brancusi, Bird in Flight, which was initially refused entry into the U.S.A. as a work of art on the grounds that it bore no resemblance to a bird. "What hunter", one customs official asked, "would want to shoot a bird like that?" (7). For Wisdom, and for us, the process of coming to accept the Brancusi as art is clear, and does resemble the one that Dickie suggests : we come to accept the Brancusi by a comparison of the case in question with other cases.

To employ again a favourite phrase of Wisdom's, what we are trying to do with the Brancusi is to locate this work within the aesthetic manifold : and (as suggested in Ch.2, Ch.3) that requires a comparison of cases. For, as was said, to know the 'nature' of something is to know how it resembles, and how it differs from other things : that is, to know what the thing in question is like (where this idiom is taken literally.) And Dickie ought, perhaps, to accept such a model. After all, it was by a comparison of cases that he attempted to explain the driftwood's being accepted as art.

Given these conclusions, we are in a position not so far removed from that suggested by the earlier (fanciful) example. To establish Bird in Space as art requires something like comparison with, among others, say Rodin's Age of Bronze.

---

(6) Blizek "An institutional theory of art" B.J.A. 1973.

(7) Story from Barrett "Are Bad Works of Art 'Works of Art'?" in Vesey ed. Philosophy and the Arts Royal Inst. of Philosophy Lectures Vol.6. 1971-72 Macmillan (1973) p.186.

If we consider the direction of this argument, we are surely forced by parity of Sclafani's reasoning to postulate further senses of the term "work of art". For just as before, a work is compared with a paradigm in order that it be accepted as art. The pardigm exemplifies "art" in one sense and, as in their driftwood case, the other work exemplifies "art" in some other sense. And this procedure will apply to our new paradigm too. Age of Bronze must in turn be 'justified' by reference to, say, Michelangelo's David, and no doubt others; and hence we have yet another sense of "work of art" and so on endlessly. (In my wicked imagination I see David being accepted as art by a comparison with the original piece of driftwood.) And, in this situation, we are not far from a bitter acquaintance with that metaphor of Neurath which Quine (8) offers us so regularly: that we cannot replace all the planks of a ship at sea at once.

Having followed a line of his argument, perhaps Dickie's error can now be diagnosed, for what we have been trying to suggest is that no cases can reasonly be taken as paradigms of what it is to be art. Of course, we won't usually argue about Michelangelo or Rodin. But their status might be challenged, just as Bell challenged (and overthrew) some of the academic painters of his day. (In fact the point is more general. There may be nothing paradigmatic about the instances in connection with which we learn most words.)

As was mentioned, Dickie can be seen as having recognised that the procedure which allows the driftwood to be accepted as art is essentially a comparative one : but without having recognised that, this being so, the procedure which admits the Brancusi and others might, and I'd say must, also be comparative. Thus it follows that every comparison cannot possibly yield a new sense of the term "art". For the status of every work is established by comparison. Since he perhaps hasn't noticed that, in the last analysis, all reasoning in aesthetics rests on the case-by-case procedure, he attempts to evade the consequence of every case being challengable by recourse to paradigms. But this move is simply not available. For when we present our 'paradigms', we are still dealing with cases all of which are challengable in principle.

So how can we begin our direct comparison of cases if no cases are above 'assault'? How can we find any cases which definitely are art? And this result extends beyond aesthetics, of course. As Wisdom puts it:-

---

(8) See, for example, Quine From a logical point of view Harper Row (1953) p.79, and Quine, Word and Object M.I.T. (1960) p.124.

. . . . Then there's another matter. When he's
endeavouring to prove "This is a case of K" - of
greyhound, tapir, goat, thirty-six glasses, morally
wrong, good scientific evidence - one might ask,
"And how does he know with regard to the other cases
that they are cases of K?" I mean, when he supports
the statement "This is K", how does he know what to
refer to "Isn't this K?" and "Isn't this K?" and so on?

(<u>V.L</u>. p.132)

It might even be claimed that we have some kind of "implicit"
definition at work here : that we <u>must</u> have one in order that we
recognise the cases of kind K <u>as</u> cases of K.   But why <u>must</u> we?
It is <u>assumed</u> by such a line that a definition of K is required
in order that we understand K : and this pernicious assumption
was attacked earlier.   (Ch.2, Ch.3).

Yet there <u>may</u> be one sense in which we have an "implicit"
definition at work here, rather in the way in which a judge might
be said to have an "implicit" sentencing policy.   It is his
biographer who finds certain similarities between all the judgements the late judge made, and all the sentences he gave.
The judge himself neither had nor needed this ("implicit")
sentencing policy.   He merely made judgements on the basis of
the cases as he found them, marking similarities with previous
cases, and the like.   The biographer, we might say, <u>constructs</u>
the sentencing policy from the sentences.   And if the judge is
not called upon to pronounce any more sentences after the
biography is written (which won't occur if, for example, he's
dead), the biographer may well be right.   But this emphasises
why such "implicit" definitions of "art" are of no use to us :
they must be constructed <u>after</u>, and <u>from</u>, our judgements as to
what is and what is not art.   <u>We</u> do not have any "implicit"
definitions, we might say; which does not mean that someone
might not find similarities within our judgements.   The point is
that we are not <u>following</u> this 'definition" so much as <u>creating</u>
it.   For we are not <u>bound</u> by such a 'definition' to act or
judge in a particular way in the future.   So talk of "implicit"
definitions now is beside the point.

To return to the art case, there does seem to be a sense
in which certain works 'stand firm' for me.   <u>From</u> these works
my judgements of other works are rendered intelligible.   And I
myself compare and contrast these particular cases with others.
Yet how can this be?   How can any works have this special status?

What has been done so far is to set up an obvious and
tempting counter-example to my argument, which runs roughly as
follows : we point to the work of certain critics and say,
"But here you are talking of judging etc. those very same works

which, as 'particular cases', were placed above judgement."
And the general diversity of critical judgement might seem to
support this line. For if, say, Picasso's "Guernica" is <u>above</u>
criticism or comment, as one of this corpus of works which stands
firm, how can there be disagreement about its status? Surely if
(the line of argument might go) "Guernica" is, to put it crudely,
the kind of thing by reference to which we learn what the term
"work of art" <u>means</u>, how can there <u>then</u> be dispute as to whether
or not "Guernica" is a work of art? And yet critics do just
that.

    To this point, one thing may be said immediately : that only
infrequently would we employ a statement like '"Guernica" is a
work of art', or 'This is a work of art'. What could be the <u>use</u>
of such statements? Well, one such case might be when explaining the use of the expression "work of art". As Rhees (9)
suggests, one way (the only way?) would be:-

    . . . . to give a range of examples of works which
we should all call art. (p.136)

And even this would be a peculiar way of doing it. After all,
so much is being left out. As Diffey (10) says, we do not:-

    . . . . go about the world just predicating it (the
term "work of art") of objects . . . . (p.114)

Diffey maintains, and surely correctly, that "work of art" is
generally a subject-term, not a predicate, in our 'language of
aesthetics' : and that only philosophers are interested in <u>just</u>
using statements like "this is a work of art". (This recalls
Wittgenstein's remark in <u>On Certainty</u> § 467 (p.61) that a man
who says "that is a tree" is a philosopher rather than a madman).
So what <u>will</u> be the use of this expression? Certainly not, and
this is the important point, to tell us anything about the
object in question, the 351.0 cm by 782.5 cm tempera on canvas
'object' in the case of Picasso's "Guernica" : although it will,
for example, rule out the objects being appraised primarily
functionally (c.f. Ch.5, Ch.7). For such a 'naming' ceremony
only has a point when I know everything, or many things, about
the object except its name.

_____

(9) Rhees "Art and Philosophy" in his <u>Without Answers</u> R.K.P.
    (1969)

(10) Diffey "Essentialism and the definition of 'Art'" <u>BJA</u> 1973.

However, our account is closely related to Wittgenstein's discussion of the status of <u>some</u> 'remarks' in my picture of the world.   For example, when he (11) asks:-

> Why is there no doubt that I am called L.W.?   It does not seem at all like something that one could establish at once beyond doubt.   One would not think of it as one of the indubitable truths.

The question is : what could doubt <u>amount to</u> in such a case? Let us ignore points about being called so-and-so, but that not being your name : which would be open to empirical confirmation. Now what <u>room</u> is left for the doubt?   Only that I've forgotten my name, or 'lost' it (like an amnesiac), or been misinformed all my life.   Or, like Shenandoah, I might have no idea.   But all these grounds for doubt rest on a contrast between what my name <u>is</u> ("really") and what I might <u>think</u> it is, but be wrong : and this contrast pre-supposes that there generally are right answers, even if they are not given.   (This is simple stuff but worth rehearsing to get our <u>foundations</u> straighter.)

Now this idea of "getting it right" in the name case isn't intelligible if every case is <u>always</u> up for grabs.   To see this we need only consider the difference between (roughly) following a rule and making a decision each time (12).   Any new decision can't be right or wrong in the way that following or not following a rule can, for by what standards could it be judged? Well, if every case isn't always up for grabs, what alternatives can be offered?

I offer four fairly plausible ones.   No doubt others <u>might</u> be defended, but these allow me to consider the points I see as salient : and give guidelines against other options.   They are:-

(a) That some particular cases are exempt from doubt, in any circumstances : for example, as paradigms.

(b) That in some circumstances, for example, majority agreement, <u>every</u> case is exempt.

(c) That particular cases are exempt in particular circumstances.

---

(11) Wittgenstein <u>On Certainty</u> Blackwell (1969) § 470.

(12) The point is based on ideas in Rhees "Can there be a private language?" reprinted in his <u>Discussions on Wittgenstein</u> RKP (1970)

(d) That <u>some</u> cases, though not any in particular are
exempt in some circumstances, although (again)
not any in particular.

What would these amount to for the foundations of our aesthetic
judgements?

We can almost take option (a) and option (c) together.
Option (a) might be taken as the claim that, for instance, some
particular class of works of art always ground our judgements.
And this view is not merely very like the view of Dickie's
already dismissed, it is also prima facie implausible. We ask,
"in <u>which</u> ones?" And we have already given the answer "none"
to that question. Option (c) has a little more to be said for
it. As Terry Diffey (13) has pointed out, visitors to the
Sistine chapel won't <u>usually</u> need to decide or guess that the
paintings of Michelangelo are art. That seems long since
settled. Indeed, these are the kind of things we might use to
explain the term "art". But (to again follow Diffey) <u>someone</u>,
and his example is the Tolstoi of <u>What is Art?</u>, might be
determined to deny what had appeared to be established 'fact'.
Indeed the championing of Cezanne by Bell might be mentioned
again in this context, for Bell also claimed that the (accepted)
academic painters of his day <u>weren't</u> painting works of art.
Considerations of this kind, and the more general ones advanced
earlier (Ch.3) against the certainty of any case, lead me to
reject option (a) and option(c). No case can stand apart from
others as absolutely above question.

Option (b) represents one common interpretation of
Wittgenstein's position (14), to the effect that right answers
must generally be given in order that practices like, to take
a popular example, promise-keeping by intelligible. By parity
of reasoning, in the name case, answers to questions about my
name must generally be right. Or what are generally picked out
as works of art must be art, if that notion is to have application.

The problem about such a line, which seems to claim that in
every case <u>whatever</u> coincides with the majority view will be the
correct one, is that while it is doubtlessly true if taken as a

---

(13) Diffey "The Republic of Art" <u>BJA</u> 1969.

(14) c.f.,for example, Malcolm <u>Knowledge and Certainty</u> Prentice-
Hall (1963) p.195, where the phrase "overwhelming
agreement" occurs.

statistical generalisation, that does not seem adequate (15).
For surely the majority <u>can</u> be wrong. Indeed the contrast
between what the majority think and how it actually is would not
be intelligible if this were not so. Only if there are standards
of right and wrong can the majority be wrong. But how are these
"standards" to be understood? How are we to know what "wrong"
amounts to? It might be argued that practices such as promise-
keeping could not have come about <u>without</u> majority agreement.
This might be psychologically interesting, but hardly philosophic-
ally. In particular, it is no reason why the "standards" should
be provided by majority agreement.

It is not really that the majority <u>agree</u> that such-and-such
is the case, if we think of this in terms of their deciding such-
and-such. A more accurate picture would be that offered by
Wittgenstein (16) in terms of "agreement in judgements". To
repeat an earlier formulation, we grow up accepting certain
things. (c.f. Ch.2, Ch.3). We accept such-and-such as an
application of, to take the appropriate example, the concept
"art". We know what it is, to put the point crudely, to call
something "art". Of course, this also allows us to recognise
(and rule out) certain misapplications of the concept too!

But more than this, doesn't option (d) reflect a more
realistic picture than option (b) of what it is to be, or to
provide, a standard? Perhaps it has not been sufficiently
emphasised that this is the role of <u>all</u> the options. Consider
the following comment of Beardsmore (17) (on morality):-

> Concepts like honesty, chastity and integrity are not
> techniques for enabling us to do something, but rather
> the standard by which we judge what we ourselves and
> others do. They are not principles for attaining the
> good life, but decide what the good life is. (p.181)

Reflection on how we could possibly come to understand, or acquire,
these crucial moral concepts, which could only be through
particular cases of honesty etc., should clarify our position.
In aesthetics, then, our standards will (at least partly) have to
be given by reference to certain works; that is, to particular
cases. And, of course, it is in connection with such cases that
we will have learnt what art is. But they will "decide" what it
is to be a work of art, in just the way that the moral concepts

---

(15) Criticism of pragmatic theories of truth often start from
here, c.f. Ayer <u>The Origins of Pragmatism</u> Macmillan (1968)
p.35 ff. for example.

(16) Wittgenstein <u>Philosophical Investigations</u> Blackwell (1953)
§ 242.

(17) Beardsmore "Consequences and Moral Worth" Analysis 1969.

that Beardsmore mentions, again rooted in cases, determine what
the good life is (18).

This account makes plain why the status of Michelangelo's
paintings usually isn't in doubt : we have grown up with them as
(crudely) pardigms of what it is to be art. But, of course,
this formulation is too crude : or rather may be misinterpreted
as an avowal of option (a) or option (c). The cases are not
paradigms, but can serve for a time in a way not so radically
different from paradigms (19). Hence option (d) leaves our
notion of a standard very much where it intuitively is. So
that I can use (almost) any work of art in a case-by-case
procedure to, say, justify the inclusion of another work within
the class of works of art. As Wittgenstein (20) puts the point:-

. . . . the same proposition may be treated at one time
as something to test by experience, at another as a rule
for testing.

In this context it seems appropriate to recall the extended
music example (Ch.2) where we used this technique in attempting
to justify "4 minutes 33 seconds", or rather to present a logical
model of that being attempted : and to reiterate that art-critics
too seem to use this kind of procedure.

When we accept this kind of picture of those works which
"stand firm for me", we might perhaps again be tempted to attempt
a definition of "art" in terms of those cases. Yet such a
definition would still be open either to falsification, for these
works are not paradigms and hence their art-status is challengable,
or to the charge of emptiness or circularity. And in some ways,
we would actually be in a worse position than the earlier writers
who "defined" art. To see why, let us consider an example.
Bell's (21) claim that art was "significant form" is clearly
subject to one or other of the refutations mentioned above.

---

(18) c.f. Newell The Concept of Philosophy Methuen (1967)
    pp. 77-8 for some discussion of the appeal to instances.

(19) Diffey in correspondence suggested calling them "temporary
    paradigms"; which catches the right spirit.

(20) Wittgenstein On Certainty Blackwell (1969) § 98.

(21) Bell Art Arrow Books (1961) p.6.

Either we can point to examples which are clearly art even though they lack "significant form", or "significant form" is specified in terms of art, with the attendant lack of content to the claim (22). Bell's 'definition' may be an ideal stalking-horse for writers on aesthetics, but its importance is far wider than that. To see why, we must begin to consider the circumstances within which Bell made his claim.

Let us repeat the details of the earlier example (23). Bell felt that the work of the academic painters of his day was poor compared to that of Cezanne. But their status was high and Cezanne's low. Bell was able to claim that Cezanne's art had something crucial which the works of the academic painters lacked. And this "something" was significant form. With this tool Bell was able to instate Cezanne as the great painter he, Bell, had always known him to be. Thus the slogan that the essence of art is significant form becomes intelligible if we view it as a slogan for reform. Bell can profitably be seen not as trying to define art, but as attempting to direct our attention to certain features of the art. That is, as attempting to introduce a new way of looking at art.

It is tempting to dismiss Bell's work as worthless, simply because his attempt at defining "art" is doomed to fail, and so it does. What he says is certainly inadequate if viewed in this way, for it does not do justice to the richness and complexity of art. But to dismiss his view is to fail to do justice to its richness and complexity. For Bell's claim does illuminate : it allows us to see certain works, for example those of Cezanne, in a different light. So we see it more clearly if we view the claim on a helpful/unhelpful scale, rather than a true/false scale.

By contrast, any definition of art which we construct by looking at what was accepted as art in the past (either by us or by others) would not be helpful in this way. Since it is to built up in this fashion, it is inevitable that such a "definition" would be a complex, highly qualified statement. And it would be foolish to assume that much illumination could come from something so long and involved. Hence it would not

---

(22) c.f. Lake "Irrefutability of Two Aesthetic Theories" in Elton ed. Aesthetics and Languages Blackwell (1970)

(23) Information drawn from Kennick "Does traditional aesthetics rest on a mistake?" in Barrett ed. Collected Papers on Aesthetics Blackwell (1965) p.10.

score highly on the true/false scale. Of course, if we'd made no mistake, it would not be falsifiable by considerion of any <u>previous</u> works of art : but it certainly would, in principle, be falsifiable by consideration of works by contemporary or future artists. Hence the idea of constructing a definition of art in this way is not merely a pipe-dream in terms of the impossibly endless task involved, but also because the definition would lack the virtues of earlier "definitions", which could at least be illuminating.

To sum up so far, we have seen how claims to ground our aesthetic judgements and our reasoning in aesthetics on paradigm cases were inadequate. No cases could have this 'paradigm' status, and not merely because there were none to be found in practice. It was in principle always possible to question the art-status of any works. We attempted to clarify just how this could be so, and how works could <u>both</u> stand firm for me and <u>still</u> be open to challenges to their art-status. That is, how they could be "temporary paradigms". So far, we might say, so good.

Yet there are numerous difficulties over the relationship of those cases we accept as art to those cases we discuss to discover if we can see them as art, using our case-by-case procedures. To present a problem autobiographically (24), on the walls of the room in which I am sitting are two paintings executed by college students, studying subjects other than art, during class time. Are these two works of art, or not? Of course, we are not aiming to answer that question, but merely to feel the temptations it embodies. For it <u>is</u>, I hope, clear that not <u>all</u> the work produced in this student art class is to be properly called "art". (I have the word of the staff concerned for this.) Yet what general differences are there between what are clearly non-art works and the two paintings on my wall? They were produced in very similar situations, with similar guidance etc. And with similar intentions, in so far as it makes sense to talk in those terms. At the other end, the works of local artists, exhibited in the local gallery, share a great many features with the two paintings on my wall, as well as with the Hockney's and Spencer's in the same gallery. If the student paintings became 'non-art', aren't we on a very slippery slope vis-a-vis the works of the local artists? Our argument for the student paintings <u>not</u> being art seems to have the unacceptable consequence that the work of these local artists isn't art either. But, as Wisdom said of a similar case:-

---

(24) My thought on this issue was considerably aided by frequent
    discussions of related points with Margaret-Mary Preece,
    to whom my thanks are due.

> Our trouble seems to be that we cannot see anything
> wrong with the reasoning used to support these
> claims. (V.L. pp. 218-9)

That is, we are marking similarities between the works under
consideration and genuine non-art cases.   (The contrast between
evaluative and classificatory senses of the term "art" might be
flourished here.   Against it, see Ch.2, Ch.7.)

In part, no doubt the role of students' futures needs to be
considered, even though at the moment it does not seem to be a
case of 'good or bad'.   If they go on to become (recognised as)
great artists, even their "juvenilia" might be considered art.
This is certainly true of the "early" works of David Hockney,
and of Eliot's undergraduate poetry.   So there does seem to be
a mechanism by which what the students go on to do can be
relevant here.

But it also seems that these works should be art <u>now</u> if they
are to be art at all, in rather the way we'd say that Van Gogh
produced works of art long before the value of his painting was
recognised.   Works can be art before the public acknowledges
them as such.   (Here too those paintings of Francis Bacon which
he destroys as soon as he has finished them have their place.
For they are, arguably, works of art which <u>never</u> achieve public
acclaim.)   What must be here recognised is that this simply <u>is</u>
a genuine borderline case.   The student paintings simply do
have a number of similarities and a number of dissimilarities
with the paintings of Picasso.   Whatever 'decision' is arrived
at, it seems to carry with it unacceptable consequences.   If
we allow that these student paintings are art, why aren't the
other student paintings?   And if we <u>deny</u> that they are art, how
can the local artists' work be art?   The answer here <u>must</u> be in
terms of some boundary being drawn.

Another borderline case runs as follows : We can accept
the Greek vases in certain galleries as art, but can't one be
used to hold geraniums?   In <u>that</u> case, it is surely not a work of
art : especially as the owner of the geraniums would no doubt
not care if it was art or not.   Yet if it ceases to be a work of
art when used in this way, what is the status of those others
which still lurk in the galleries?   Do they cease being art too?

Now there is a (fairly) clear sense in which this argument
has it rather backwards.   We can generally see that a flower
vase isn't art, so it is the ones in the galleries that really
need explaining.   Or rather, the <u>number</u> and <u>kind</u> of similarities
between the non-art vases and the ones on exhibition in the
gallery can seem far more important than the dissimilarities, or
the similarities with other works of art, or whatever.   What are

being stressed here are the kinds of comparison which lead us
away from viewing the Greek vases as art. But the other
comparisons, those which lead us towards seeing them as art,
might also be stressed. And it might be pointed out that the
art-status of many objects we wouldn't want to challenge might
be called into question if the vase falls outside the art
category. Well, is it art or isn't it? Here again we have a
borderline dispute, where acceptance of either view (art or non-
art) seems to carry with it unacceptable consequences.

Of course, the point is not so much to solve borderline
disputes of this kind as to see what such disputes are like, and
how they might be approached. Exactly how are these 'borders'
to be drawn? If we can answer this question we will have
cleared up the logical difficulties the borderline disputes
appear to cause, and merely be left to sort out these disputes
themselves.

But these two tasks may not be so separate. For, from
what has been said earlier (especially Ch.3), it should be
obvious that our answer to any question about how the boundaries
or "borders" of concepts are to be drawn will rest on the
direct comparison of cases. That is, we will say that the
business of "ascertaining" whether or not a thing is of kind K
is a case-by-case procedure. And when deadlock is reached -
when you claim that it is of kind K on the basis of certain
comparisons and I claim it is not on the basis of others - we
will resolve our problem by each challenging the consistency of
the other's position. You will claim that I treat obviously
different cases in the same way, ignoring differences; and I
will claim that you treat obviously similar cases in different
ways. That is, each will 'twit' the other with inconsistency
(as per Ch.3).

A variety of solutions to our borderline disagreements seem
suitable here. We may be in a situation where our disagreement
is purely verbal, purely about what words we should use. We
can usefully discuss such an impasse, which may be clarified by
an example. It may be that you'd call any object 'made' with
a certain amount of skill "a work of art". So you'd call wallpaper that was well put-up a work of art, and deny that the same
wallpaper badly put-up was a work of art. And I don't call the
wallpaper "art" at all. Here we mean something quite different
by the term "work of art". In a case like this, it will be
good my trying to show that only some of Shakespeare's plays, or
only some of Donne's poems, are works of art, once you have
accepted that both those and the others were constructed with
the required amount of skill. When we have agreed on that, we
will have settled the question as to whether such-and-such is
or is not a work of art in your sense. Of course, you may not

agree that all the poems or plays are appropriately skilfully constructed, but once you do that settles the question of their being art for you. But the expression "work of art" is not usually used just in this way.

Before continuing it is worth putting aside one difficult issue raised by this example : that we may be in dispute as to what is or is not the appropriate amount of skill. It might, for example, be insufficient to point out the strictly canonical form of the first movement of Webern's "Symphonie" Opus 21. You might not be willing to accept that as the <u>kind</u> of skilful organisation required for music. But ultimately you may be forced to admit that the <u>appropriate</u> form, the <u>appropriate</u> method of construction, etc., for any particular work is not specified in advance of that work itself. (See Ch.7 for a discussion of the "Heresy of Paraphrase".) Students at art school may be taught that no painting can be considered skilful if it has exposed patches of canvas, bare of paint. As a rule-of-thumb this is no doubt so. Yet Van Gogh's "Church at Anvers" breaks this 'rule' quite successfully. This is a point to which we will return, but for now let us note that it is <u>generally</u> a criticism of a work as art that it accords with a formula or recipe. And if we do not have a formula for the construction of art, which can be followed or not, we cannot judge the skill of execution of works in any hard-and-fast way. The techniques of Picasso's "Guernica" may not be appropriate for a contemporary painting about the horrors of war in South-East Asia, but they were 'appropriate' for "Guernica". We know that fact because we judge that work the way we do.

Recognition of this point allows us to tie the aside into the main body of our argument. The question "What is the appropriate kind of skill, or technique, or whatever for work of art X?" may itself turn out to be a borderline question. We will have room for argument as to whether such-and-such <u>is</u> well constructed, as to what are the <u>appropriate</u> 'rules' for construction etc. And such argument will usually be of an explicitly case-by-case kind.

To continue, the situation where you use the word "art" in one way and I use it in another is essentially an unusual, and in many ways misleading, situation. For even though you choose to make a <u>different</u> distinction with the term "art" from the one I mark, you may still require some way of marking the distinction I mark when I use the term "art". That is, you may, for example, need to distinguish <u>fine</u> art from other kinds of art. So borderline disputes which turn out to be merely verbal will be untypical.

However, the point of that example was to illustrate how we __might__ come up against a purely verbal dispute in considering a borderline case. In addition we might come up against what can be called a __pseudo__-borderline case : one which further information makes clear cut. For example, suppose I had not realised that what I took to be shapeless (non-poetry) free verse in Pound's "Hugh Selwyn Mauberley" IV was in fact a careful imitation of the late Greek pastoral poet Bion (25). What had seemed beyond the border of poetry for me, I can now recognise as poetry; and we no longer have a borderline case.

Again, it might be that some deductions, from facts of which I'm well aware, haven't been made, some conclusions haven't been drawn. This can create a pseudo-borderline case of a different kind. I have the information but fail to 'use' it. Since I __can__ begin to use it, such cases are also 'solvable'. That is, solutions could easily be found.

What we are centrally interested in here are cases which are not 'borderline' in these ways, and hence which are not soluable in these ways. We can agree on all the features of the student paintings, and on all that follows from (is entailed by) our agreement that the works have these features. Yet it still seems open to me to claim that they are art and for you to deny it, or vice versa. But I am suggesting that this is not merely a verbal dispute. Here we might begin to go over these features in detail, drawing comparisons and contrasts with works we both accept as art and with works we agree are not art. What must be noticed first is how beneficial such a process of detailed consideration could be. In the course of the discussion, one side may come to grasp the other's conception of art for the first time, and this seems more than a purely verbal achievement. But also it is not one achieved by further information or further deductions. You do not merely find out how I use the term "art" but begin to recognise what features of works of art I see as of importance, which features have value or significance for me.

It is in this way that such discussions do often lead to some kind of resolution of the difficulties. One side may come to see more clearly what is involved in upholding the position they had been advocating, and become inclined to reject it. Or they may not have recognised the strength of their opponent's argument, and come to see __it__ as more tempting. In short, they may be made to mark some affinities or disaffinities between the case under discussion and cases which they __do__ see as clear-

(25) Information taken from Davie "Pound's 'Hugh Selwyn Mauberly'" in Ford __ed.__ The Modern Age Penguin (1961) p.325.

cut. This may not resolve their difficulties, but at least it
gives them some reason for changing their opinion. It must be
stressed that what is in operation here is reasoning : reasoning
directly from the features of one example of kind K towards
acceptance of the other object in question as of kind K.

Such a picture of reasoning strikes many as unfortunate for
a number of reasons, but primarily because it emphasises the
role of particulars. We argue from similarities between one
particular case and another, also noticing the differences.
The 'results' of such a procedure may be the enlightenment of
one party with regard to the work of art under consideration.
And this picture is not always acceptable as a picture of
reasoning. How, it is asked, can we argue constantly through
particulars, without generalising? Our answer to this question
will consist, crudely, in the rejection of the question. We
do, and we must, employ the case-by-case procedure in reasoning,
or other procedures which come down to the case-by-case
procedure (as argued in Ch3). And this form of reasoning
simply does operate through particulars. However, we might
offer some reasons for this point by showing how the generalisations are actually only as well-founded as the cases on
which they are based. Hence an argument through those cases
is no weaker than one using the generalisations. (See Ch.3).

Since we often use explicitly case-by-case procedures in
our discussion of borderline cases, and since we accept that
such cases are not generally soluable, the case-by-case
procedure itself may seem dubious. But when we recognise (as
in Ch.3) that all reasoning in the end comes down to this
procedure, the objection can be seen to be valueless. Since
all reasoning cannot be defective in principle, it follows
that at least some instances of the case-by-case procedure are
acceptable. And it seems appropriate that to further
establish this conclusion, we would begin to employ the direct
comparison of cases.

It seems particularly necessary to note one consequence
of our argument here which may well have escaped notice.
Since we have acknowledged that the process of 'twitting' with
inconsistency, which we employed in the borderline cases, is
genuine reasoning we have given the reactions of those involved
in this business a special status. If the connections I draw,
because of my reactions to such-and-such, are to be part of an
argument as to whether such-and-such is of kind K then clearly
my reactions have somehow acquired the status of reasons.
Yet equally clearly it is not the case that any reaction is as
valuable as any other. And, correspondingly, not all judgements of art have the same value. If they did, I should have
no reason to prefer the remarks of a Leavis on poetry to the

remarks of the philistine.   Indeed a man's philistinism
might well consist of his inability to come to grips with the
poetry under discussion.   And hence his views would deserve
less weight.   The difference is, roughly, that the judgements
of one show understanding, or show more (or a richer) understanding.   It is for this reason that a critic must establish
his credentials (see Ch.6), must make us see that his judgements,
and hence the comparisons he draws and also his reactions, are
to be given more weight than those of the philistine.

To repeat our earlier conclusion, in discussion of borderline cases we often use an explicitly case-by-case procedure :
and we can come to grasp another's conception of art in this
way, come to see what is involved in upholding his position.
And, of course, what is involved in upholding ours too! It may
even involve us in learning about our own reactions to things.

What is being advocated is the direct comparison of cases
as a method in philosophical aesthetics.   Those who, like
Diffey (26), claim that art cannot be defined because it has a
history might get some support from here.   Afterall, if (say)
the changes of style in art do not rule out direct comparison of
cases, and given that this fact is logically (or epistemologically) interesting but not as a means of providing definitions
or looking for essences, where can our interest in these
comparisons lie?   Not in any one style itself, since we are
comparing styles, nor in some underlying 'essence' : then where?
Diffey answers that:-

    . . . . there are conceptions of art which animate
    the minds of artists, critics, art historians,
    conceptions it is the business of aesthetics to
    make explicit. (p.117)

His suggestion, then, is that our interest lies in the
uncovering of what it is that animates the artists and the
critics, what they understand by the term "art".   Of course,
there does seem to be some room for comment on their views too.
It is one (important) thing to feel the temptations embodied in
Plato's aesthetics, but in the last analysis we realise that
this could not be the impartial business we'd once hoped for.
I criticise Plato's aesthetics from the standpoint of here and
now, of England and my aesthetics.   (We shall return to this
point in Ch.6).

---

(26) Diffey "Essentialism and the definition of 'art'" B.J.A.
     1973.

Yet such a view fits well with Diffey's; for our investigation sheds light on what animates us too. Moreover those of us who regularly attend lectures on art appreciation will no doubt be familiar with the sensation (usually temporary) of feeling that one has finally come to see what Plato's aesthetics, or Hume's aesthetics - or equally Picasso's painting or Webern's music - is 'all about'. We become able to draw connections between whatever it is and other things. We begin to make sense of the motivations etc. for ourselves. But we recognise how partial this insight is. We are not seeing a work of art in the way Picasso did, or Plato did, since we are not even seeing it from the perspectives of their society, let alone from their personal perspectives. That is to say, within a particular society or group, certain things are seen as inherently valuable - be they magic, or sonnets, or serial music, or democracy. To understand the art of a society, and hence to understand the appreciation of that society, we too must begin to see these things as valuable. In part we can do this by seeing these things in relation to things we see as valuable. For the rest, it is impossible. Wittgenstein (27) makes this point succinctly in a passage already quoted. (Ch.2):

> It is not only difficult to describe what appreciation consists in, but impossible. To describe what it consists in, we would have to describe the whole environment. (I.20 p.7).

And later he gives what can be seen as the reasons for the impossibility of adequately describing the appreciation, or taste, of a society:

> What belongs to a language-game (like appreciation) is a whole culture. In describing musical taste you have to describe whether children give concerts, whether women do or whether only men give them, etc. etc. And that children are taught by adults who go to concerts, etc., and that the schools are like they are, etc.
> (I.26 p.8)

---

(27) Wittgenstein <u>Lectures and Conversations on Aesthetics,</u> Psychology and Religious Belief. Blackwell (1970)

That is to say, we must fill in all the details of what we have called (Ch.2, Ch.3) the process of 'growing up with' certain standards. We can only fully grasp the taste of a society when we have completely described it in this way because only then will we have a _chance_ of understanding as valuable what that society saw to be of value. Hence questions of the 'nature' of art will involve historical questions (28).

Here again there is a tie-in with the case of the judge and his sentencing policy mentioned earlier. He did not have any such policy in his mind, but the eyes of history (in this case, the eyes of his biographer) 'see' this policy there. That is, see the policy in what he has done. In a not dissimilar way, the art-historian and the writer on aesthetics might arrive at some thoughts on what art had been, if art were no longer being created : for, as with the judge, current artists are not bound by the precedents of what art has been when they come to answer, in practical terms, the question of what art is to be. That is, when they come to create art.

---

(28) c.f. my "Conceptual Change and this History of Art" in _Chelsea Papers in Human Movement Studies_ (Philosophy and Movement : collected lectures by Graham McFee) 1977.

CHAPTER 5.   "Objects of Aesthetic Appraisal" : an omission
recorded.

To focus solely on art when talking about the aesthetic will
seem absurd, even if the practice has a long history in
philosophical aesthetics.   After all, there is something in what
Urmson (1) says:-

> But to me it seems obvious that we derive aesthetic
> satisfaction from artifacts that are not primarily
> works of art, from scenery, from natural objects,
> and even from formal logic.   (p.14)

One part of our reply to any such remark about our limited scope
should be clear : that <u>in the end</u> any such similarities or
differences between works of art and other things must be brought
out by a case-by-case procedure.   But there does seem to be a
misleading tendency in Urmson's very plausible claim.   My own
<u>generalising</u> and grouping of cases in this chapter is dangerous,
since it will tend to gloss-over important differences, but it
is useful here if only to show how larger "important differences"
may easily be glossed-over.

However, our discussion will leave out, or at best suggest,
another important point, closely related to the point under
discussion.   For, as has been argued by Beardsmore (2), it is
as wrong to try to explain our appreciation of nature in terms
of our appreciation of art, as it is to explain our appreciation
of art in terms of, or in the same way as, our appreciation of
nature (3).

However, I will concentrate only on the seond of these
positions, for our intentions are to show that art did require
separate treatment, and that nature would too.   As Beardsmore
(4) says:-

(1) Urmson "What makes a situation aesthetic?" reprinted in
Margolis <u>Philosophy Looks at the Arts</u> Scribners (1962).

(2) Beardsmore "Two trends in contemporary aesthetics" <u>BJA</u>
1973.   Since my first writing "Art, Nature and Aesthetic
Appraisal" (unpublished paper and the basis of this
chapter) Beardsmore has been kind enough to send me his
article, which argues for similar if more far-reaching
conclusions.   But to consider them would take us beyond
the scope of this chapter.

(3) Following Beardsmore, I find the first of these views in
Wollheim <u>Art and Its Objects</u> Penguin (1968), and the second in
the Urmson article previously cited.

(4) Beardsmore "Two Trends in contemporary aesthetics." <u>BJA</u> 1973.

. . . . there are aspects of the love of nature which make no sense if one has before one's mind the way in which people respond to paintings and sculptures.
(p.351)

To make good this claim, it would be useful to focus on the art/ nature distinction in a way not so radically different from that undertaken here. In both cases, the differences between appreciating art and appreciating nature must be emphasised. So perhaps some thoughts on this issue of the unique character of our appreciation of nature will be suggested by the discussion which actually occurs.

The place for us to begin is with the notion of an object of aesthetic appraisal. For Urmson's claim may be taken in the following way: that there are objects of aesthetic appraisal which are not works of art but which are appraised in ways <u>like</u> the appraisal of art. Since works of art must surely be (almost) <u>paradigm</u> objects of aesthetic appraisal, Urmson is then suggesting that the difference between our appraisal of works of art and of, say, natural objects is at most one of the degree. However, this strikes me as importantly misleading for reasons to be given.

Any account wishing to disagree with Urmson's must draw distinctions within the class of objects which Urmson treats as <u>not</u> different in kind. That is, they must mark relevant differences. So let us begin by attempting to distinguish between works of art on the one hand and, on the other, one group of "objects of aesthetic appraisal", namely natural objects. We will in effect be attempting to distinguish between art and nature (5). We begin by a consideration of the importance of <u>understanding</u>, of what we might call "the cognitive content", in our appraisal of works of art. The poem or the symphony can be understood, made sense of, and so on. And that allows for someone to 'get it wrong' : by denying that the fourth movement of Beethoven's "Ninth Symphony" was <u>about</u> joy (where this was not intended wholly as a remark about the title) to take an extreme example.

The object of natural beauty, say the rose or the sunset, the soaring eagle or the waterfall is not the sort of thing we can understand or misunderstand, make sense of, or fail to make sense of. For there is no 'sense' to be made of it. Understanding the form of development of a symphony is different from

(5) This ground has been helpfully trodden by Rhees "<u>Art and Philosophy</u>" in his <u>Without Answers</u> RKP (1969) and Beardsmore <u>Art and Morality</u> Macmillan (1971) whose conclusions form the basis of this discussion.

understanding the development of a sunset. The sunset might be 'understood' in some scientific fashion. We might know why just this conglomeration of colours came about. To know why this conglomeration of notes (for the symphony) came about would clearly not be the same thing. The reason for just that set of tones in that ordering, in that time-sequence and so on, being the symphony might be something the composer or his biographer could provide. And to do so he would mention other pieces of music too, in order to explain the symphony to us. For if he were to start from scratch, he would need to explain what a symphony was, in addition, and how it was related to other pieces and other types of music (See Ch.2).

But the sunset has no "composer" in this sense, no one who could provide this kind of explanation. Of course, how the conglomeration of notes came about could be explained in a way similar to that used for the sunset. We might, for example, mention the properties of air when passing through reeds and tubes, of horsehair moving across cat-gut, etc. But the sunset cannot be accounted for in a way which parallels talk of a composer.

This kind of point might be put in terms of standards or traditions : that art has a background of traditions etc., which can be accepted, rejected or changed, and that innovations in art take place and are intelligible against such a background. And against this background the composer's concerns and intentions are intelligible too. As Rhees (6) puts it:-

I should not even understand the significance or power of that formal arrangement . . . . (p.138)

in a sonnet if I had no idea what poetry was, had never seen nor heard a poem in my life, and so on. I render what I see or hear intelligible by reference to what has gone on before. These traditions of poetry, of sonnet construction etc. carry with them the possibility of informed judgements, and of under-standing (and misunderstanding). In contrast, the (only) 'rules' in nature are the so-called 'natural laws', the laws of the sciences. These cannot be rejected or contravened, for if they can be broken or ignored they are not really laws in the first place. (c.f. "All Swans are White". Ch.3).

So the work of art, we are suggesting, must be seen as a work of art. That is, against the background of the standards, traditions etc. of the arts. This might entail, for instance,

(6) Rhees "Art and Philosophy" in his Without Answers RKP (1969)

not viewing the work as a means to an independently specifiable end (7). For to see it as a means to an end is to see it as one means, among others, to that end : and such a picture, on which works of art can be "paraphrased", is counter-intuitive. It will not do to say of one poem that it means or signifies exactly what another means or signifies, for this would amount to saying they were the same poem. (See Ch.7 for a discussion of this idea of "Heresy of Paraphrase"). And again, we would not be viewing the work as art if our interest were in its accumulating value, or its usefulness as a door stop, or its ability to conceal damp patches on the wall. Such "ends" at least would be ruled out, if we are to see the work as art. What is it like to see a work as art? Well, this will characteristically involve us in ignoring the surroundings of the work (but see example (ii) later), for it will be the same work in the garage or the gallery. We will concentrate on the work alone, while of course seeing it against the general background of the traditions, etc. of art.

Now there is a sense in which the natural object is, as the work of art is not, inseparable from its context. (Or, perhaps better given the difference in what "context" amounts to in these cases, is inseparable in a different way.) If I am entranced by a sunset or a waterfall, that it is a sunset or that it is a waterfall is important. This seems to lead me in disagreement with Oliver Johnson (8), who replies to the question (of a sunset) "In what does its beauty consist?" by saying:-

It consists in the visual spectacle the sunset affords.
(p.169)

He goes on to generalise:-

Beauty, whether it be of a sunset, a mountain, or the starry sky, whether it is natural or man-made, depends for its existence on sensory qualities . . . .
(Johnson p.169)

If we ignore my being entranced by descriptions, or films or some such, of a sunset or whatever, it seems beyond question that I could not be entranced by a sunset I had not seen. So Johnson is right to that extent : but surely he has not said enough. My reaction is a reaction to a sunset, with a

---

(7) c.f. Beardsmore Art and Morality Macmillan (1971) passim.

(8) Johnson "Aesthetic Objectivity and the Analogy with Ethics" in Vesey ed. Royal Inst. Philosophy Lectures Vol.6. 1971-2 Philosophy and the Arts Macmillan (1973).

particular relationship to night, etc.   Just <u>that</u> light, but
man-made might still be arresting - as a simulated sunset, for
example (9).   But a simulated sunset is not a sunset.

Again, when a waterfall (say, the one at High Force in
Cumbria) holds my attention, this <u>is</u> a waterfall and I am aware
of such water at other times, quick higher in streams, slow lower
down, although I may know <u>nothing</u> of this stream.   What is being
stressed is the importance of the <u>relationship</u> of the waterfall
to hills, streams and so on.   We see the waterfall as a part of
the natural scene, and of nature in general.   Again Rhees puts
this idea clearly:

> This is the nature I know and have known.   It is what I
> have watched and lived in.   I may never have been here
> before, or seen anything quite like it.   But there are
> trees and rocks and rivers and hills, as there are where
> I have lived.   I'd not have to wonder what to make of it.
> (Rhees p.142-3)

The reason we do not have to wonder what to make of nature and
natural objects is that the same nature provides the background
to so much of our everyday life.   And that kind of background
doesn't go with anything else.   As we saw, the traditions of
art do not work in quite that way.   And it is difficult to see
how whatever "traditions" are associated with other candidates
for the title "object of aesthetic appraisal", like a fountain
or a firework display, could either.   Part of being arrested
by nature, it is suggested, is being arrested by <u>nature</u> - by
something with a special relationship to what is around it and
through it etc.   (And around us too.)

Of course, that it is a part of nature isn't sufficient to
make something arresting, or to make it worthy of holding my
attention.   This can be seen by considering an example (from
Rhees p.142) : that a dead eagle is a part of nature too, yet it
<u>usually</u> wouldn't make me stop and contemplate as the mountain,
the sunset or the soaring eagle might.   <u>Just because</u> an object
belongs to nature, is a part of nature, it doesn't follow that
it is an object of aesthetic appraisal - although it might be -

(9) Here many people's reaction to "processed-meat" made from
soya beans is interesting they appear to be concerned with
the "processed-meat" not as a meat <u>substitute</u> but only as an
attempt to <u>simulate</u> meat.   That is, their concern is with
the appearance of the dish rather than with its food value.
It appears that "processed-meat" is judged by how well it
can be assimilated into nature in the place of meat.

any more than it is because it belongs to music that a song is beautiful.   Much of nature would not turn my head.

But its place in nature is important, of course, for this is what distinguishes the soaring eagle or the waterfall from something which is just nice to look at: say, a fountain or a firework display.   Can such a distinction between the natural object and something which is just nice to look at be maintained? After all, couldn't we just say that the waterfall was nice to look at?   But this is to ignore the kind of importance for which we have been arguing in the case of natural objects, that they must be seen as parts of nature.   And we might say similar things to distinguish between a song and a collection of pleasing sounds. In addition, we can imagine someone who did not see this difference between the waterfall and the fountain as important. But wouldn't we feel he was missing something?

One apparent counter-example to the contentions thus far advanced, namely that our appraisal of art and of nature are radically different, might come from the case of landscape gardens (10).   These seem to be both nature and art.   But two considerations can be advanced here.   In the first place, it is possible that case-by-case procedure would resolve these apparent borderline cases.   This is neither the time nor the place to undertake such an investigation but, should it prove possible, the art/nature distinction here drawn would be saved.   The second point relates to some other counter-examples, to be considered later.   The discussion of them does at least suggest just what is involved in seeing landscape gardens as art.   For a landscape garden is not so far from being a kind of "total-environment" work of art, a view reinforced by the need to 'see' landscape gardens as art.   Do we really see the landscape garden as a part of nature or the natural order?   It is my guess that we tend to admire them, at least partly, as an escape from the natural course of events.   In this kind of way, it is hoped that the distinction between art and nature suggested above could be sustained, in the absence of a complete case-by-case procedure which would make similarities as well as such differences.

Now we are led into discussion of another group of objects of aesthetic appraisal, or candidates for that title.   The   · object of "natural beauty", which certainly need not be beautiful in the ordinary sense (recall Wordsworth talking about the terrifying and awful aspects of nature in the Prelude), is

_____

(10) I owe this example to both Brian Smart and Terry Diffey
     who independently offered it in connection with the
     unpublished paper on which this chapter is based.

obviously an "object of aesthetic appraisal". But are the
fountains or the firework displays, mentioned earlier?
Fountains, like those at Trocadero in Paris, may be striking or
not. We might be entranced by them as a spectacle, and think
"How cleverly executed!" I could not react in this way to, for
example, High Force waterfall in Cumbria, and not merely because
talk of the waterfall being "executed" seems out of place. Of
course, we might have said of a work of art "How cleverly
executed!" but if that were all we said, it would be difficult
to see how we regarded it as art. For there is surely more to
art than craftmanship.

To return to the waterfall as compared with the fountains,
we might say that the fountains are superficial. And this would
not be a criticism, but rather a comment on the relative
unimportance for fountains, and our appreciation of them, of the
kind of relationships mentioned earlier. Of course, the
relationship of a fountain to its location might be important,
but we can imagine just that fountain divorced from its present
location. For how long will it be before fountains too join
bridges in being shipped from Europe to the U.S.A.? There they
might even be fitted with different pumping apparatus. But a
change in the pumping apparatus will not affect our appraisal
of the fountain unless it were, for example, to change the
force of the fountain. But how could a waterfall be separated
from its context? If it were not connected to a stream, how
could it be a waterfall at all? This is just to reiterate
what was said about the relationship between the natural object
and nature, about what in fact it is to be a natural object.
And such a relationship would be impossible for the fountains or
the firework display. The pumping arrangements of the fountain
or the chemical composition of the bangers is not important.
A change in these details would be irrelevant to the onlookers.

Neither can I make sense of a fountain, where this means
anything more than understanding all about the pumping arrangements and the like; nor understand it. So the fountains and
the firework display do not offer understanding, which is the
province of works of art. And they are not striking in the way
in which natural objects can be, for they are not part of nature
nor intimately related to such a background.

What then do the fountains or the firework display provide?
Crudely, what Johnson picked out in terms of "sensory qualities"
(Johnson p.169) : that is, something which will produce certain
fairly specific responses in us, for instance, excitement or
stupefaction. And this can't be our interest in works of art,
for two reasons. Firstly there could be recipes or general
rules for the production of such responses in a way which (as
will be argued later) is impossible in art. Secondly because

were it so the emphasis would be taken <u>away</u> from the work, towards
the specific response, which would again suggest that works of art
would be "paraphraseable" in a way they are not (see Ch.7). So
what can we say of the firework display?   Clearly it will not do
merely to record our hoots of glee.   But what <u>else</u> is there?
Perhaps we can approach the point indirectly, via an art example.
If you ask me why I prefer the poetry of Stevens to that of
McGonagall, I <u>could</u> offer reasons.   At least it should be fairly
obvious by now what would count as justifying such a judgement,
what a reason would look like in this case.   If I pointed out
how McGonagall writes doggerel, to then ask <u>why</u> I didn't like
doggerel would, except in some special contexts, be to misunderstand poetry.   So even if I didn't give <u>all</u> my reasons, we
would at least know where to start.   For the point here is not
one of my <u>liking</u> doggerel at all, but of my judging it to be bad.
Or, rather, of my knowing that doggerel is not poetry.   Now how
would we justify our claims to prefer one firework display to
another?   Perhaps in terms of the number of fireworks in the
display.   In any case, <u>not</u> in terms of the greater value of one
rather than the other.   Indeed, I suspect that in most cases we
would not even <u>bother</u>, for such claims do not stand in need of
justification.   They are, to employ Beardsmore's (11) formulation of the distinction, matters of preference not of judgement.

In addition we can see how good poetry, good art in general,
might come to affect my views or attitudes on certain things,
although it <u>need</u> not.   For example, Picasso's "Guernica" might
alter my perception of what war is 'all about'.   (This idea
will be discussed again in Ch.8).   Does this feature, which is
of course <u>related</u> to the fact that art is the sort of thing
which can be understood and misunderstood, appear in the case of
the firework display?   That is to say, can the firework display
be understood or misunderstood, as opposed to merely
misperceived?

Let us rule out of consideration certain arcane cases,
where a spy is using a code in fireworks, for example, and
consider <u>how</u> we could make sense of the idea of 'understanding'
a firework display.   Even though we have given the <u>answer</u> to
the question earlier, it is still helpful to consider the
question, "What is there to understand?"   So what is there
to understand?   Suppose someone famous in the field had made
a particular firework display : wouldn't we be willing to at
least consider the possibility that it could be understood,
or could change our attitude or perspectives?   So there does
not seem to be any straightforward logical bar to our understanding firework displays.   But <u>who</u> would this creator of

(11) Beardsmore <u>Art and Morality</u> MacMillan (1971) p.39.

displays be?   How would he get us to see the firework display
as an object for understanding or misunderstanding?   Or to put
that question another way, what sort of thing would need to
occur before we would call a firework display "art"?   For, I
suggest, any reason we had for saying that the firework display
altered a man's views or attitudes would be a reason for saying
that it was a work of art.

What had been stressed earlier is the cognitive content, as
we called it, of works of art as against objects of natural beauty.
It has also been pointed out that natural objects have important
relationships to nature in general, which distinguishes them from
the fountain and the firework display.   Here we are beginning to
deal not with an art/nature dichotomy but with a trichotomy,
which is by no means intended to exhaust possible types of
"objects of aesthetic appraisal".

Now we can return to a main thread of this chapter by
agreeing that, in general, the sort of account provided earlier
of the difference between art and nature enough : and yet that
certain apparent counter-examples can readily be produced:-

(i) Objets Trouvé : found natural objects may be exhibited in
just the way that Duchamp's Ready-Mades were.   Of course, these
do involve selection by the artist, exhibition (both of which
also apply to the landscape garden mentioned earlier as a
counter-example), and also divorce from their natural environment.
Thus they share many features with works of art with Minimal Art
in particular.   However, the idea can surely be taken further,
to produce examples such as:

(ii) "The Ring" by Austin Wright (a young contemporary English
Sculptor) : That is a large rough-metal circlet mounted atop a
hill.   The structure might be regarded as sculpture, except
that one cannot avoid seeing large chunks of scenery through it.
In a way it provides a focus or frame on nature.   Now does this
work of art have just the kind of relationship to nature as was
earlier argued a characteristic of the natural object?   Moreover, this idea can be extended still further:

(iii) A waterfall to which someone makes a path (12) : Here
there is a sense in which natural beauty is being exhibited,
as happens at High Force waterfall in Cumbria for example.   But
someone, who had already established his credentials as an
artist (see Ch.6) might choose to call this exhibited object a

---

(12) This example is loosely based on one from Blizek "An
     Institutional Theory of Art" B.J.A. 1973.

work of art. To do so would, again, be to challenge the art/nature dichotomy as set out previously.

Let us consider these three 'counter-examples' in turn. It seems likely that whatever rubric lets Ready-Mades into the class of works of art also allows in the objects under example (i). For example, these objets trouvé are, like the Ready-Mades, selected by artists. Hence we need not give too much weight to objections based on this example. Austin Wright's "The Ring" is a very interesting piece of sculpture, designed for exhibition in a particular place and with those surroundings carefully taken into account. But it has enough in common with, for instance, Rodin's "The Kiss" for little argument to be required to explain its being accepted as a work of art. That is to say, we could compare cases directly, marking similarities between Wright's "The Ring" and Rodin's "The Kiss", perhaps using a work like Giacometti's "Man Pointing" as an intermediary. All these have been structured in a medium, by an artist, and the like. And again like the others, "The Ring" could be moved from the location for which it was designed to a gallery, say. Something would certainly be lost, but not everything.

Our maximum attention must be given to example (iii), the most taxing and also the most informative. Does it succeed in closing the gap between art and nature, making our earlier discussions relatively valueless? And if it does, can we really continue denying that objects of aesthetic appraisal are of one type, when our most promising distinction breaks down?

One tack is clearly denied us immediately : we cannot simply refuse to call such a waterfall a work of art. Whatever else is true in the history of art, that history is an illustration of the fact that whatever boundaries writers on aesthetics or art-theory draw for the concept "art", artists can always push art over those boundaries. This point should be familiar by now (see Ch.2, Ch.4). We are not, after all, seeking to define "art" by stipulation. Indeed we are dealing with a chief reason why such an undertaking would be little but wasted energy.

The question we must ask is this : why is this waterfall a work of art and not an exhibited object of natural beauty? (If we can still work with this distinction.) Someone might reply that it is a work of art because one man, the artist, selects the waterfall and does the exhibiting. But the construction of the path to High Force waterfall might well be the work of one man, who also selected it as a fit object for appreciation. And the exhibiting of the "art" waterfall, as with any work of art, might be the work of a number of men (artistic collaboration).

Should we look at the artist's intentions in order to answer our question? Taking such a line may be a step into largely discredited psychologising terriory (13), for it is certainly true that many responses directed to works of art are irrelevant to them as art. Just as the spectator's reasons for wanting the Picasso may be as an investment or to cover a wet patch on the wall, as mentioned earlier, and hence what he says about it be irrelevant to seeing it as art, so the value of the artist's pronouncements as to what he intended might be questioned. We are, someone might say, interested in what he has done not what he set out to do. Cavell (14) characterises this view as follows:-

> . . . . it no more counts towards the success or failure of a work that the artist intended something other than is there, than it counts, when the referee is counting over a boxer, that the boxer had intended to duck.
> (p.181)

Nothing is more common among art-critics etc. than to cast a question about why a poem or painting is as it is in the form : "Why did so-and-so put that after that?" But surely the poems of, say, Sylvia Plath speak for themselves. We do not question her sincerity, the sincerity of an actual person, by asking if she intended such-and-such. It is there, and that is enough. Thus we are beginning to agree with many modern critics that the author's intentions are of no importance in understanding or evaluating a work. For that we must look to the work itself.

However, even the most austere of critics will eventually be compelled to admit that this claim does not do full justice to the situation. We could put the point in a number of ways, one of which is to ask just what constitutes "the work itself". Take a poem like Thomas Carew's "Ask me no more", to provide a simple example : is the fact that this work is in seventeenth century English a part of "the work itself"? It seems that facts such as this must be admitted. After all they do have explanatory value. Does the fact that the author was a courtier also have explanatory value of this sort? Does such biographical material generally? In some cases, it clearly will. Yet this is just the sort of information that those who insist on looking only at "the work itself" are seeking to rule out.

---

(13) See, for example, Wimsatt and Beardsley "The Intentional Fallacy" in Margolis ed. Philosophy Looks at the Arts Scribners (1962)

(14) Cavell Must We Mean What We Say? Scribners (1969).

Or we can put this same point by seeing that the artist's biography, and hence talk of historical as well as implied intentions, is often informative. And if this is true of something fairly circumscribed in terms of where "the work itself" will end as in the case of a poem, how much more true it will be of, say, paintings. So a rigid ruling - no information of this sort to be admissible - is inappropriate. How much biographical etc. information will be appropriate to interpretation of works? As expected, that question must be answered by a case-by-case procedure, taking each case separately.

Perhaps, then, something in the way of reflected light on the question of why the waterfall counts as art will be gained by considering the artist. If we ask how the artist understands this 'object', the waterfall, as art, his first answer will probably be that he does : that is, he just sees it as art. But neither our question nor his answer were about his perception or his psychology. Our question was a logical one : why was this 'object' acceptable as art? The difficulty with such a question is that it really only allows one answer. The only justification that could be given for calling it art, the only explanation the artist could give of how he is able to see it as art, would be by some reference, however oblique, to what had gone before as art : to the history and traditions of art. Of course, this does not mean adherence to traditions. How could it, when I am prepared to use Picasso as an example? But it does mean that the new in art is seen as art by reference to, or in revolt against, what had gone before. Wittgenstein (15) puts such a point of view, at its crudest, when he says:-

> You can say that every composer changed the rules, but the variation was very slight; not all the rules were changed. The music was still good by a great many of the old rules. (I.16, p.6)

We might go on to ask how else it could be good if not against the background of such "rules", the traditions of the art-form in question.

Of course, if the "rules" or the traditions were seen as recipes for making art, this point would be difficult to grasp. It might seem that there could not be any such "rules", since to say there is a recipe for such-and-such would seem to be a good reason for saying that the products were not art. But this picture misunderstands the nature of these "rules". If we think of the "rules" as recipes, the idea of innovation (where you 'get it right' without following the recipe) is not

(15) Wittgenstein Lectures and Conversations on Aesthetics, Psychology and Religious Belief Blackwell (1971)

intelligible. For "right" would be explained by reference to the recipe. Yet in art there clearly is innovation. And when further innovations come to be explained, they can draw on those very cases which had previously been contentious, as in the extended music example (Ch.2). So not merely do innovations in art require the traditions, standards etc. of art in order to be intelligible, but they also add to and enlarge those traditions. We might say, in summary, that an early work in this tradition becomes accredited by reference to that tradition, and so on.

We have been arguing that only by reference to those traditions etc. could anything be accepted as art. Yet can we make any hard-and-fast distinction between works of art and exhibited natural beauty? For if this distinction stands, whatever grounds it will be the basis for calling the 'art' waterfall a work of art and High Force waterfall an exhibited natural attraction. However, no real argument can be offered for this distinction. Crudely, we might say that it is drawn. In addition the practice of conservationists and foresters cannot surely be assimilated to those of artists, even though neither need cash the aims of their respective activities in terms of the results : that is, extrinsically (See Ch.7). National parks, however, well constructed, are not works of art in the appropriate sense.

Perhaps we might return to the reply our artist first offered to the question, "Why is this waterfall a work of art?". He said that he just saw it as art. In this context, we might recall Wittgenstein (16) saying:-

> If a theme, a phrase, suddenly means something to you, you don't have to be able to explain it. Just this gesture has been made accessible to you.

If we were careful not to take the form of words too seriously, we might talk of the phrase or whatever having or acquiring significance for you. (An example of taking the form of words too seriously would be to ask what significance. This is one version of a mistake common in aesthetics, as diagnosed by Wittgenstein (17) in terms of taking an intransitive expression transitively. See later). Putting our remarks in that form makes it easy to understand what it is to see an object as a work of art. It is to see its significance.

---

(16) Wittgenstein Zettel Blackwell (167) § 158.

(17) Wittgenstein The Blue and Brown Books Blackwell (1958)
                    p.160 ff.

Consider 'philistine' judgements of art : the man who sees, for instance, Picasso's "Guernica" and makes a medicine-face. He does not seem to see the "meaning" of the art, the point of it Or, perhaps better, he does not see the significance of the object. It has no connections with things he sees as valuable. So what might such a man 'see' in a work of art he considers "nice"? Perhaps he would be looking at it as just something nice to look at, in the way he looks at the fountains or the firework display. Or he might be viewing it in the way he would a natural object. Here he is surely missing something. We might say : if you are looking for "natural beauty" in art, you are not looking for art. One reason would be the importance of detail, which must surely be of primary importance for the work of art, but largely irrelevant to the natural object. (see Ch.7) The point might be put as follows: that the artist uses just those materials, and these could not be changed without seriously affecting the work of art. For to see the significance of say, a poem is to see why only those words will do to express what the poem expresses, for "what the poem expresses" can only be put in those exact words. We will return to this point again, to see the inaccuracy of stating the condition so badly. But for the moment, remember Strawson saying (18):-

> The only method of describing a work of art which . . . .
> is entirely adequate for the purpose of aesthetic
> appraisal . . . . is to say "It goes like this" - and
> then reproduce it. And, of course, this is not a
> method of describing at all. (p.185)

Recall too the voluminous literature on the so-called "Heresy of Paraphrase". (See Ch.7). Since we would not (generally) talk of the natural object as "expressing" anything, changes in detail would not have the same effect in that case.

But it is equally difficult to see how the 'philistine' could really be looking for natural beauty in any work of art, even an objet trouvé art-work made of a piece of driftwood for instance. How could even such driftwood 'art' be seen as a part of nature? For it would, for example, be in a gallery, its ties with the natural world cut.

Perhaps what such a man will see in art is, for example, some pleasing collection of colours. But these will be nothing more than something nice to look at, with no significance at all. It is only a small exaggeration to suggest that a similar effect

---

(18) Strawson "Aesthetic Appraisal and Works of Art" reprinted in his Freedom and Resentment and other essays Methuen (1974).

might be achieved by carefully placing an electrode in the brain. If all we are concerned about is the effect, how it is produced, its method of 'production', cannot be important.   All that is important is that it is produced.   (This reiterates an earlier conclusion in a different form).

Or his philistinism might consist in his use of work of art solely as, for example, reminders of his past.   He is not seeing the works as art at all.   On another interpretation, the 'philistine's' response is a reaction to the technical brilliance of the execution of the work.   Two points can be made in reply. The first reiterates a point made in passing earlier (Ch.4) : that an appropriate technique cannot be fully specified apart from the work involved.   So questions about the appropriateness of techniques really cannot be asked, or answered.   The second point is more important here.   As Rhees (19) puts it:

> . . . . we could hardly understand how achievement in painting or music was any different from a superb performance by a trapeze artist . . . . (p.136)

if we thought craftmanship was what was important in art.   Of course, there is the use of the expression "work of art" noted earlier, where well hung wallpaper, for example, is a work of art even though the same paper poorly hung would not be.   In such a case the expression "work of art" would be cashed in terms of fine execution.   But that is not the 'sense' of the term employed here.   That art is not to be explained in terms of craftsmanship follows from our remarks on the connection between detail and significance in works of art.   If all that ever mattered in art was how much...., or how faithfully...., then photographs from a fine camera would always be preferable to paintings.   (After all, there is no problem with perspective..)

Perhaps all this discursive discussion sheds some light on the vexing question raised by our attempts to relate the notion of 'significance' and the exhibited natural object.   For if we admit that we can see the object as significant we have admitted that it is a work of art.   On the other hand, if we deny that it can be seen as significant, it is difficult to see what reason we could possibly have for calling it anything other than an exhibited piece of natural beauty.   Another example may clarify the matter.   A girl in a bikini would not usually be considered a work of art (in the appropriate sense.)   To imagine a situation or context in which a girl in a bikini does constitute a work of art is to imagine a society where she can be seen as significant in the way works of art are.

(19) Rhees "Art and Philosophy" in his Without Answers R.K.P.
       (1969)

Of course, all this talk of "significance" is intolerably woolly : for it certainly could not be explicated except in terms of works of art (20). But the grain of truth it contains could make clearer the initial contention that it is misguided to lump together, as Urmson seemed to, our appraisal of works where the notion of "significance" was crucial (that is, art) and our appraisal of objects where it was not, for example, the natural object or the fountain. For what allows us to distinguish the work of art from, for example, the natural object is just what prevents us from assimilating one kind of appraisal to the other : and hence universal of flourishing the expression "object of aesthetic appraisal."

This chapter so far may be divided into three parts. The first part endeavoured to characterise the art/nature contrast, and the second attempted a similar thing for a contrast between objects which were nice to look at and natural beauty. In the third part discussion or problem cases led to some clarification of the first contrast. The possibility of exhibited objects of natural beauty, which assigns such objects a status different from that accorded works of art, suggested the viability of the art/nature contrast : and the notion of 'significance', linked with ideas of changes in understanding, was seen as inapplicable to nature. This amounted to a claim which can be put (over-simply) as follows : nature cannot 'tell us anything'.

An apparent loop-hole in the insistence that works of art, but not natural objects, 'tell us something' should be clear. For it is surely true that the flower I send to my darling conveys an important message. And, just as with a work of art, the message need not be completely specifiable independent of the flower, for example the red rose.

But in fact this case illustrates two points towards which this chapter has been directed. The first is that, in order to give this rose any 'message', any significance, it must be brought within the compass of the kind of 'rule-relatedness' mentioned earlier. That is to say, it must be _invested_ with significance by being seen in relation to things which have significance for us. And, as with the practice of putting lilies on a child's grave (21), the 'code' or the practice in question need not be restricted to just us. In any case my

(20) What this seeks to emphasise is the important connection between art-forms and the possibility of comment on the central issues (moral, religious, etc.) of life. See later especially Ch.8.

(21) This example is drawn from Beardsmore _Art and Morality_ Macmillan (1971) p.43, where it illustrates a different but related point.

action in sending the rose could then be understood; or misunderstood if, for example, my beloved does not remember this 'code'. That is to say, it can be taken in the right way or (if, for example, she does not remember the agreed message) in the wrong way.

The second point is that details will still not (usually) acquire the same sort of importance for us in such cases as details have when dealing with works of art. To put it oversimply, a sightly off-colour rose would still convey the message because, we might say, the message is a red rose and not this particular red rose. In a similar way, a fountain might have a message for someone. And one example of this would be if it were the fountain where we met. Here our earlier conjectures about the 'shallowness' of fountains are borne out. Very often what is valued is not the fountain but, for example, the memory. And if some avant-garde artist, following in Duchamp's footsteps, exhibited the fountains as work of art, it would not be because of our message but because he saw them in relation to the traditions of art.

The reason for the plausibility of Urmson's claim, alluded to earlier, should now be clearer. What we have done in this chapter is to begin with one of Urmson's candidates for a non-art-work object of aesthetic appraisal, the natural object, and begin marking some difference between objects of that type and objects of other types. We began by contrasting them with works of art, and then with objects like the fountains and the firework display. It is arguably true that what allows us to even consider glossing over these obvious differences between the work of art and the natural object is that the natural object is in the same 'pigeon-hole' as the fountain and the firework display, under the title "object of aesthetic appraisal". If we can ignore those radical differences it seems just as reasonable to suppose that we can ignore the differences between the appraisal of works of art and of these other kinds of object.

But "object of aesthetic appraisal" is a philosophical technical term. And if it extends across boundaries, as it does by covering at least these three diverse types (art-work, natural object, and fountain-type), its usefulness must be suspect. How could similarities here be important? In the most crucial respects these "objects of aesthetic appraisal" are extremely heterogenous. What sense can be made of the notion of aesthetic appraisal if it covers all these?

Perhaps it was a mistake to say that works of art were virtually paradigm objects of aesthetic appraisal, for that was one step along the road to agreeing with Urmson. What must we do in order to disagree? Surely not assent to the unfortunate

sounding suggestion that works of art are not objects of
aesthetic appraisal. It does not, either, seem practical to
expunge the expression "object of aesthetic appraisal" from our
philosophical vocabulary. Perhaps we must just keep this
weapon in our armoury but recognise the dangers of it back-
firing. This becomes a viable suggestion if we recognise that
a complete case-by-case procedure will bring out differences as
well as similarities from within this class. If our discussions are to proceed in a case-by-case fashion, we have nothing
to fear.

It might be tempting to some readers to offer as what is
common, or at least similar, in our appreciation of art and of
nature some distinctive way of viewing the 'objects' in question.
Some of Urmson's (22) remarks, indeed, seem to suggest this is
his view. Hence we should be focusing on 'ways of looking
at . . . .', rather than on 'objects of . . . .'. Hence we
would be focusing on some kind of aesthetic attitude. Now
there is certainly a place for a view on which a special way of
apprehending or judging things is seen as centrally important.
That is, to put it simply, that our perceptions of these objects
be under the concept "the aesthetic". Such a view will be
mentioned later (Ch.7).

What is, I suggest, to be avoided is any account in which
what is distinctive about art or the aesthetic is (roughly) the
mental attitude with which we approach it. Of course, such an
'aesthetic attitude' theory is too complex to receive detailed
treatment here, but a refutation of a caricature of the theory
can be suggested. For such a theory will not do justice to the
fact of our experience that we really do not look at Picasso's
"Demoiselles D'Avignon" and listen to Webern's "Symphonie"
Opus 21 in 'the same way' - whatever that could mean. There
may be similarities between my attitude to these works of art,
my way of approaching them, but it is hard to think that these
similarities could really be as important as the huge variety of
dissimilarities. To take the most obvious, we are using a
different set of sensory apparatus. Can I really have the same
mental attitude in both these cases? (23) Can I really be, for
example, as disinterested in my looking as in my listening?

(22) In Urmson "What makes a situation aesthetic?" in Margolis
ed. Philosophy Looks at the Arts Scribners (1962)

(23) Indeed, we might question the coherence of the idea of "the
same mental attitude" here? For what is the criterion of
sameness? It is at least arguable (see later and Ch.7)
that it is the work of art itself. c.f. Best Expression in
Movement and the Arts Lepus (1974).

I'm just not sure. The point here is that with such a diversity of art-forms, and a diversity of reactions to them, an "aesthetic attitude" theory seems rather unlikely to have any explanatory value. If asked what is common to my perception or judgement of various works of art, my answers may well come down to no more than that in every case I am perceiving or judging works of art : that is, a return to interest in "objects of . . . .". And if the situation is so complex <u>before</u> we introduce natural objects as "objects of aesthetic appraisal", how much <u>more</u> complex will it be afterwards?

In addition, and more crucially, we encounter a related logical difficulty if we ask what we can say about the aesthetic attitude. That is, if we ask what kind of "access" we can have to this aesthetic attitude. For I will only be able to recognise the aesthetic attitude by reference to characteristic <u>objects</u> to that attitude, and to <u>characteristic</u> ways of acting vis-a-vis such objects. These are things Wollheim (24), for example, might be taken as accepting as distinctive of the aesthetic attitude. Indeed he recognises that the aesthetic attitude is, so to speak, the end of the line, a 'something' about which nothing can comprehensively be said. He makes the point by reference to a contrast of Wittgenstein's, alluded to earlier, between intransitive and transitive uses of a term. Wittgenstein (25) had said:-

> Now this is a characteristic situation to find ourselves
> in when thinking about philosophical problems. There
> are many troubles which arise in this way, that a word
> has a transitive and an intransitive use, and that we
> regard the latter as a particular case of the former,
> explaining the word when it is used intransitively by
> a reflexive construction. (p.160)

The suggestion here is, roughly, that to say for instance "Art is expressive" <u>seems</u> to invite the question "Expressive of what?", if we take the term "expressive" transitively. And it has a transitive use, but that is not the use of the term here. The question itself would be unanswerable once we have acknowledged that what a work of art says or expresses or means can only be completely specified by the work itself. (See Ch.7 on the Hersy of paraphrase). As Wittgenstein (26) succinctly

---

(24) c.f. Wollheim <u>Art and its Objects</u> Penguin (1968) pp.111-2.

(25) Wittgenstein <u>The Blue and Brown Books</u> Blackwell (1958)

(26) Wittgenstein <u>Philosophical Grammar</u> Blackwell (1974)
      I § 121.

characterises the situation:-

> "What the picture tells me is itself" is what I want to
> say. That is, its telling me something consists in its
> own structure, in its own forms and colours. (p.169)

In a similar way, to speak of an aesthetic attitude is to use the
expression intransitively : which is another way of saying that
no complete characterisation of the aesthetic attitude can be
given.

It may appear that we have wandered from our original
intention, for we set off with the aim of showing why any
serious aesthetic should not ignore nature. And we seem to have
talked centrally about inadequacies of the expression "object of
aesthetic appraisal". Yet in fact we have suggested that nature
needs a kind of treatment <u>separate</u> from that accorded art, for we
have marked differences between them. And this is not to deny
that there are similarities too, for a direct comparison of cases
would involve recognition of both affinities and disaffinities.

However, we have attempted to explain and justify our
emphasis on art : that a similarly extensive treatment would be
required into most of these "objects of aesthetic appraisal",
for which we have no time. And, utilising earlier conclusions
(Ch.3, Ch.4), such investigations would take the form of a
direct comparison of cases. The time has come to begin some of
our own preliminary investigations. And the starting place for
any investigation into aesthetic judgements must surely be their
fountain-head : the critic.

Who is "the critic"?   What are his credentials?   How does
he establish them?   Let us begin with what is often seen as one
of his essential credentials:-

> Personal preferences may, in fact, be <u>irrelevant</u> to what
> is good in art.   Many a critic has been known to make a
> most sensitive appraisal of a work of art in which he has
> made careful and subtle distinctions with great feeling
> and having extolled qualities of form, texture, balance and
> harmony, has, in spite of all these declared: "But its not
> my cup of tea".   This I would suggest is the highest form
> of objectivity one can achieve in aesthetic judgements....
> (p.22)(1)

This statement brings together a cluster of views which are of
interest here.   Let us put aside the question of "objectivity"
for a moment, and consider our <u>reaction</u> to this critic's
pronouncements.   Is he <u>indifferent</u> to the work?   Or unmoved by
it?   That such a fine critic is indifferent to, or unmoved by,
a particular work seems a kind of comment on it.   And isn't this
at the heart of what 'feels' wrong with Gordon Curl's claim?
The critic, in drawing his subtle distinctions etc. has offered
us <u>reasons</u> for evaluating the work;   and yet he can withhold <u>his</u>
evaluation.

It might seem that this critic is not, in fact, <u>withholding</u>
his evaluation at all.   Someone might argue that he is giving
us his <u>evaluation</u> of the work based on his reasons, but that this
is radically different from telling us how he feels about it.
And that this last is, in some sense, not a matter of his reasons
for such-and-such as of his reactions to it.   There are two
important misconceptions embodied in such a view.   The first is
the implied radical separation of questions of reason from
questions of feeling.   Thus it is seen an important that a
critic be able to produce a coherent critical 'account' of a work
of art in terms of rational areas of concern (matters of reason)
in spite of, or in the absence of, his own reactions (matters of
feeling).   Much of this chapter is an attempt to break down
such a rigid dichotomy, to illustrate the interpenetration of
what one feels and what one thinks.   The second misconception,
a related one, was mentioned earlier (Ch.4, Ch.5).   The
reactions of the critic seem to have a particular importance.

---

(1) From Curl "Aesthetic Judgements in Dance" in <u>Collected
Conference Papers on Dance</u> A.T.C.D.E. (1974)

A critic, working within his field of competence, cannot merely offer a remark on a work without this amounting to some kind of judgement of the work. Anything he says about a work will assume some sort of weight if only because _he_, the fine and sensitive critic, said it.

His remarks will, in effect, be offering us such-and-such as reasons for a particular judgement of the work, even if they do so covertly. Of course, _we_ may not accept _as_ reasons what he offers us as reasons, and so we need not accept any evaluation he offers us. But that _he_ should not accept them as reasons, or as reasons sufficient to justify his evaluation, seems decidely odd. Are there _other_ reasons for our evaluating it differently? If so, surely he must tells us _them_ too. The work may, after all, be flawed. And if this is not so, why doesn't the having of these reasons, and having them _as_ reasons, entail a certain evaluation? To repeat, we may not see that what the critic offers us as reasons _are_ _indeed_ reasons. (We'll be returning to this shortly.) That the critic himself should not do so seems decidely odd.

Faced with such a situation, _I'd_ want to ask the critic just what _was_ his "cup of tea" : and find out if he really _meant_ all those fine discriminations in his "sensitive appraisal". (Although to call what this critic does "appraisal" seems odd, since he _refuses_ to appraise.) Perhaps he was just playing to the audience. Or trying vainly to keep up with fashionable critics. For if he _means_ us to accept as _reasons_ for an evaluation those things he has offered us as reasons, why doesn't he accept them himself? We _might_ come to understand this by reference to the situation where he is evaluating a work. If he is saying of the work which **isn't** his "cup of tea" that, for example, it is a work of technical virtuosity, but flawed in some way, I could understand. It is in this vein that Leavis writes (2):-

> Today it is assumed that if one withholds one's
> admiration from the <u>Pisan Cantos</u>, it must be because
> one's dislike of the Fascism and Anti-Semitism in
> what Pound says prevents one from recognising the
> beauty and genius of the saying. (p.173)

(Leavis goes on to say that, in this case, the versification itself is flawed, to say the least.) One of the critics of the type Leavis mentions might well say that the <u>Pisan Cantos</u> weren't his "cup of tea". And we'd be quite clear that this

---

(2) F.R.Leavis <u>New Bearings in English Poetry</u> Chatto and Windus
   (1932) Penguin (1963)

was a kind of condemnation. Oh, the verification may be quite something, but...... As Barrett (3) put it, there but for something goes a great work of art. But it does seem odd to say of a man that he has reasons for a view but _he_ doesn't accept them as reasons when he offers them to others (to us) _as reasons_.

Of course, critics won't usually offer all their reasons for a particular judgement. Indeed on some occasions they may, in practice, scarecely offer any reason at all. What is being suggested is that, if pressed, they should be able to offer such reasons. And hence that Curl's imaginary critic might be called on to explain _why_ this work isn't "his cup of tea". Here too it is necessary to bear in mind that we have seen (in Ch.3) how what is usually taken as the sort of thing which _could_ be a reason does not exhaust the field of what can properly be called _reasons_ for a particular judgement. Not all reasons are the kind of thing from which conclusions follow deductively, for example, even though the relation of being a reason for such-and-such is a logical relation. Hence it may not follow that because such-and-such a verse-form is employed in two poems and is my reason for taking one of them to be a rather inferior poem, I will judge the other one similarly. Indeed the verse-form might even be a reason why I thought _that_ poem rather fine. What is required here is some understanding of how the critic's _reactions_ to works do indeed constitute reasons, or "evidence", as a basis for _judgements_ of those works.

We can take a step forward by asking what it is like to have a _reason_ for a judgement. Now _your_ reasons for your judgements may not be _my_ reasons for similar judgements. Bennett (4) puts what at first may seem a rather obvious point very well:-

> A problem exists for me only if I have it; evidence which solves the problem exists for me only if I have it. Someone else may have evidence which bears upon my problems, but I cannot take such evidence into account until I have it too. (pp.129-130).

In order to understand an argument or a work of art, _I_ must understand it. We might capture the difference between my grasping it and my not grasping it by saying that in the first of these cases I have _internalised_ the data. The central claim,

---

(3) Barrett "Are bad works of art 'works of art'"? in _Philosophy and the Arts_ Royal Institute of Philosophy Lectures Vol.6. 1971-2 Macmillan (1973) p.193.

(4) Bennett _Kant's Analytic_ Cambridge (1966)

that understanding rests on such internalisation of data, is more
of an insight than it appears.   For, since the critic's intention,
and presumably his audience's too, is that understanding of works
be promulgated, the general hope must be that people <u>come to see</u>
such-and-such as art, or <u>such-and-such</u> features as important, or
as reasons for X being of value, or some such.   No doubt to the
critic these connections are <u>self-evident</u>.   But his audience
must be "brought to see" what are for him self-evidences.   His
hope must be that they come to understand : that is, that they
internalise the data for themselves.   It was for a similar
reason that, in Ch.2, the argument of the extended music example
took place, or was intended to take place, through listening to
<u>the music itself</u>.   There the intention was that the audience be
"brought to hear".   The situation is not so radically different
for the literary critic.   The critic <u>offers</u> his reasons, offers
an account of the things which make a work important and meaningful (or, equally, mediocre and meaningless) for him.   Or he may
offer an account of features he hopes or expects <u>we</u> will find
helpful in coming to understand a work.   But if he does no more
than describe a work in this way, we will expect his judgement
of the work to coincide with the one he offers us.

An example of a critic at work may prove helpful here.
After quoting a passage from Eliot's poem "Portrait of a Lady",
Leavis (5) says:-

> The flexibility and the control of this(passage)are
> maintained throughout the poem.   The utterances of the
> . lady are in the idiom and cadence of modern speech, and
> they go perfectly with the movement of the verse, which,
> for all its freedom and variety, is nevertheless very
> strict and precise.   The poet is as close to the
> contemporary world as any novelist could be, and his
> formal verse medium makes possible a concentration and a
> directness, audacities of transition and psychological
> notation, such as are forbidden to the novelist.   (p.62)

We are left in no doubt of Leavis' opinion of the poem in
question, and he achieves this by pointing to features in the
poem, for example by references to the movements of the verse.
Here Leavis is offering a comment on the work.   He is <u>literally</u>
criticising it.

Thus far we have been focusing on a <u>central</u> 'function' of
the critic, one without which he would not deserve that title.
There are, however, a number of other things which critics do,

---

(5) F.R.Leavis <u>New Bearing in English Poetry</u> Chatto and Windus
     (1932) Penguin (1963)

to greater and lesser extents. One such would be to impart
such relevant information as the critic may reasonably expect
his public to lack. For example, information about Donne's
personal life, about his imprudent marriage and subsequent fall
from favour, may well help us to understand works such as
Biathanatos (his book on suicide) or the "Nocturnal upon St.
Lucy's Day". Yet even here the critic will generally select
what he sees as relevant from which is known of, say, the life
of so-and-so. Much of that biographical information won't in
general have bearing on the matter in hand. Or if it does, it
can be included. But we can easily imagine a critic who, for
example, saw no biographical information as important, and yet
was a first-rate critic. So while the giving of information is
the kind of thing critics will often do, it is not a sine-qua-
non of the critic. What, it is argued, is required of the
critic is that he offer judgements and interpretations of works.
And the example taken from Leavis seems to support such a view.

If this example from Leavis does indeed pick out the kind
of thing critics do, Curl's claim for the objectivity of the
judgements of his imaginary critic might ring queer, and
especially Curl's holding him up as a paradigm of objectivity.
Of course, we don't necessarily want critics with strong biases,
but in practice their criticism, of literature at least, has
been as illuminating (perhaps even more illuminating) than the
work of critics who have been seen as scrupulously fair. And
aren't we just as likely to 'come to see' (that is, to internalise
data) by being presented with a view we despise? It seems to
work in practice, and now we can offer some theoretical account
of that fact. For what we want from a critic are opportunities
for, and examples of, the internalisation of data : for, in my
jargon, the internalisation of data is no more nor less than
coming to understand for yourself. A critic who points out the
good features of a work he abhors may help us in this understanding. If he only or primarily presents the good features,
as I take it Curl's critic does, he may even get us to appraise
the work favourably, to see it as a fine work. But if he also
presents us with his reasons for despising it, he may not.
And if he does not offer us these reasons too, he is dishonest,
not objective.

We can see, of course, why Curl considered this critic
objective : for, on Curl's view, this critic had managed to
separate his rational concerns as critic (matters of reason)
from his personal reactions to the work in question (matters of
feeling). Instead we are claiming that such a separation is
mistaken; that merely because our reactions can certainly
explain why we judge as we do, in some circumstances, it does
not follow that our 'judgements' are merely statements of, or
"expressions" of, our feelings, Philosophers (and others) tend

to ignore the importance of feelings and reactions in their accounts of rationality; and we are attempting to rectify that situation.

In addition the superficial distinction often drawn between thinking and feeling inclines us to forget, or to ignore, the fact that our feelings are 'mediated' by concepts : that is, that we feel, perceive etc. under concepts – and that it is in terms of these concepts that we spell out the objects of emotions etc. (See Ch.3).

In fact the whole idea of objectivity here is an odd one. This imaginary critic of Curl's is someone who attempts to withdraw himself and his opinions from his judgements. And to do this is to withdraw all force from these judgements too, as they could no longer be seen as the judgements of any person. But is the problem not better viewed when we realise the inappropriateness to the 'art' situation of our usual models of what it is to be objective, models drawn from the sciences. To oversimplify, there is room for an objective/subjective contrast to the situation where, for example, I can 'measure' the temperature of something in both ways : which might be a thermometer ("objectively") and by touching it with my hand ("subjectively"). But if the only possible way it could be 'measured' were by touching the thing in question with my hand (and this was so "in principle", not merely due to some lack of knowledge on our part), it would simply be inappropriate to dismiss this practice as "subjective" and to search for an "objective" procedure. We have already said that no such procedure could possibly be found.

Neither would the procedure actually undertaken by the critic be appropriately called "subjective", at least if this were taken to imply an "anything goes" situation where a critic can offer just anything as an interpretation of a particular work. The interpretation must, to put it roughly, be answerable to perceivable features of the work. In defending my interpretation of a work against your interpretation, I will point to features of the work you had missed or had seen in another way. You will do the same sort of thing, and we will accuse each other of inconsistency. If you offer an interpretation which is not answerable to, or based on, perceptible features of the work of art in question, you are offering an ("objectively") incorrect interpretation. A critic who accepted that his interpretation of a work was not based on features of that work and yet continued with this 'interpretation' would not really be judging the work at all. His reaction would be beyond the pale of reason, and hence truly subjective.

In this context, it is interesting to consider one excellent critic's view of another (6):-

> The first credentials of a critic are his taste, but to praise another's taste amounts really to saying it agrees with one's own, and therefore I would prefer not to claim that Eliot excels by his taste. I would say, rather, that he excels by his insights into the evidence of taste, and by his loyalty to the relevant. (p.239)

Greenberg does not claim "objectivity" for Eliot, but those things which we most respect in a critic - sincerity to his response and to the works he considers.

However, Greenberg's claim for Eliot (with which I heartily agree) does seem to me to involve an important and revealing equivocation on the term "taste". For the sense in which we praise a man for his taste when it agrees with one's own seems to me just the sense in which he has a taste for chocolates or buxom red-heads (7). Since there cannot be <u>reasons</u> for such taste (except perhaps in the individual's psychology) we do not consider them as judgements. We do not see in them evidence of understanding. And if we "appreciate" the arts in this way, wagging our tails at pleasing noises or sights, we are exercising taste and not Taste. In a particular mood I would prefer to listen to Schoenberg's "6 little piano pieces" Opus 19 rather than Beethoven's "Hammerklavier" : not because I <u>rate</u> one more highly than the other, but because I am <u>in the mood</u> for one rather than the other. On that particular day <u>this</u> rather than <u>that</u> is my taste. And this clearly accounts for the <u>preference</u> I express on that day. But I am not offering a judgement or a criticism of the works. I am not claiming that, for example, my understanding leads me to rank them in a particular order.

A genuine critic can only say "It's not my cup of tea, but I don't have any reason at all for saying that" if either he is abdicating from his responsibilities or he <u>does</u> have some sort of 'reason' to prefer one today - for example, his mood - which he doesn't consider worthy of mention. And neither of these reactions is the reaction of a critic acting in that role. Of

---

(6) Clement Greenberg "T.S.Eliot - A Book Review" in his <u>Art and Culture</u> Thames and Hudson (1973).

(7) This is a less clear exmple, of course, just because he may be making this 'preference' on the basis of genuine inductive arguments based on his experiences with women.
c.f. Beardsmore <u>Art and Morality</u> Macmillan (1971) p.39.

course, a critic may be unable to articulate those faults he finds with a work, but this again is a different case. He <u>does</u> see faults even if he cannot say just what they are. His understanding of the works leads him to value one more highly than the other. Clearly a critic who cannot see any features of, say, Picasso's paintings as important will offer judgements of those paintings which differ radically from those of a critic who sees many of the features of Picasso's works as important. One has internalised certain data, the other not. But it would be a mistake to explain this difference as a matter of taste. It is rooted in the very different <u>understandings</u> these critics possess : that is, in the different things they see as important and the different comparisons they would draw.

If this situation does not reflect a difference of taste, in what circumstances do we say "Its just a matter of taste"? Primarily when we have reached an impasse in discussion. (And a shrugging of the shoulders will often accompany the exclamation.) But as we saw (in Ch.4) to reach the end of the line in a discussion is not necessarily a sign that the matter was not one amenable to rational argument. Disagreements can survive agreement about the circumstances (and probable outcome) of a line of action : and there can be borderline disputes about matters of facts. We can bring out this point with an example. For once we have acknowledged the place of reflection in all our investigations, we will have shown how questions of fact can be seen as launching a kind of two-pronged investigation.

To ascertain that the creature in the cage is a greyhound, we might both need to produce a list of its features and then to recognise those as the features of a greyhound. (Such a situation might occur when I could see into the cage but was not familiar with the features of greyhounds, and you were familiar with the features of greyhounds but could not see into the cage.) And there might be a dispute about the "reflective" phase of this procedure for ascertaining a matter of fact. The person next to you claims that, for example, these features I describe are not the features of a greyhound but of, say, a whippet. And this might happen even when we have agreed on the "descriptive" phase of the procedure; that is, agreed as to just what features the creature possesses. Such a disagreement would be a borderline dispute about a matter of fact. For the creature before me may well be some taxing whippet/greyhound cross, for example.

And now recall our discussion of the "borderline" cases at the end of Ch.4 : for in the end we came to a position where all we could do was to 'twit' one another with inconsistency. But it is a mistake to call this "<u>all</u> we could do", as though more <u>could</u> be done, if only we had the right kind of know-how. For

the situation here is that we can offer a case-by-case procedure
and then dispute the admission of cases and the acknowledgement
of parallels.   And since all argument will in the end come down
to this pattern, we will have reached rock-bottom.   To put that
point another way, in the end we draw the boundaries or borders
for our borderline disputes by the comparison of cases, and by
'twitting' with inconsistency.   In this way we ascertain that
a thing is of kind K;   that, for example, the whippet/greyhound
cross has the features it has, and draw the contours of our
concepts accordingly.   To repeat, we come in the end to a case-
by-case procedure, for we can do no better than compare cases in
this way.

And when we realise that there genuinely _is_ nothing more to
be done, one reaction may be the retreat (already discussed)
into the claim that "Its just a matter of words".   Yet what is
required here is not any such shrug of the shoulders or flip of
a coin, or any consoling phrases about "merely a matter of words"
Well, what _is_ required then?

Again, I can do no better than quote Wisdom (8):-

. . . . it is submitted that questions which neither
further observation and experience nor yet further
thought will settle may yet present real problems
and even problems about matters of fact.   It is
submitted that questions which 'have no answers' may
yet present problems which have solutions, that
questions which 'have no answers' can and, mostly,
do evince some inadequacy in our apprehension of things,
and that when this inadequacy is removed by thought,
which while it is helped by precedent is not bound by
it, we gain a new view of what is possible and sometimes
of what is actual.

But it must be acknowledged that to call the kind of searching for
similarities and dissimilarities required here bits of thought, or
of reasoning, or of reflection, may seem a little odd to those
unfamiliar with the case-by-case procedure.   Those who do not
recognise that all reasoning in the end comes down to a case-by-
case procedure will no doubt be perplexed.   But we have seen (in
Ch.3) that a piece of reasoning which uses this direct method of
the comparing of cases is not bad for that reason (nor good, of
course).   There is some very interesting insight in the claim
that comparison of cases is not a disreputable method : and again

---

(8) Wisdom "Introduction" to his Paradox and Discovery
    Blackwell (1965).

Cavell (9) pin-points it:-

> . . . . just as people tell us what we ought to do when
> all they mean is that they want us to . . . . private
> persuasion (or personal appeal) is not the paradigm of
> ethical utterance but represents the break down (or
> transcending) of moral interation. (p.23)

No doubt these same things could be said of aesthetics.
What needs to be recognised in this case is that reasoning
which employs the case-by-case procedure does not <u>necessarily</u>
become nothing but private persuasion or personal appeal, does
not <u>necessarily</u> represent the breakdown of interaction.
When I am 'twitting' another with inconsistency, I am not so
much telling him how he <u>ought</u> to judge a work, or how I'd <u>like</u>
him to judge it, as displaying how he <u>does</u> judge it.   I am
giving him a chance to <u>recognise</u> how things stand with him.
To use an expression suggested earlier, I am giving him a chance
to internalise some data.   And, of course, telling him how
things stand with me.

This kind of argument is found in Wittgenstein's work, and
thus Cavell(10) accurately characterises Wittgenstein's method
as confessional.   And the critic must surely do just that : say
"how it is with him".   This will allow the audience to internalise (in the sense suggested) his remarks, and find or recognise
"how things are with them" in what he says.   It is useless in
practice to rest solely on telling people to react in such-and-
such a way.   The critic's best hope is that the reader can
begin by sharing his initial doubts and confusions, and be led
to see how such doubts might be resolved.   The readers must come
to recognise the comparisons the critic offers as valuable
comparisons, and to recognise some biases and fraudulences as
exist in their own positions.   (For me Cavell's book <u>The World
Viewed</u> (11) would be an extremely good example of "saying how
it is with me", in the sense in which I intend that phrase (12).)

---

(9)   Cavell <u>Must we Mean What we Say?</u> Scribners (1969)

(10) Cavell <u>Must we Mean What we Say?</u> Scribners (1969) p.71

(11) Cavell <u>The World Viewed</u> Viking (1971)

(12) I believe my attention was focused on it by a review of
      Cavell's work, but I cannot now find whose review it was.

Of course, we need to consider the importance of interpretation. Here the essential point is captured by Wollheim (13):-

> The spectator will always understand more than the
> artist intended, and the artist will always have intended
> more than any single spectator understands.   (p.135)

I do not see what _arguments_ might be produced for _or against_
this view.   It does seem to capture a fact of our experience of
the arts.   And yet not just _anything_ can count as "what the
spectators understand".   (We can naturally call these their
interpretations of the work.

Interpretation is, roughly, the business of making sense of
a text, or whatever, and of making it your own : that is, of
internalising it (in the sense in which that phrase has been used.)
And this immediately places a variety of constraints on interpretation.   If I am to render the text, or whatever, intelligible I must do so by reference, in some way, to what has gone
before in that art, for only by reference to what has gone before
can I genuinely see this part of the work as ironic, that part
as satirical etc.   (c.f. Ch.2, Ch.5). That is to say, if someone really knows _nothing_ of a particular art-form, say poetry or
the novel, to what considerations could he appeal for an interpretation, or its justification?   As suggested in Ch.5, the
kind of thing to which he could appeal (say, formal features)
will only be reasons if he can see them as reasons : and if he
can see them as reasons, he _does_ know some things about poetry
or the novel or whatever.

Moreover, as suggested earlier, an interpretation of a work
of art must be answerable to the perceivable features of that
work of art; and any which is not grounded in this way will not
be an interpretation of _that work_ at all.   Thus some 'interpretations' will be beyond the pale, as it were.   For example,
it seems highly improbable that anyone could produce an interpretation of "Guernica" which claimed it was an amusing painting.
And, in order to do so, a critic would need to offer us a new
way of looking at the _features of the painting._   So that even
if he succeeded in convincing us that this interpreation was
justified, still others would remain unjustified.   So while the
number of possible interpretations may be large, it is certainly
not unlimited. It is a consequence of this feature of 'answer-
ability to the perceivable' that judgements in the area of the
aesthetic are not, as is commonly supposed, "subjective".
Or, at least, it is mistaken to claim that 'anything goes',

(13) Wollheim _Art and Its Objects_ Penguin (1968) § 51.

-109-

that any opinion, judgement or interpretation is as good as any other. For only interpretations answerable to the perceiveable features of the situation will render intelligible that text, or whatever.

If, in addition, it is crucial that I render the text intelligible to myself as well as to others, I must draw on what I have, what I know, what I have experienced. I will call on those kinds of comparison which allow me to understand. I will draw comparisons between the work before me and others in order not merely to make sense of the text or whatever, but in order to understand anything of it at all. Of course, there is the general point (made in Ch.3) that any description implicitly involves comparison. But more than that. In order that I recognise the features of works as important I must be implicitly comparing those features with the features of other things and other works.

We all begin our interpretations from who we are and where we are. To re-employ a popular metaphor, our journey may be of any length and duration but it can only begin from where we are. Just so an interpretation of a work of art. If I am unfamiliar with any works since 1900, I may find in Picasso's "Demoiselles D'Avignon" a number of distorted travesties of the human form. If later I come to have some way or ways of drawing connections between that work and things I know, I may begin to offer a quite different account of that work. And a critic could provide me with just those connections. Or, to return to our music example (c.f. Ch.2), I may be unable to make very much of Cage's "4 minutes 33 seconds" - and so be offering one interpretation of it - when a critic points out, and gets me to see, connections between it and Mahler's Song of the Earth", perhaps viz some chain of such "connections". This might completely change my interpretation of Cage's work (14).

Two points must be made here. The first emphasises that this is still my interpretation. I come to see these connections or I don't. The critic cannot force me to see them, but can only hope to bring me to see them. And, of course, I may see other connections, rather than the one's he suggests. In any case, it will be my interpretation. This is not to say that it won't coincide exactly with yours or with someone else's, but merely to reaffirm that it is based on my internalisation of data. The second point is to recognise that this procedure of "coming to see" works both ways. If I come to see connections between "4 minutes 33 seconds" and "Song of the Earth", I also see

(14) c.f. D. Best Expression in Movement and the Arts Lepus (1974) p.130, for a slightly different account of this same business, in terms of "interpretative reasons".

connections between "Song of the Earth" and "4 minutes
33 seconds". So my interpretation of either work may be
affected by these connections. Indeed, we can readily imagine
someone who saw the connections so strongly that they subsumed
"Song of the Earth" under the kind of disapprobation which
they'd had for "4 minutes 33 seconds". And every comparison
is reversible in this way. To point out an unnoticed
similarity or difference between this and that may help you in
the overall placing of either of them. This is perhaps why
running over the features of, for example, Picasso's 'new
anatomy' in "Demoiselles D'Avignon" helps us to understand better
not only that anatomy but also the more usual one in, say, the
works of Poussin and Ingres. Picasso's work allows us to see
the familiar anatomy in a new light, and it is only through the
familiar anatomy that we can make sense of the 'new anatomy'.

If we confine ourselves to literature for a moment, certain
things at least are obvious.

Writers create texts : readers interpret texts

as Peter Jones (15) puts it. These texts from the artist are
then the critic's subject matter; and he will have or provide
his own interpretations, based on what he sees as important or
significant. And this in turn will be based on what he has
grown up to view as important, who he is, and the like. This
means that we have (almost) as many interpretations as we have
interpreters, within the constraints mentioned earlier. Thus
it is misleading to talk of the meaning of a work of art, for
'meanings' of works of art are inseparable from interpretations
of those works. There will be as many 'meanings' as there are
interpretations. How many possible interpreters are there?
Well, we all are, or can all be, interpreters. So are we all
critics? In a sense, the answer to that question will be "Yes".
But that hardly seems to explain the pre-eminence of certain
critics. Perhaps we can come to understand that pre-eminence
indirectly.

We often recognise that people differ in their grasp of a
particular concept. The first-year university economics
student's grasp of inflation isn't the same as mine, or as his
professor's. This tempts us with misleading idioms like "we
have a different concept". And a consequence of accepting such
an idiom literally is that we aren't talking about the same
phenomenon when we discuss inflation. For myself, well, perhaps
I'm not. They, at least, are : and that they can argue and
learn from one another demonstrates the fact. Yet they can
learn. There is still room for a better, or a different, grasp
of the concept.

(15) P. Jones Philosophy and the Novel O.U.P. (1975) p.182

A more revealing idiom here is our talk of the "richness"
of so-and-so's understanding.   We can see the kind of thing this
amounts to - that more affinities and disaffinities are marked,
more cases brought to bear.   What we are saying here echoes
Cavell's (16) claims that the art critic's purpose in comparing
and distinguishing works is:-

> . . . . that in this crosslight the capacities and
> saliences of an individual object in question are
> brought to attention and focus.   (p.103)

For we will come to understand the work in question by just this
kind of comparison.   Indeed, this suggests that the critic will
often use an explicitly case-by-case procedure, rather than one
which is merely equivalent to, or in the end comes down to, such
a procedure.   To explore why this should be so will tell us more
about what the critic does, and help us to focus on the critic's
credentials.

What do these other processes, say deduction, offer?
Mill (17) answers this question succintly when he refers to
general propositions, which function as the major premises in
deductive arguments, as:-

> . . . . merely registers of such inferences already
> made, and short formulae for making more.   (p.126)

That is to say, these procedures offer a generalising, or scope-
providing, facility.   Many cases are quickly brought to bear.
(And also deduction tends to be used in places other than borderline cases.)   Also, the conclusions of deductive arguments have
the appearance of generality and of conclusiveness.

The case-by-case procedure will not perform in this way.
Unless we present the whole case-by-case procedure, we will not
have the same degree of generality or range.   So what has the
case-by-case procedure to offer the critic?   As Wisdom remarks:-

> The case-by-case process gives vividness, not scope.
> (V.L. p.82)

And such "vividness" will surely be just what, for example, the
literary critic will require.   For the critic's work won't
(usually) be damned by the uncovering of some fallacious

---

(16) Cavell Must We Mean What We Say? Scribners (1969)

(17) Mill System of Logic (1843) II iii 4. c.f. Toulmin
     Uses of Argument Cambridge (1958) p.120.

arguments, unsupported premises, or inconsistencies.   These may still be seen as <u>defects</u>, but they can be discounted.   For the critic's job is to show, persuade and enlighten.   The same goes for dark sayings - they may well illuminate.   (One is reminded of Wisdom's (18) emphasis on the paradoxical character of metaphysical statements, and their offering <u>genuine</u> insights and <u>illuminations.</u>)

Let us take, as an example, a quotation from Stravinsky. Stravinsky (19) called Webern's music "his dazzling diamonds". There are clearly many ways in which Webern's musical works <u>do not</u> resemble diamonds : they are not literally hard, will not cut glass, lack the appropriate crystaline structure etc.   Yet all these features might serve as illuminating <u>metaphors</u> in connection with Webern's works.   For his works are small and 'hard' in some sense.   (They might be called "intellectually austere", although this misses a lot).   They were, as Stravinsky goes on to point out, 'mined' at great personal cost. And to call their structure "crystaline" might well be similarly informative.   What is being stressed is the <u>usefulness</u> and the <u>vividness</u> of Stravinsky's apparently cryptic comment.

There are many situations where a recognition of the utility of such expressions is advantageous.   When we talk (as we did in Ch.4) about the <u>illuminating</u> effect of, for example, Bell's account of art and aesthetics, we should bear in mind how illuminating it can be to claim that all a child's behaviour is sexual (c.f. <u>V.L.</u> p.98), or that a person has committed adultery if he so much as looks lustfully at a woman (c.f. <u>V.L.</u> p.94).   As <u>definitions</u> these would be valueless : for they would turn out to be either false or empty (and this is a line commonly taken against Freudian explanation).   But the <u>illumination</u> they produce is not dimmed by this fact.   (This will be a point taken up again in Ch.8).

Now if the (literary) critic's job is indeed to produce some such "crosslight" (Cavell's phrase) of comparison, we can see why successful critics are often erudite and scholarly men, in various positions in higher education.   (George Steiner is currently (1975) professor of English and Comparative Literature at the University of Geneva.)   Of course, people other than those with university educations and the like will make good critics, but the odds in modern times would always be in favour

---

(18) c.f. for example Wisdom "Paradox and Discovery" in his <u>Paradox and Discovery</u> Blackwell (1965)

(19) From Forward to <u>Die Reihe Vol.2</u> published in English 1958 and revised, ed. 1959 Theodore Presser Co. (information from Michael Finnissy.)

of those with, for example, this kind of grasp of the history etc. of the area of study. It is not <u>required,</u> anymore than we could require a knowledge of linguistics in order to understand the sentences a man uses. But when we want a detailed analysis of those sentences, wouldn't we be inclined to turn to the linguist first? There may be no genuine experts in criticism as such, but a realisation of the role of comparison and the need for <u>materials</u> for such comparisons, that is, knowledge of particular cases, does surely go some way towards explaining the pre-eminence of, for example, Leavis, or Steiner, or Eliot as critics.

But while it may go <u>some</u> way, it clearly does not go <u>all</u> the way. Just what makes their criticism valuable, as against the interpretations of the rest of us? Here any adequate answer must be **an extremely complex** one, for the issues are extremely complex. However, a broad outline can be drawn, again picking up an insight of Cavell's (20), which he expresses as follows:-

> . . . . Asking anyone about his intentions is asking whether he is meeting his responsibilities, asking an explanation of his conduct. And what gives one the right? In morality the right is given in one's relation to what has been done, or to the man who has done it. In art it has to be earned, through the talent of understanding, the skill of commitment, and truthfulness to one's response - the ways the artist earned his initial right to our attention. If we have earned the right to question it, the object itself will answer; otherwise not. There is poetic justice.
> (p.237).

(How this sounds like Greenberg's account of Eliot!)

What such a line emphasises is the need for critics (**and for** philosophers) to be serious, truthful to their responses and on guard against the soothing effect of their own pet theories. And this is not only something we should <u>expect</u> from the critic (or philosopher) but something he must show us is true of him. That is, we must be able to see that he is serious (in a way which does not rule out jokes), truthful to "how it is with him", and aware of the seductive tendencies and traps of theories; and he must <u>make</u> us see him in this way. To put that another way, he must establish his credentials as critic. If he fails to do so, we will <u>not</u> be able to see him as a critic, we will have no reasons to take his judgements and his reactions seriously. To give us such a reason <u>is</u> to establish his credentials. We can

---

(20) Cavell <u>Must We Mean What We Say?</u> Scribners (1969)

see that point clearly if we consider just why we should take
Stanley Cavell's word for the position of the critic.   After all,
no one is right merely because he says he is.   So why should we
give Cavell's views any consideration at all?   But Cavell has
established his credentials both as critic, with essays such as
"The Avoidance of Love" and "Ending the Waiting Game", and as
philosopher with the other essays in his book Must We Mean What
We Say?

If, then, to "have earned the right to question" is, among
other things, to have displayed one's own truthful to "how it is
with me", one's seriousness, etc. where does that place the
author of this work?   After all, how can we begin if, in order
to be understood, we must first establish our credentials?
And clearly any answer to such a question will be a complex one.
In part, no doubt, academic training of a particular sort will
have to be admitted as one good reason for taking a work seriously
to begin with.   (This is true in art as in philosophy.   A great
many arguments against Picasso's work have been blocked by the
realisation that Picasso can execute works in an academic style).
And then we come to the work itself.   So that this work, and all
such work, in part justifies itself (if it does), by establishing
its author's credentials.

Just as the critic must, in some way, "establish" his
credentials, so must the artist.   The character who exhibited
the waterfall as art (in Ch.5) had already established himself
as an artist, in some way.   That he was an artist gave a certain
amount of credibility to his later claims that what he was doing
or making was art.   (Taken in this way, Kurt Schwitter's claim
that his spital was art does not sound so extreme (21).)

Two points must be emphasised here.   The first is that we do
not always approach the work of an artist, or of a critic, with
knowledge of the artist, or critic, himself.   We may, or may not.
If he is our contemporary, we are likely to; but if he lived in
the Middle Ages we are likely not to.   If we do not, then such
knowledge won't be able to function in the way I was suggesting it
might, to make us give the work serious consideration.   (The
knowledge won't be able to function in this way because we won't
have the knowledge.)   The second point has already been
mentioned.   The affect of recognising a man's credentials in
any field is not to make us accept his work as valuable, but
merely to make us give it serious consideration.   Or, rather, it
is one reason (and one often ignored) why we should give a man's
work serious consideration.   Just because it is a Picasso, it

---

(21) Example drawn from conversation with Charles Prosser.

doesn't follow that such-and-such is a work of any value.
However, **one** reason why we give new works of Picasso a fair
hearing will be that Picasso has, in the past, produced works
of value.

And both these points tie-in with the other prong of George
Dickie's (22) definition of art.   In Chapter Four we discussed
his artifactuality arguments, and now we can briefly look at
another central part of it.   To remind ourselves, Dickie says:-

> A work of art in the classificatory sense is (1)
> an artifact (2) a set of the aspects of which has had
> conferred upon it the status of candidate for
> appreciation by some person or persons acting on
> behalf of a certain social institution (the art world).
> (p.34).

Hence Dickie stresses the importance of what he, following
Danto (23), calls "the art world".   It is from this feature
that our discussion begins.   He describes this art world as:-

> a broad social institution in which works of art have
> their place.   (Dickie p.29)

And he emphasises (as we have done in Ch.2, Ch.5) how continuities
within the traditions of an art-form allow us to see innovations
as art.   **Again,** he is keen to admit the role of both artist
and audience as parts of this "art world".   To use a provocative
phrase of Gombrich's (24), he acknowledges "the beholder's share".

But when he talks of the conferring of art-status on works
(that is, of their becoming candidates for appreciation by this
conferring) it seems he must have made a mistake.   His account
of such conferring begins with an example, from Dada, which
seems to admirably support his case.   Duchamp's exhibited urinal
(and Schwitters' spital too) can best be understood in terms of
stories like those that Dickie tells : that they (Duchamp and
Schwitters) were artists, and hence were in a position to confer
status on these objects.   And that is a revealing way of putting
the point, because it forces us to ask about their creditability
as artists.   It is easy to go alone with Dickie's explanation
of why we should at least give "Ready Mades" a chance as art,
but hard to see why Duchamp thought they were art.   Perhaps
Duchamp is able to confer this art-status for us on the urinal.
What I am trying to get to is : who confers the art-status

---

(22) Dickie Art and the Aesthetic Cornell U.P. (1974) p.34

(23) Danto. "The Art-World" J.P. 1964.

(24) Gombrich Art and Illusion Phaidon (1960), where it is
     the title of Part III.

for Duchamp?   Perhaps we can return to the waterfall-artist
(Ch.5).   I put into his mouth the claim that he just saw the
thing, the waterfall, as art.   And I can perhaps imagine
Duchamp agreeing that he saw the urinal as art.

To accept such a picture is to set up certain serious
worries for Dickie's account.   The conferrers can only do their
conferring on works they see as art: which means that the
picture Dickie's words suggest, a picture where people decide
what is and is not art, is an inaccurate one.   For although there
are kinds of decision at work here, they are not made on the basis
of a leap into the dark.   To leap into the dark is to arrive at
a 'conclusion' arbitrarily, for in such a situation no considerations or reasons are operative.   But in the case of judgements
of the arts we have seen that our reactions can come to have the
status of reasons for our judgements;   seen, in particular, how
the reactions of artists such as Duchamp can acquire this status.
For it is scarcely misleading to view his coming to see such-and-
such as art as a judgement.   And this is not arbitrary.   It
is not the case that any conclusion could have been reached here.
For what a particular person can see as art is not arbitrary.

Also these conferrers do not confer status in the way that
the status of common-law wife (Dickie's example p.37) is
conferred by a legal system.   For while the legal system may
merely be confirming a situation which already exists, it does
at least change the legal standing of that situation.
Perhaps the woman can now inherit, for example.   The legal
standing of the woman changes.   Not so in the art case.
In most cases, although certainly not in all, the art object
does not have its status changed by any conferring.   In fact,
no such conferring generally takes place at a time and in a
spatial location (as Dickie acknowledges).   The most usual
situation will surely be that where an artist comes to see
certain formal features or certain formal changes as
significant.   That is, he comes to see such-and-such as a work
of art.   And this is why these are not leaps into the dark, for
he will see them as significant by reference to, crudely, the
past history of the art form in question (as argued in Ch.2,
Ch.5).   It is surely in this vein that Schoenberg's (25)
following claim is to be understood:-

I personally hate to be called a revolutionary
which I am not.   What I achieved was neither
revolution nor anarchy.

(25) Quoted Davies Paths to Modern Music Barrie & Jenkins (1971)
p.71

Part at least of Schoenberg's claim must rest on the way that his innovations are understood, made sense of, by reference to what had gone before. Neither Schoenberg nor anyone else conferred the art-status on his music. Instead, they learned to hear its "discords" as music.

Such a picture allows us to see how people can have reasons for calling such-and-such art, that is, for their "conferring" : and how they don't (necessarily) decide that such-and-such is art, but rather come to see it as art. If the art- world had to decide anew in each case, to what considerations could appeal be made? As asserted in Ch.2, the aim to make all things new will involved us in incoherence, for to make all things new is to removed the reason-status for all things. And then we cannot even a reason for wanting all things new.

It might seem though the "minimal art" (26) examples Dickie offers in support of his remarks about the conferring of art-status rebut my claims. This cannot be so, for two reasons. First, and already mentioned, is the fact that even in such cases the artist coming to see such-and-such as art is logically prior to any conferring : and second, it has not been claimed that art-status is never conferred on objects (although I have suggested that such a view is not without complications) but merely that the status is not always conferred. Only if we are looking for a neat and complete answer, as it seems Dickie is, will we be disappointed.

However, there is at least one clear sense in which the art-status of works is conferred. To leave an object where it is, unchanged in any way, to say no magic words over it and yet some-how think of it as art is an absurd suggestion. As Dickie clearly points out (p.38) one person claiming X as art is at least some reason for thinking of it as art. And if I so much as tell you that X is art, or erect a sign to that effect, I am doing (in a minor way) just the kind of conferring of which Dickie approves. But to concentrate wholly on that side of the business is, I was suggesting, to over-rate "the beholder's share" : or, rather, is to over-rate the share of those who would take someone's word for such-and-such being art without seeing it as art themselves. If we give some attention to those who see the work as art, we will recognise that they do not decide that it is art. To repeat an earlier simplification, they grow up with it as art. And this claim isn't affected by cases, like Duchamp, of a person coming to see such-and-such as art : for he sees it as art by reference to what he already sees as art.

---

(26) An extremely interesting and informative view of "minimal art" is to be found in Wollheim "Minimal Art", reprinted in his On Art and the Mind Allen Lane (1973)

The critic's position vis-a-vis Dickie's "art-world" should be a little clearer by now. To repeat (from Ch.3), it is only when two people share certain reactions, opinions, convictions and the like, that is, when they share a common understanding, that one person can show the other something he had not seen before, by means of a new comparison. Without the shared understanding, the "receiver" will not even know how to take the comparison. So the critic must be operating within a context of shared understanding, to a greater and lesser extent. And a large part of this "shared understanding" will turn on what has gone before in art, on what we have called the traditions and standards of art, as well as the critic's own perspective. Dickie sees critics as the kind of people who could be <u>agents</u> in, and of, the "art-world". While it is certainly possible for critics to be arbiters of taste and to introduce "fashions" etc. as Ruskin's treatment of Turner's work illustrates, we have seen that this agentive role must not be overplayed. Like the rest of us, the experienced critic must <u>come to see</u> such-and-such as art, or so-and-so as valuable, for himself. He must internalise the appropriate data, we might say. And to do this is not to <u>decide</u> so much as to come to see.

In conclusion, a number of points were emphasised by our discussion of the critic and his functions. He is centrally involved in "getting us to see", which he will do with vivid comparisons among other means. And this will involve him, like the artist, in first "coming to see" for himself. The proficient critic will be able to bring to bear a battery of comparisons, which amounts to the same thing as employing a "rich" concept. Through his connections with what has gone before, he will come to understand certain things as <u>reasons for</u> particular evaluations of art. Hence the critic's work rests firmly and directly on case-by-case procedures. His work is not to be dismissed as "subjective", despite the many places where who and what he is are of crucial importance in our exposition of his work. No more "objective" situation is possible. The reactions of the critic, based as they are in understanding of art, have the status of <u>reasons</u> for his judgements. And this is one reason why a critic's credentials need to be established.

CHAPTER 7   The Evaluation of Art

At first glance it might seem that when we have discussed the _evaluater_ of art, the critic (as we did in Ch.6) we have said all we have to say about the _evaluation_ of art. Or that any additional information or material should really have its place in that discussion. However, our focus there was on what one had to do in order to be counted as a critic. The emphasis, we might say, was more on _who_ he was than _what_ he did, although these two cannot be rigidly distinguished. And such an emphasis can be changed.

There is no one difficulty which deserves the title "_the_ problem of evaluation for art", but rather a number of related problems. We will concern ourselves with three of them or, perhaps a better way of putting it, with three faces of the problem. The first argues from a premises of the _uniqueness,_ in a sense to be explained, of each work of art to the conclusion that evaluation of works of art is impossible, since evaluation is a comparative procedure and its uniqueness entails that there is nothing with **which** any work of art can really be compared.

It is certainly worth saying something about the idea of the uniqueness of works of art, for there are two important ways in which works of art should be seen as unique. The first is simply that which denies that the work is derivative or copied. These would be condemnations, would be reasons for thinking that the work in question was not art after all. It is more important for us to note the second sense of "unique", for it runs partly counter to what is often meant by the term. It would clearly be nonsense to say that works of art are unique in the sense that only one 'example' of each work exists. This claim would be simply and obviously false for many novels, poems, films, etc. And yet there _is_ a sense in which the volume The Alexandria Quartet by Lawrence Durrell on my bookshelf and the volume on your bookshelf are the same book - Durrell's _Alexandria Quartet_ - and no other book could be exactly the same book as _this_ book, without having the same status of your volume and mine. That is, there may be many _volumes_ but there is only one book. We might bring a type/token distinction (1) into play here, and say there were many tokens of the one type. We will return to this point later, and so we can return to our specification of "problems of evaluation."

_____

(1) The distinction is Peirce's. See Collected Papers of
    C.S.Peirce Harvard U.P. (1933) Vol.II § 243. Also see later
    for a fuller discussion, based on Strawson's "Aesthetic
    Appraisal and works of Art", reprinted in his Freedom and
    Resentment and other essays. Methuen (1974)

The second such moves from the claim that evaluation must be a generally accessible procedure, through the claim that such accessibility requires the kind of rules which do not exist in the arts, to the conclusion that "genuine" evaluation of the arts is impossible. The third problem simply claims that, perhaps for reasons given under the other two, nothing has the status of a genuine general <u>reason</u> for any evaluation of a work of art. Hence any claims to evaluate are merely expressions of preference.

The third of these, to take them in reverse order, is already refuted. We have seen how its notion of a "genuine" reason is a bogus one, and how the <u>reactions</u> of the critic have the status of reasons for his judgements. Evaluations of works of art may be personal, but they are not to be dismissed as "subjective" on that score. Hence this third formulation need not concern us.

The second formulation turns out to be about a rather larger issue. For it asks how, and if, any facts have aesthetic import. Once facts, or features, are acknowledged to have this kind of value we can argue from those facts, or the possession of those features, to conclusions about the value of the work. But it is denied that any facts have this kind of import. And the argument is more or less the one against the possibility of moving to moral values from 'facts' : that is, we are discussing the fact/value dichotomy. The problem here is posed by those writers who assert that we cannot move from descriptive ("fact") premises to an evaluation ("value") conclusion without involving any evaluative premises. And since evaluative premises are not <u>entailed</u> by (that is, are not logically deducible from) any set of descriptive premises, general rules cannot be constructed. We can never, to put it simply, say that every work of art with ("factual") properties X, Y, Z . . . . is a good one. Yet it might seem that such writers, and Hare (2) is a good example, are simply mistaken from the start. Is it not just <u>true</u> that in our society certain facts do have aesthetic significance? For it is certainly true that when we describe a dance as graceful, we are both describing <u>and</u> evaluating it. The 'fact' of gracefulness has evaluative implications. And, if so, can't we move from such 'facts' to our evaluative conclusions?

However, those who favour a fact/value dichotomy have a reply. They claim that the difficulty of some 'facts' already possessing aesthetic import is at best a psychological rather than a logical difficulty. In logic, they inform us, we can distinguish between <u>what</u> a work of art is like ("facts") and <u>our attitudes</u> to it ("value"). Hence, they go on to say, the problem is how we can

(2) Hare <u>Freedom and Reason</u> OUP (1963) p.140 ff. p.167

move from the evaluation-neutral 'facts' to any evaluation. And they attempt to explain this transition in terms of some decision on our parts. Yet, as we saw (in Ch.6), the notion of deciding is not appropriate here. On what basis could such a decision be made? To what considerations could appeal be directed? And the answers must be "none", for the only possible considerations would be 'factual' ones and these have been described as evaluation-neutral. The point here is that, as a matter of logic, if all available facts must be neutral (that is, evaluation-neutral) we can never move from them to evaluative conclusions. Such 'facts' would be picked-out as unable to entail or support evaluative conclusions. Hence if we can ever provide factual support for evaluative statements, the distinction cannot be as rigid or as hard-and-fast as the position suggests.

That is to say that non-evaluative descriptions of works of art are not possible. Fried's description of the Caro piece Prairie (Ch.2) would be a good example of one such. What is involved in upholding a rigid fact/value dichotomy is the mistaken picture of what it is to establish a factual conclusion mentioned earlier (Ch.3). We must free ourselves of this cramped notion of what facts are.

One potentional misunderstanding of our position can be cleared up right away. We are not claiming that facts have some irremovable aesthetic import. That would obviously be false, given the changes in what is seen as valuable in art, and in our attitude to the arts in general. As Wittgenstein (3) puts the point:-

> Suppose Levy has what is called a cultured taste in painting. This is something entirely different to what was called a cultured taste in painting in the 15th century. An entirely different game is played.
> (p.9)

We are merely urging that in our society, and in the fifteenth century society Wittgenstein mentions, some facts do have aesthetic import. Of course, which facts these are may differ radically. And that later societies may not see any of these features as important is simply beside the point.

We have been urging that evaluative statements can ever be supported by factual statements only if there is some way of bridging the proposed 'gap' between factual and evaluative statements. Unless such a bridge can be found, nothing could

---

(3) Wittgenstein Lectures and Conversations on Aesthetics, Psychology and Religious Belief Blackwell (1970) I.29.

have the status of evidence for, or be a reason for, a particular evaluation. It is easy to see why this is so. For the factual statements can only acquire the status of evidence if they can be seen to bear upon the evaluative ones in just the way that is denied. It may be advantageous to consider the situation vis-a-vis moral claims. For example:-

Smith is a despicable person.

Since what we are interested in is how claims such as this are related to evidence, or to reasons, we can ask how such claims, which are obviously of a moral nature, can be rationally supported. And we are, in effect, asking whether any ethical judgements could be verified ("conclusively verified"), whether or not disputes as to the applicability of ethical predicates could be settled, whether we can offer reasons for our value-judgements and the like. As with aesthetics, we are in the end asking whether or not our judgements can be rationally justified (c.f. Casey quoted in Ch.1). Claiming that they can be so justified requires an explanation of, or at least an example of, such a procedure at work. And denying that such judgements can be justified leaves us in need of an explanation of the position of moral or aesthetic judgements. How are they _judgements_ at all?

The situation in ethics is clearer only because we are more familiar with the course of disputes in ethics. Both sides accept _certain_ descriptions of what has occurred, but not _all_ the other side's accounts are accepted. We accept, for example, that the car struck the body. I offer the description "man-slaughter", while you press the description "murder" on the events. While our descriptions are incompatible with each other, neither of them is (logically) incompatible with the agreed or 'neutral' descriptions of the happening. To use either of our descriptions with this 'neutral' one is not to contradict oneself. But we have now ruled out both _inductive_ and _deductive_ inference as modes for justifying our ethical judgements. For there is no room now for some deduction from the 'neutral' description, nor any need for further evidence. And this dispute is not merely verbal, as the treatment of the culprit will depend on the outcome. How can such judgements be justified, if not inductively or deductively? (4)

---

(4) c.f. Newell The Concept of Philosophy Methuen (1967) pp.122-9 for a discussion of the claim that there is some _special_ problem about the justification of ethical statements, which Newell (following Wisdom) denies. In particular, the view that in ethics or aesthetics _feeling_ or _reaction_, rather than reason, is operative is to be combatted. See my "Critics have feelings too" and "The Myth of 'The Response'" in Chelsea Papers in Human Movement Studies (Philosophy and Movement : collected lectures by Graham McFee), 1977.

The answer to this question lies in our actual practice in such cases; an example of which has been carefully catalogues by Beardsmore (5):-

> 'Smith', one man remarks, 'is a despicable person'. Someone else disagrees. He has always found Smith to be perfectly upright in his dealings with him. When this happens, each party to the dispute will probably try to defend what he has said by giving reasons. One points out that Smith is always polite, never goes back on his word, and pays his debts; the other claims that Smith tends to ignore other perople's feelings, is insensitive to suffering and so on. (p.ix)

What is presented here is a direct comparison of 'moral' cases, and no coubt some 'twitting' with inconsistency might follow. So what we do in actual cases is to appeal to instances, to the case-by-case procedure. And this is reasoning, does justify.

Yet a sceptic might remain unconvinced. Even if reasons can, in some way, be involved in the making and justification of aesthetic (and moral) judgements, it does not follow that thie problem of evaluation is overcome. After all, any claim made by artist or critic is in principle challengable (as we saw in Ch.4). The claim that such-and-such is art, or is good, or whatever can always be denied. Hence any evaluation of art is biased or partial. While it may not be merely a preference, given the earlier arguments (Ch.6), it is hard to see it as very much more.

Yet this line of argument takes us nowhere because any claim at all is challengable in this way, even (as argued in Ch.3) the claim to have recognised a thing as a such-and-such. This is one place where we can clearly recognise a cramped notion of what it is to establish a 'truth' of fact. For it had been assumed that such truths are conclusively establishable in a way that does not involve appeal to instances. And this was just not so.

We have argued this point before (Ch.3) : that we can always ask "why?" of any statement we are offered, any claim that is made. And if I claim to have identified a certain animal as a greyhound, its dissimilarities to other greyhouds and its similarities to whippets can always be pointed out. That is to say, for every statement such as "This is of kind K" it is always possible to produce some other reason which relates to the claim, some other case which bears upon this case.

---

(5) Beardsmore Moral Reasoning RKP (1969)

If this feature were seen as a defect in reasoning, we __would__ be in that situation (outlined in Ch.3) where __no__ reasoning was sound, since even if we had some special case to which final appeal was made (or some paradigm. See Ch.4) we would still need to justify __this__ case as being or not being of kind K.   And the production of **further** instances would enlarge, rather than palliate, the problem.

We misunderstand what it is for recognitions to be certain if we assume that because my claim that such-and-such is a spade is always challengable, by the production of other reasons or cases, there can be no certainty.   When (in Ch.4) we espoused a line which involved what Diffey called "temporary paradigms" (option (d)) we were attempting to accommodate just this possibility. There is certainty but this does not rule out the challenge. For when a challenge is successful the shift is from one certainty to another, not from doubt to certainty: nor, as it would __have__ to be if there were no certainties, from one state of doubt to another.   Hence any doubting of claims __rests on__ notions of certainty, although certainty of a kind to be explained.   As Wittgenstein (6) puts it:-

> If you tried to doubt everything you would not get as
> far as doubting anything.   The game of **doubting** itself
> presupposes certainty.

Still, might someone not go on to urge that all such claims to __know__ that such-and-such is a spade, or a work of art, are hypothetical? Clearly not.   The term "hypothesis" is useful only if not __every__ claim is hypothetical in that sense.   So that when Wittgenstein (7) asks:-

> . . . . isn't it as if you wanted to say : "If such-and-
> such is not the case, it makes no __sense__ to say it is the
> case"?

he can be seen as drawing attention not merely to the effect on the concept "certainty" were it the case that the certainty of all cases was simultaneously questionable, that they were all hypotheses, but also the effect on the concept "hypothesis".

Thus we can reject outright the claim that the assertions of, for example, art-critics and of persons discussing the arts are always hypothetical.   They may, of course, offer conjectures or

---

(6) Wittgenstein __On Certainty__ Blackwell (1969) § 115.

(7) Wittgenstein __Zettel__ Blackwell (1967) § 132.

hypotheses or theories. Equally, they need not. And when we have recognised this fact, we should have overcome our fear that what the critic or whoever offers us is less valuable merely because it can be changed by events or just by the passage of time.

The point of this further discussion of the place of reasoning and reflection in aesthetics has been to suggest that these notions apply to what had been called "descriptive" statements as well as "evaluative" ones. And so to combat the view that evaluative conclusions were necessarily less well-established than descriptive ones.

This in turn places strain on the idea of a descriptive/ evaluative dichotomy. Certainly there are 'pure' descriptive remarks about art, such as that of Fried quoted earlier (Ch.2). Equally certainly claims like "That is tremendous!" might be seen as purely evaluative. But why should it be possible to draw any hard-and-fast line here? Don't they just shade into one another? In the context of a particular discussion, say with the buyer for an art museum wanting characteristic pieces of a period, it might be obvious that my saying of some object "Oh, yes, its a work of art" is merely descriptive. I need not be ascribing any aesthetic value to it. The problem here is to see why, except for convenience, anyone should seek to argue with the contention that there are continua of usage in operation here, rather than a descriptive/evaluative dichotomy. Of course, a dichotomy would be neater. And this explains why it could be a pedagogic aid : it may facilitate our finding our way about in the unfamiliar terrain of aesthetics and of criticism, when these are unfamiliar. But its usefulness in this should not be over-emphasised. In stressing the dissimilarities between evaluating and describing to create a dichotomy, and in choosing extreme examples in support of this view, the similarities and the relating cases may be forgotten. And these similarities may be just as significant as the dissimilarities.

The most reasonable procedure is, perhaps, to accept the value of a dichotomy-view as an aid to teaching or explaining, but to realise that this view is, at best, very likely to mislead. In practice, and here I mean when directly comparing this case with that case, we will have little or no use for such a dichotomy anyway.

To recap, our point has been that if all facts were evaluation-neutral, it would be impossible to ever get to evaluative conclusions. Not merely would there be a logical gap, which we might overcome with, say, a decision : but a chasm, for nothing would count as a reason for or against any such decision.

But there is more to it than that, as we can see if we ask
how we render art intelligible to ourselves. As suggested earlier
(Ch.5, Ch.6) this can only be done by reference, explicit or
implicit, to what has gone before as art. Only in this way could
art possibly be understood, or even misunderstood. And this
point is further reinforced by consideration (See Ch.3) that such
understanding is itself a case-by-case procedure. Hence if art
genuinely is the sort of thing which can be understood and misunderstood, or generally made sense of, it follows that certain things
do have the status of reasons for particular judgements (within a
form of life). And if this is possible, it follows that there is
no hard-and-fast dichotomy between evaluating and describing such
that the latter can never entail the former (although this puts
our conclusion rather baldly.)

Now this in turn deals with the first of our three "problems
of evaluation", for if we can perform the direct comparison of
cases required for a case-by-case procedure, it follows that there
can be no argument against the evaluability of art which requires
that comparison of cases be impossible.

The form of our argument so far has been roughly this : that
there can only be a genuine "problem of evaluation" if certain
conditions hold. And if they do hold (a) the "problem" is
insoluable, and (b), since nothing could then have the status of a
reason for any judgement, art is not the sort of thing which can
be understood or misunderstood. But this last contention is both
false and counter-intuitive. From a recognition of that fact, we
can see how the "problem of evaluation" disappears. For what is
required in order that we understand works of art is precisely
what is required to solve this "problem of evaluation" : namely,
the possibility of case-by-case procedures.

We have agreed that all reflection in the end comes down to
the case-by-case procedure. It follows that the possibility of
understanding (which must involve reflection is some wide sense)
requires that case-by-case procedures be applicable. Yet the
central "problem of evaluation", as we have presented it, revolves
around the uniqueness of works of art : and hence their
inapplicability to comparisons. Now we can see that comparisons
must be applicable after all. So if we really can depend on the
case-by-case procedure, this "problem of evaluation" will disappear.
The crucial difference between this work of art and that work of
art will not necessarily be important, ruling out comparison.
Indeed, even to say that such-and-such a work differs from another,
or is a different work from the other, is to compare them. Of
course, there will be differences between works. If there were

not, we should not call them _different_ works, but the very fact
of differences will not rule out comparisons (8).

Yet a _vestige_ of the old difficulty remains.   The question
arises as to how there can be any _important_ similarities to play a
part in comparison.   That is, how anything can get the status of
'important', for formal similarities are compatible with an
entirely different 'meaning' if we accept the so-called "Heresy of
Paraphrase" arguments mentioned earlier.   The time has come to
give this important argument brief scrutiny.   Indeed rather too
much seems to hang on this argument, for it has cropped up in our
discussion of a number of issues.   But it must be acknowledged
that the best that can be said here will be extremely sketchy,
since it will be brief.

One of the proponents of the "Heresby of Paraphrase" argument,
Cleanth Brooks (9), says of a poem:-

> The poem communicates so much and communicates it so richly
> and with such delicate qualifications that the thing
> communicated is mauled and distorted if we attempt to
> convey it by any vehicle less subtle than the poem itself.
>   (p.256)

Now this is one way of making the point, the professional critic's
way : but philosophical critics (like us) might not feel happy to
let the matter rest on subtlety alone.   After all, could a
language with finer discriminations be constructed one where all
the subtleties of the poem could be marked without mauling?   I'd
want to say "no", and this reaction illustrates my feeling that
there is more to this matter than subtlety exactly.   And we are
reiterating a point (from Ch.3) that there is no _complete list_ of
features of such-and-such to be marked, for at any stage new
comparisons could be offered.   This being so, it is not merely
the complexity of a work of art which prevents "what it says"
being precisely put in any other way.

If we consider a particular poem, with a very obvious theme
and 'message', like Wilfred Owen's "Dulce et Decorum est", we
can see the _point_ of a "Heresy of Paraphrase" argument.   For
just what does this poem 'say' or 'mean'?   That war is a nasty
business?   And that we should not trick the young, with war

---

(8) c.f. Sue Jones "The evaluation of art : a dialogue" in
    Chelsea College of Physical Education Yearbook 1976 for a
    discussion of this point.   Much of this section owes a debt
    to that paper.

(9) Brooks "What does poetry communicate?" reprinted in
    Beaver _ed_. _American Critical Essays_ (1959)

films and the like, into thinking it is a glorious one?   But
put like that, the point sounds trite.   And even when seen in
relation to poems like Brooke's over-famous "The Soldier", which
do just what Owen deplores, one is left asking why Owen bothered
so much to say so little, why he fiddled with small details of
of the verse, why he opted for just that formal structure.   Of
course, the reply is that Owen says far more than that trite
summary.   But what more?   As we go on to fill in precisely
just what the poem is 'saying', we see why it would be absurd to
say to someone who could not get a copy of "Dulce et Decorum
est" : 'Well, read another of Owen's poems – it is "saying"
exactly the same thing' (10).   For it simply would not be
saying exactly the same things.   Or, to draw an example from the
visual arts, Picasso's "Guernica" does not 'say' the same thing
as Douanier Rousseau's "War", or "Dulce et Decorum est" for that
matter : although it might appear that these works all amounted
to the same thing if we considered some rough (and trite) account
of "what they said".   For, in part, "what they said" is
determined by the formal features of them as art, as well as
others.   If, as suggested before, we introduce a type/token
distinction (11) here, we can see just why the idea of two works
is a nonsense, putting the point in the following way : that the
uniqueness of a work of art rests in the uniqueness of its
"meaning", or of "what it says".   For any work with just that
same meaning precisely would merely be another token of the same
type, just as all the Union Jacks hanging in Whitehall are the
same (type-) flag, although they are different token-flags.

We can put this point in Strawson's way:-

It seems a clear tautology that there could not be two
different works of art which were indistinguishable in
all respects relevant to their aesthetic appraisal.
            (Strawson p.185)

This is a "clear tautology" just because to say that these were
two different works of art would be to say that they differed in
some respect relevant to their aesthetic appraisal.   For otherwise they would merely be like the volume Durrell's Alexandria
Quartet on your shelf and the one of that novel on mine : that
is, different physical objects but the same work of art.

---

(10) c.f. Beardsmore Art and Morality Macmillan (1971) pp.17-18
      for discussion of this and related issues.

(11) c.f. Strawson "Aesthetic Appraisal and Works of Art"
      reprinted in his Freedom and Resentment and other essays
      Methuen (1974)

One aspect of our argument protected by putting the case in Strawson's way, one completely avoided, is that we have not been forced to offer a decision as to whether or not all works of art could, in principle, be tokens, or whether some are irrevocably particulars. For example, it might be held that the relationship of "Guernica" to its painter, Picasso, is an aesthetically relevant feature, and hence any work without this feature but (otherwise) indistinguishable to perception would not be "the same work of art". This may be so (12) : or it may not (13). Either way, our argument stands in the same position since it talks in terms of aesthetically relevant features, without attempting to suggest what these might or might not be. And in the last analysis, what is or is not relevant to the appreciation or appraisal of a particular work of art will be the subject for case-by-case consideration.

This highlights a further point. Just as the problems over evaluation were seen as generated by a craving for generality, so the very general nature of our account of the "Heresy of Paraphrase" must make it immediately suspect. If, as is a part of the argument of this work, recognition that all reasoning comes down to the case-by-case procedure attacks our acceptance of general answers, this general account of the Heresy of Paraphrase" must ultimately rest on the direct comparison of cases. That is to say, while we may produce a general line in an argument like that presented here, it will probably still be susceptible to counter-examples in particular places. That possibility should not concern us once we are aware of it. Our aim is to provide helpful remarks, helpful guide lines. And it may not affect their helpfulness that they may not be true in their full generality.

One of these reminders would (as suggested in Ch.5) be to recognise the inadequacy of the question "What does such-and-such a work of art mean?", as it suggests the use of reflexive constructions to gloss intransitive expressions. But the commonness of the question "What does such-and-such mean?" makes this recognition of little practical use. Except, of course, as a reminder against taking that form of words too seriously.

However, we can certainly hope to avoid what seems like one common over-extension of the "Heresy of Paraphrase" argument. From the fact that exactly what a work says or expresses is given

---

(12) c.f. Wollheim "Minimal Art" in his On Art and the Mind
        Allen Lane (1973)

(13) c.f. Strawson "Aesthetic Appraisal and Works of Art"
        reprinted in his Freedom and Resentment and other essays
        Methuen (1974)

only by the work itself, that is from the fact that the features
of the work are (logically or epistemologically) related to "what
the work says", it seems to follow that no feature could be
changed without change of "what the work says". In part, we
recognise that what are and are not features of a work is an open
question. For some poems, for instance George Herbert's "Easter
Wings", the printed words on the page clearly are an integral
part or feature of the poem. To say this is to say that they
must be seen as well as, or even instead of, heard in order that
their full 'meaning' be presented. What they look like is
important. And yet for other poems, for example Thomas Carew's
"Ask me no more ...." and most poems, the printed (or whatever)
words on the page will not be parts or features of the poem in
this way. Nothing will be lost when the poem is read. Of
course, sensitive reading might perhaps add to a person's grasp
of the poem, but at least a person would have missed nothing if
he had not read the poem for himself.

So it is rather difficult to say generally what changes in
a work will or will not constitute its becoming a different work
of art : that is, will change its 'meaning'. For instance, is
Blake's early draft of "The Tyger" from the Rossetti Manuscript
the same poem as "The Tyger" from the published Songs of
Experience (14)? I am inclined to say that it is not, for it
seems to be about different things. For example, the "dread
feet" of the Experience version (p.73) are presumably the tiger's,
while the "dread feet" of the Rossetti Manuscript version (p.94)
are related to the "dread hand" and a question is asked about
fetching "from the furnace deep" : which must imply that the feet
are some smith's. Such a change of sense is a radical example
of what happens when changes occur. Many examples would provide
more subtle changes than this one.

The changes in the two versions of the Blake poem, or
differences between the two poems, were substantial, clearly
affecting the sense of the work(s). But if we take an example
at what must appear another extreme, what happens when we change
one comma in Tolstoi's War and Peace? Clearly its 'meaning' or
'message' is almost certainly not affected by this change.
After all, a comma might easily be changed in the type-setting,
and so the presence of the comma which this version leaves out
might itself be a misprint. Hence, it seems we could 'paraphrase' War and Peace with the one-comma-different version :
but it is hard to see that this really warrants the name 'paraphrase' at all. However, what might seem to be suggested by
considering the 'misprint' case - that whatever counts as the

(14) c.f. The Complete Poetry and Prose of Wm. Blake. ed.
     Keynes Nonesuch Press (1927), to which references are given.

same work with misprints is the same work - cannot be so. We may recognise a work despite misprints which destroy its sense and its beauty, just as we may recognise a glossy reproduction of a matt painting as a reproduction of that work but also recognise what has been lost. Perhaps we can capture this realisation by saying that what the work is will affect what, if any, changes can occur without it becoming a different work : that is, one with a different 'meaning'. The situation will probably be different if, for example, we are dealing with a long novel or a short poem.

Here someone might object that since the content of Picasso's "Guernica", or of the Owen poem "Dulce et ......" could be written down, two works could share this content : just as, to borrow an example of Rhees (15), two news reports of for instance an accident get the same points across though in a different style. And, in so far as we regard works of art as conveying information of what we can call a factual sort, about the working conditions of meat packers or mine workers for example, this objection is well-founded.

But we can meet it, and display the misunderstanding an objection of this sort embodies, by introducing a contrast between the extrinsic and intrinsic 'point' of art. While we are dealing with matters which can be shared, or put into other forms, we are dealing with matters extrinsically connected with the work in question. That is, with matters which are externally related to the method of presentation. And it cannot be denied that the extrinsic value of a work could be paraphrased or shared. But to concentrate on the extrinsic is to miss why the artist chose just those words in a poem, or just those lines and colours in a painting, to create his work. That is, to concentrate on the extrinsic is to ignore what makes it art.

When earlier we considered the question of the 'meaning' of "Dulce et ......", we recognised that the artist's labours result in the production of something which could not be put in any other form. Something of what it means might be shared, say by another poem of the same author such as "Mental Cases", but precisely what it means could not. And this is because the artist is not choosing one route among many. To say just that, he must use those words, that formal arrangement etc. To recognise this is to see how the details of a work, its form and its structure, are related to its 'meaning'. To produce just that result, we must use just those words, lines or whatever.

---

(15) Rhees "Art and Philosophy" in his Without Answers RKP (1969) p.154 c.f. also Beardsmore Art and Morality Macmillan (1971) p.15 ff.

There are a barrage of related issues. We will mention one
such : what are we to say of translations? Perhaps we must say
that we enjoy Scott-Moncrieff's novel <u>Remembrance of Things Past</u>
as well as Proust's <u>A la recherche de temps perdu</u> : or perhaps the
situation closely parallels that in (some) music and (some) dance,
where the work is designed to be interpreted by performers. That
is <u>a part</u> of the artist's creation : and his orders implicitly
include the order to interpret. Or, perhaps a better way of
putting it, that it is inevitable that such interpretation takes
place. Then we might admire Scott-Moncrieff's Proust just as we
might admire Karajan's Beethoven. In the last analysis, each
case must be treated separately, comparing similar and dissimilar
cases, to answer questions such as these. But at least some
guidelines have been suggested.

To conclude our discussion of the "Heresy of Paraphrase"
argument with some sort of summary, we have suggested both (a)
the sense in which works of art are unique, which is rooted in
their intrinsic qualities but does not prevent comparative
judgements; and (b) the sense in which what works 'say' or
'mean' can be shared. But the possibility of this 'sharing'
does not mean that works are paraphrasable, since to claim that
would be to ignore the imporance of the formal features and the
details of a work, the part they play in determining what it
can 'say' or 'mean'.

And one consequence of a general acceptance of such a
position should be noticed : that it relates the central <u>point</u> of
art to its intrinsic features. Thus if we point out that works
of art can titilate, or infuriate, or convert to religion, we are
not talking in terms of what art <u>qua art</u> is 'about' : for we are
talking in terms of functional (and hence extrinsic) values for
art. The "Heresy of Paraphrase" argument emphasises that the
central point of art <u>qua art</u> must be intrinsic. The point was
succintly put by Solzhenitsyn (16):-

The artist cannot set himself political aims;
they may come out as a by-product.

We entered into the discussion of the "Heresy of Paraphrase" in
part in order to be clearer about problems of evaluation. And
now we can see that the fears which led us to discuss this
argument are groundless. For in explaining <u>how</u> the formal
features of works of art could acquire their significance, which
would be in relation to what had gone before in art, and hence
in explaining <u>just how</u> the essential uniqueness of meaning of

---

(16) Solzhenitsyn talking to Michael Charlton "Panorama"
 (B.B.C.1 T.V) March 2nd, 1976.

works of art operated, we employed the very kind of comparative procedure whose applicability worried us.

That deals with the last of our three "problems of evaluation". However, we can bring out a related issue in the following way. If we were to ask "What is aesthetics?", no doubt the number of answers would be nearly as large as the number questioned. But some general views can be gleaned. That Monroe Beardsley can call a book Aesthetics : problems in the philosophy of criticism (17), displays clearly what at least was his view. And such a view might be expected to focus on our appreciation of the arts; not much on what are or are not work of art but on what reasons we have for thinking this a good or valuable work of art. The focus of Dickie's Art and the Aesthetic (18) suggests a quite different answer. He is very concerned to pick out those 'features' which make works art, leaving aside questions of the value of these works. Indeed his definition begins:-

A work of art in the classificatory sense . . . (Dickie p.34)

While these views may be seen (with but little inaccuracy) as representing poles or extremes, such views as these are to be found in many writing on aesthetics, sometimes one and sometimes both. Clearly these ways of looking at aesthetics have affinities with the problems of appreciation and of definition respectively (See Ch.2). And the discussion of these problems did something to suggest the inter-connectedness of these two problems, and hence of these issues. What may be less clear is that the problem of definition centres around providing a classificatory, none-evaluative, account of art : and, therefore, often rests upon a fact/value dichotomy. But this can be seen to be so once we recognise that reasoning, or judging the object, is supposed to be kept out of the picture. For the model proffered is one on which we are attempting to find out what such-and-such is, rather than giving our opinion, attitude to, or judgement of it. If we take such factors as these as consideration, we are seen as invoking problems of appreciation. To put it oversimply, the problem of definition is seen as essentially a factual problem, while the problem of appreciation is seen as essentially concerned with values.

---

(17) Beardsley Aesthetics : problems in the philosophy of criticism. Harcourt Brace (1958)

(18) Dickie Art and the Aesthetic Cornell U.P. (1975)

The inadequacy of the fact/value dichotomy, as demonstrated, might be one reason for uneasiness at this picture. To put the point over emphatically, the definition/appreciation contrast, and its brother and ally the classificatory/evaluative contrast, seem to derive from a Positivistic fact/value dichotomy, like a philosophical **coelacanth**. And, even in Anthony Flew's (19) 'aquarium', this distinction smells like a stuffed fish.

Invective is to no purpose, if we are still left with the same problems. And one at least still looms large. For there does seem to be a certain <u>oddity</u> in claiming that such-and-such is a bad work of art, an oddity which is removed by the announcement that the expression "work of art" is there used in a purely classificatory sense. The reason the expression "bad works of art" strikes our ears as odd, the argument runs, is that we take the expression work of art as <u>evaluative</u> : and taken in <u>that</u> sense, the expression "bad work of art" would be an alienans, like "counterfeit money" (which is not money at all.) Here the evaluative/classificatory contrast is doing useful work, so what price our rejection of it?

Two lines may be offered in reply. We can briefly sketch the first, which denies that "work of art" can be used <u>other than</u> evaluatively, before going on to consider a way of attacking the problem itself. We can begin with a clearer statement of the difficulty. Consider for a moment, as glosses of the expression "it is a bad coin", the following:-

(a) It is a coin, but a counterfeit one : that is, it is not really a coin at all. (This is an alienans use of the term "coin".)

(b) It is a coin, but a worthless one, as an old threepenny piece might be. Here the object would be of little use or value as a coin.

We are asking of the expression "bad work of art" is an alienans like (a), or if it really amounts to something more like (b) : that is, that such-and-such <u>is</u> a work of art but not a very good one. And the doctrine of the two senses of the term "art" comes from here. If we take the term "art" as evaluative, indicative of positive evaluation, "bad work of art" will be an alienans. If we take the term "art" as classificatory, the question "good or bad"? is left open.

---

(19) Almost the complete works of Anthony Flew involve fact/value dichotomies. But c.f. his "On the interpretation of Hume", reprinted in Hudson <u>ed</u>. The Is/Ought Question Macmillan (1969), and more recently his "The Jensen Uproad" Philosophy (1973)

Now we can turn to one attempt to resolve the difficulty. This argument against the possibility of a non-evaluative account of art comes from Cyril Barrett's (20) article "Are Bad Works of Art 'Works of Art'?" He begins by setting up an 'acquiescent' use of the term "work of art" in which:-

> . . . . one makes no special claim that a work is or is not a work of art, but simply goes along with accepted usage . . . . (Barrett p.188)

He opts for this since it seems to <u>rule out</u> questions about <u>why</u> the person sees the object as art, for any answer to this question might be seen as involving evaluations of the object : and Barrett's objections to an acquiescent account do stem from this point. (See Barrett pp.189-191). The chief objection is that the tolerance of even acquiescent users of the term "art" is limited, even when huge. Garden gnomes, for instance, are cited (Barrett p.190) as being the kind of thing which few would accept as works of art, even acquiescently. But how could they be excluded? On what grounds? The answer here must be on some kind of <u>aesthetic</u> grounds; that is, on grounds of their <u>value</u>. Hence, as Barrett puts it:-

> Since their exclusion would be based on judgement of their aesthetic value, the term "work of art" would then be used honorifically. (Barrett p.190)

There is much to recommend this view. It does seem odd to claim that such-and-such is a work of art without ever, at least minimally, judging such objects to be of value. And its reasonableness is reinforced by Barrett's conclusion that the expression "bad work of art" <u>has</u> a place, roughly and plausibly glossed as "flawed work of art". For Barrett has already pointed out that not all the things we might call bad works of art are pseudo-art. That is, they are not a variety of <u>putative</u> art at all. We are willing to give the paintings in, for example, the Royal Academy summer exhibition <u>some</u> credit even if we do not rate these works very highly. They are <u>art</u>, and that is a great deal more than can be said for a number of works, which would not even have qualified as <u>bad</u> works of art. (And Barrett quotes with approval a remarks of an Oxford tutor to C.S.Lewis, to the effect that on a particular occasion his ideas had risen to the dignity of error : and therefore above mere incoherence. See Barrett p.184. Presumably such a picture is to be offered as bad works of art.)

(20) Barrett "Are Bad Works of Art 'Works of Art'?" in Vesey ed. Royal Institute of Philosophy Lectures Vol.6. 1971-2 <u>Philosophy and the Arts</u> Macmillan (1973).

For all its temptations, it seems to me that Barrett's argument too is fundamentally misconceived. After all, he accepts that how the expression "bad work of art" is to be taken represents a problem. And while this may be intuitively accept-able, reflection should make us think otherwise. For where does the problem come from, if not from the "two sense of 'art'" doctrine? And we had attacked that doctrine earlier in this chapter.

Of course, there is some oddity in the sound of the expression "bad work of art". But consideration of some cases may well convince us that we can explain this oddity without recourse to any general scheme on which the expression appears to be (or roughly to be) an alienans, or to any on which it is explained as classificatory or evaluative. And the way to do this is, of course, the direct comparison of cases. We look at other cases of the expressions "a bad X", "a good X", and see what similarities and what differences we are making : and if this helps us to gloss the expression "bad work of art".

What must be acknowledged is that this good/bad contrast is an odd tool elsewhere as well as in the art case. Good thoughts are not usually good __as__ thoughts, as examples of thought, but are thoughts on good matters. To think bad thoughts is not a stage barely removed from not thinking at all. On the contrary, bad thoughts are often schemes of devilish ingenuity. Hence "bad thoughts" is not an alienans, but neither is it an expression we use for something which is barely a thought. A bad argument is, roughly, a poorly constructed one : and that is not one which is bad at convincing. Indeed the term "rhetoric" is often used perjoratively for persuasive 'arguments' which are nonetheless poorly constructed in just such a way. Here we say: "That was a bad argument but ...." (If we are politicians, we do not __mention__ that the argument was other than sound.) Or perhaps we even go so far as to say: "That was no argument at all." Here we are moving in the __kind__ of direction that seemed appropriate for the art case.

Bad grammar is another case again. For there is a sense in which it is not grammar at all. That is, a sentence which is not grammatically accurate is not really an example of bad grammar but of non-grammar. And we would actually call it ungrammatical. But we do have ideas of appropriate and inappropriate grammar. So that some sentences are marginally grammatical and hence may be examples of bad grammar. (Good grammar is what Henry James has and I do not.)

To take another example, a bad apple might be bad for your health, and so might a bad work of art. They might both make you want to vomit, for example. But nausea-inducing might also be a

property of some great art too. (Or of jokes like that.)
Even when we look at the expression "bad masterpiece", is the
situation all that clear? At first it seems that this must be an
alienans : but might it not be glossed in the following way:
"It is a masterpiece alright, but there are finer ones"?
That even such cases are not absolutely clear suggests to me that
the project of asking "classificatory, evaluative or alienans?"
is misconceived. We should simply acknowledge the variety of
our uses of the term "work of art", as it seems we should have to
with "masterpiece".

However, what must be recognised is that all these uses of
the term "art" or the expression "work of art" can be seen as
connected, but the kind of connection here would be that they all
fall within the scope of "the aesthetic";   that is, they can all
be used in making aesthetic judgements. When we have seen that,
we have done something to undermine the strength of any picture
of a classificatory/evaluative contrast as exhaustive. For we
have a large number of uses of the term "art", and we use it in
many of these ways at once. And exactly the same process which
might lead to judgements which upholders of the contrast would
call "classificatory" judgements, might also lead to what they
would call "evaluative" ones.

Let us look at an instance where this might occur. In
presenting the extended music example (Ch.2) it was assumed that
if we accepted "4 minutes 33 seconds" as music, we had accepted it
as art. And this was reinforced by a line which said that it was
not thereby good art. Such a line might be seen as employing the
evaluative/ classificatory contrast : and claiming that calling
such-and-such "music" places it within the compass of the classif-
ication "art". But were we not doing this by relating it to works
we considered as well founded examples of music, examples which we
heard as valuable? And in drawing connections between what we
heard as valuable and the piece under consideration, were we not
providing ourselves with reasons for finding it valuable too?
Clearly we were : for if it is like such-and-such, and if such-
and-such is valuable . . . . Again consistency, and a consistent
judgement, is asked for.

Are we then using the term "music" evaluatively? Perhaps we
are;   but at the best with only minimal evaluative content. If
you heard the similarities between "Song of the Earth" and "4
muntes 33 seconds", along a chain such as that suggested earlier
(Ch.2), and you considered "Song of the Earth" valuable you would
have a reason for a similar judgement of "4 minutes 33 seconds".
That is, we might say, you come to evaluate "4 minutes 33 seconds"
to be music. But if you heard "Song of the Earth" as only
minimally music, the same process might get you to judge "4 minutes
33 seconds" as minimally music. Here, we might say, you would be

classifying it as music. But this is the same process. You are
brought to a particular judgement by coming to hear such-and-such
connections. We might say, you are taught to react in such-and-
such a way. And it simply seems beside the point to attempt to
pigeon-hole the results of this process, in most cases, as a
classificatory or an evaluative judgement, especially to view this
contrast as an exhaustive dichotomy. Of course, there may sometimes be a point in flourishing the contrast : say, a pedagogic
one. But often there won't.

The discussion in this and the previous chapter allow us to
look, briefly and belatedly, at the claim which this work has in
its title : "Much of Jackson Pollock is vivid wallpaper". We
have seen how such a statement can indeed be seen as a judgement
and as based on reasons. Of course, these reasons will, in part,
be the reactions of the critic, Steiner in this case. But we
have suggested that the reactions of the sensitive critic do have
the status of reasons for his judgements. And Steiner's judgement
of Pollock's work is 'objective' in just this sense : that it is
based on reasons which might be shared. For we can assume that
it is answerable to perceivable features of Pollock's corpus. In
particular these features might come to be seen as reasons through
the process of investigating the visual arts in general, and
especially Pollock's work. For in this process of comparing and
considering works of art we may begin to see what Steiner sees in
these works. And in this way come to react to the work as
Steiner does. Not that it is not necessary that everyone see
these 'reasons' of Steiner's as reasons. It would be enough that
those who understand, or are accepted as understanding, such works
can see them in this way. For it must surely be acknowledged
that not everyone understands art equally well. And this is what
we should expect, given the variety of possible comparisons which
might be drawn, between works of art and other things as well as
within the class of works of art, the variety of cases which
might be brought to bear.

Of course, it may also occur that Steiner's view persuades no
one, that his reasons are not seen as reasons by others, that
others are unable to find in themselves views or reactions like
this. Here his views may still be interesting and illuminating.
(It might, for example, stimulate writing on "aesthetics"). We
would not assume that much of Jackson Pollock's work was merely
vivid wallpaper just because Steiner said so. In the case under
consideration, we would disagree with him. We would offer our
own judgements, our own comparisons and our own reasons. But
even in the situation where we agree with Steiner, we do not take
his word. We consider his opinions and his reasons as a way of
finding in ourselves such opinions or judgements. And that is to
say we do our own judging.

This discussion illustrates how, from Steiner's claim, we have built up a fairly comprehensive picture of the bases of aesthetic judgements. And we have seen these as rooted in the direct comparison of cases. Consequences of the **adop**tion of such a picture provide one theme in the next chapter.

CHAPTER 8

Philosophy and Literature

> Not merely philosophy but also the fine arts work at
> bottom towards the solution of the problem of existence.
>   (Schopenhauer (1))

Our concentration on the comparison of cases will have an
effect previously alluded to : philosophical aesthetics as such
will disappear.   For how can <u>aesthetics,</u> which must surely be
conceived of as dealing in generalities and the universal be
accommodated within the framework of case-by-case procedures?
To adopt such a procedure, the direct comparison of cases, is
surely to deny the very generality which the study presupposed.
Of course, the philosophical problems will still exist : temptations to be understood, explicated, resisted and the like.   But
these will no longer be appropriately called <u>aesthetic</u> problems.
And the actual business of comparing cases will not really be
appropriately entitled <u>philosophy.</u>   As criticism, it may be more
or less philosophical, which means it will be concerned to a
greater and lesser degree with the construction of 'realities'
and the like by artists.

To provide an additional focus to this chapter, the emphasis
will fall on literature and literary criticism, although some
examples from the other arts will be interpolated.   We already
have a picture of the critic (from Ch.6) and hence some ideas on
his subject matter.   This suggests one appropriate place to
begin this discussion of philosophy and literature : with a
consideration of what philosophy is.   But "What is philosophy?"
is itself a philosophical question, and we should expect our
consideration of it to revolve around those kinds of methodalog-
ical points (about the case-by-case procedure) made earlier.

One way of investigating philosophy is suggested by some
constructive and interesting work in aesthetics : Wollheim's
"The Art Lesson" (2).   Wollheim asks:-

> Suppose that a proper understanding of the art lesson
> will give us an insight into the nature of art - where
> does this lead us?   What in point of fact do we learn
> about the nature of art from the art lesson?   What does
> go on in the art lesson?   Or, to try and put that last
> question a little more searchingly : what continues to go
> on in the art lesson when its content changes?   What is
> its perennial character?   (p.145)

---

(1) Schopenhauer <u>The World as Will and Representation</u> 3rd ed.
     1859, Dover ed. in 2 volumes 1969.   II. p.406.

(2) Wollheim "The Art Lesson" in his <u>On Art and the Mind</u>
     Allen Lane (1973)

What Wollheim attempts to do is to find the "perennial character" of the art lesson : and this involves him in a fascinating study of the idea of a "perennial character" for art. So can we perhaps learn what philosophy is, or is all about, by looking at the philosophy lesson?

It must be admitted that there is no such <u>one</u> kind of thing as <u>the</u> philosophy lesson. If we look at any of our universities or whatever, its my guess that we'd find that philosophy is taught in a variety of ways : and often in more than one way within a particular institution. So to look for <u>the</u> philosophy lesson seems a fruitless search.

Yet perhaps we can look at <u>some</u> of these ways of teaching philosophy (or, as I'd rather say given the arguments in Ch.6, of getting people to learn philosophy) and see if that tells us anything about philosophy. It seems to me that an examination of one such teaching procedure will allow us to reiterate some methodological points. But the reverse of the coin of the famous truth that "What is philosophy?" is a philosophical question, affecting methodology, is appropriate here : that what we do when doing philosophy will reflect (and affect) our answer to the question "What is philosophy?"

So how can we begin to pick out some interesting features of philosophy lessons? One place to begin is with <u>great</u> teachers of philosophy, and it is at least arguable that one of the century's greatest was John Langshaw Austin.

As an aside, some support may be given to the line of our investigation by Warnock's (3) claim that, even **when** teaching, Austin was very much a <u>philosopher</u> as well as a teacher. Warnock says:-

> He (Austin) was not a purveyor or explainer, however competent or critical or learned, of philosophy; he was a maker of it . . . . (p.45)

So Austin was a great teacher and yet not a purveyor. What, then, was Austin's technique?

To continue in an egocentric fashion, when I first heard of the practice of Austin's I wish to consider, his practice of reading aloud passages of the works of other philosophers - and (often) scarcely bothering to comment!! - I was horrified.

---

(3) Warnock "Saturday Mornings" in Berlin ed.<u>Essays on J.L.Austin</u>
    OUP (1973)

Warnock (4) describes this procedure, by saying of Austin's voice:-

> It was also, on occasions, an effective polemical instrument; for he could, and sometimes did, reduce philosophical propositions to helpless absurdity by simply reading them aloud. (p.20)

And my horror increased tenfold when I learnt that he applied this practice to the work of **Wittgenstein**, too.   Pitcher (5) records Asutin drawing <u>Philosophical Investigations</u> from his shelf with the words:-

> 'Let's see what Witters has to say about that.' (p.24)

(Here Austin does at least go on to <u>discuss</u> what Wittgenstein had said.)   My reaction was predictable : how <u>dare</u> he read passages of the great man in an unsympathetic fashion.

However, I then **recalled** Wittgenstein's (6) advice to the Malcolms:-

> To practice reading aloud <u>well</u> i.e. carefully, teaches one <u>a lot</u>!   E.G. how rotten and slapdash most people, and the newspapers, write; and they write as they <u>think</u>.

But this was advice for the early education of the Malcolms' son. As a psychological or a pedagogic aid, no doubt reading aloud was helpful.   Yet Austin seemed to be treating it as a technique for teaching philosophy, and for doing philosophy.   This did not seem right.

Yet when we have qestioned the value of flourishing these contrasts between the psychological and the philosophical on which the rejection of Austin's technique was based, we begin to wonder if we cannot come to understand something about philosophy by looking at this feature : that reading it aloud can, although it need not, enlighten.

Now we ask <u>why</u> Austin read these texts aloud.   Clearly he did it because he thought or hoped that such reading <u>would</u> reduce the propositions in the texts to "helpless absurdity", if indeed they were helplessly absurd.   That is, reading aloud

---

(4) Warnock "John Langshaw Austin, A Biographical Sketch" in Fann <u>ed</u>. <u>Symposium on J.L.Austin</u> RKP (1969)

(5) Pitcher "Austin : a Personal Memoir" in Berlin <u>ed</u>. <u>Essays on J.L.Austin</u> OUP (1973)

(6) from a letter, quoted Malcolm <u>Ludwig Wittgenstein : a memoir</u> OUP (1958)

could make the listeners <u>notice</u> features of the texts which they
had missed. And such an idea is not so far from the one
Bouwsma (7) picks out so clearly:-

> If there are questions which have already struck one as
> queer and these questions are heard now side by side with
> the other question, the queerness of these questions may,
> as it were, be communicated to the question, like
> vibrations. (pp.187-8)

Is Austin, then, trying to expose the queerness of these
philosophers propositions? If so, should he not be using some
kind of <u>comparative</u> procedure, showing us first one thing then
another?

It is important to realise that this is just what he is doing.
And just how he aims to expose the queerness (or the good sense)
of the propositions he quotes. For they are compared with a
whole variety of sentences previously heard, both those earlier
in the same lecture or whatever, which share with the propositions
under examination the property of being a philosopher's creation,
and those used in other conversations in other parts of life.
We will return to this point.

In addition, the consideration of Austin's technique should
have exposed another feature of the teaching of philosophy : that
what is required is the pupils 'coming to see' that these propositions are helplessly absurd, or that they are not. To have
informed them, as words from the mountain, that such-and-such was
so would not have been to teach philosophy. For the aim of
philosophy teaching must surely be the furtherance **of** <u>understand-
ing</u>, not the acquisition of <u>information</u>, to put the point in a
crudely over-simple but understandable form. The internalisation of data, as we called it (Ch.6), must occur.

Philosophy does not display self-evidences, but 'gets
people to see' what then becomes self-evident. What reading
aloud can do, and what the presentation of cases too can do, is
to 'teach' those self-evidences; to make the pupil himself see or
hear them as self-evident. And not only for the self-evident
and self-contradictory, but more generally the "queer". By
training the pupil's 'ears' in this way, the teachers are allowing <u>them</u> to begin making discriminations. And this reiterates
our earlier discussion (Ch.3, Ch.6).

---

(7) Bouwsma "The Blue Book" in his <u>Philosophical Essays</u>
    University of Nebraska Press (1965)

Cavell (8) seems to have his finger on the pulse of
philosophy when he talks of:-

> . . . . what the teaching of philosophy perhaps must be -
> the personal assault upon intellectual complacency, the
> private evaluation of intellectual conscience.   (p.XXIV)

(Here it does not matter that he accuses Austin of failing to
confront this fact in his writing, for we have seen how Austin's
teaching method might force it upon his pupils.) Such a personal
assault will, of course, involve us in the internalisation of
problems : that is what makes it personal.

It is perhaps more accurate to say that we are given a chance
to internalise these problems.   More crucial here, although they
are related, is the other point we had noticed previously : that
the sentences, or whatever, read out in the philosophy lessons are
compared (implicitly or explicitly) with a whole host of other
sentences, both those fairly similar (the teacher's and Plato's,
for example) and those less similar (the charlady's and Plato's,
for example.)   But why should this comparison be helpful in the
teaching of philosophy?

Perhaps repetition of a phrase of Wisdom's (9) clarifies the
issue.   He talks of needing to place this particular enquiry:-

> . . . . in the manifold of all enquiry.   (p.101)

If we are interested in placing our enquiry (into Mill about
the term "desirable", or Locke about truth, or Berkeley about
God, or Wittgenstein about private language (10)) in the manifold
of all enquiries, it makes rather a lot of sense to display our
enquiry clearly, and expose it to these kinds of comparison.   For
as we have argued (Ch.3, Ch.4), to know the 'nature' of something
is to know how it resembles and how it differs from other things :
that is, to know what the thing is like.   And this is as true of
enquiries or arguments as it is of spades or greyhounds.

Because this consideration of Austin's technique might be
seen as exposing the role of comparison, of the case-by-case

---

(8) Cavell Must We Mean What We Say? Scribners (1969)

(9) Wisdom "A Feature of Wittgenstein's Technique" reprinted in
    his Paradox and Discovery Blackwell (1965) from Proceedings
    Aristotelian Society Supplementary Volume XXXV 1961 pp. 1-14.

(10) The examples are Stanley Cavell's from his Must We Mean
    What We Say? Scribners (1969) p.111

procedure, in the placing of enquiries and the like within the
manifold of all enquiries, its consequences can indeed be
methodological.   If one of the things philosophy must do is to
present these comparisons which allow us to place our enquiry
within any given "manifold" (and no doubt to present them in
such a way as to facilities internalisation of data), which it
must since to do this is to bring people to understand, one method
in philosophy will be to make these kinds of comparison as
explicit as possible.

We seem to have accepted the 'doctrine' that to understand
something is to place it within a particular manifold : but the
arguments are those for the case-by-case procedure as grounding
all reasoning and understanding, even that involved in
recognition (See Ch.3, Ch.6).   Such a view fits rather well with
the fact of our experience that one's grasp of a concept becomes
richer and more vivid the more comparisons and contrasts one can
bring to bear on it.

What, then, would be the consequences of accepting the view
of philosophy which is being offered? One at least would be
liberation from cramped views of what it is to reason.   Of
course, case-by-case procedures might be thought not to be
reasoning at all, or (at best) to be rather poor reasoning.   We
have argued against this view earlier (Ch.3).   And to accept
our view of philosophy is to accept that all reasoning in the end
comes down to the case-by-case procedure.

But what shape does the doing of philosophy begin to assume
if we do accept it?   Philosophy will then consist in the
examination of the similarities and dissimilarities of particular
cases.   It will deal less and less with generalisation and more
and more with the marking of what are seen as relevant similarities.   And not just any similarities will do.   But, as
previously argued (Ch.2, Ch.3 esp.), what similarities we see as
relevant will be a product of our experiences (and more than
that), and our culture.   We would be in the realm of what
Wittgenstein (11) succintly characterised as:-

. . . . agreement in judgements.

So far in this chapter we have been looking at a methodological procedure in philosophy and hence at philosophy itself.
We may have noticed that this way of working has the consequence
of making philosophy look very much more like, for example,
literary criticism (although criticism in the other arts too), in

(11) Wittgenstein Philosophical Investigations Blackwell (1953)
§ 242.

related ways in particular.   The first is in dealing in the
direct comparison of cases.   The second is that the point at
issue is not so much to _decide_ any question as to feel the
'temptations' which give rise to it.   Yet surely, if something
purports to answer some question, or some argument _claims_ to
lead to some conclusion, this needs checking.   If such-and-
such a theory or account (say, Bell's) does indeed rest on a
mistake, do we not need to be able to say so?   Do we not need
to be able to call these things true or false, as well as
illuminating or unilluminating?   In a word, do we not need to
be able to _decide_ issues?   On the account offered it is far
from clear that we could ever possibly be in that position.

This is an oddity which I cannot resolve theoretically, and
which I suspect betrays my own 'craving for generality'.   For
why should there be any _general_ resolution of this difficulty?
In some cases it will be right to treat arguments as fallacious
or invalid, or statements as false.   That will be the way to
clear up some of our problems.   So that to see where Bell's
account of the aesthetic emotion leads is, or can be, illuminating.
And to see where it leads is to see that it will not do to provide
some general account of art.   Our coming to feel the 'temptations'
it embodies, our illumination, may well _involve_ our seeing it as
false;   which will be to 'decide an issue'.

On the other hand, we won't need this across the board.
To appreciate that some consequences of logical or philosophical
behaviourism lead to unintelligibilities (if they do) may appear
to 'decide an issue'.   But only if we think the natural home of
behaviourism is philosophy.   Its value as a methodology of
psychology may be quite another matter.   Indeed, one way to
appreciate the value of behaviourism as a methodology of
psychology is perhaps to feel the 'temptation' inherent in it as a
philosophical doctrine.

Yet the similarities between philosophy and literature by no
means stop at the similarities between philosopher and critic.
Consider the situation where we ask someone what his work
achieved vis-a-vis a particular person, and he replies:-

I have changed his _way of looking at things_.

If this were the remark of some novelist or of some critic,
we would understand what he meant.   In fact it is Wittgenstein
(_Philosophical Investigations_ § 144).   Again I think we know
what he means.   And it does not seem to be so very far removed
from what the novelist or the critic might have meant.

Two points may be stressed here, both providing useful continuations from this part of our discussion. The first point, to which we will return, is briefly and crudely that both philosopher and writer are concerned with understanding 'reality', or with making sense of the world. This kind of generalisation is worthless except in so far as it allows us to consider the specific roles of specific works of novelist, poet or philosopher. So that we do know how to take the remark of the novelist, Julian Mitchell (12), that:-

We read to gain new information about life . . . (p.10)

While this may not be literally true of all the novels we read, we can take the spirit of what Mitchell says. And particularly when he goes on to assert that the truths which can be learnt from novels are moral truths; that novels are:-

. . . . a way of understanding individuals in relation to each other. (Mitchell p.15)

This is a very important idea, since it goes some way towards explaining the kinds of thing that may occur in some novels, poems etc. And just as some philosophers will want to understand the values etc. of peoples, and want to capture and shed light upon this feature of life, so will some novelists. (We must see later how these are, or are related to, epistemological concerns.)

The second point takes up a detail of this first, for it relates to how our understanding may be affected by both philosophy and literature, to how people's way of looking at things may become altered. It is a simple fact of our experience that there are changes in what we can call the geometry of such-and-such. To say in this context "It could never again be the same for me" amounts to claiming that when I have seen some comparison, or had some similarity pointed out to me, my grasp of the manifold has changed.

That amounts to a change in the geometry of such-and-such. We noticed (Ch.6) how people may differ in their grasp of concepts and how this grasp may change, especially when a greater range of cases and comparisons can be brought to bear, or becomes available. We can recall our discussion of how illuminations may be produced when our grasp of a concept changes; when we 'see' looking lustfully at a woman as adultery, or we 'see' all a child's behaviour as sexual, for example. The critic's job, it was argued (Ch.6), could be seen as the production of such illuminations. But the artist too is clearly as a producer of

_____

(12) Mitchell "Truth and Fiction" in Vesey ed. Royal Institute of Philosophy Lectures Vol.6 1971/72 Philosophy and the Arts Macmillan (1973)

these illuminations.   He too can bring about changes in the
geometry of a concept.   For example, one is left with the very
strong feeling that after, say, Shakespeare's <u>Hamlet</u> the term
"tragic" just did not <u>mean</u> the same thing (13).   Or, what seems
to me a less misleading way of putting the point, that the
geometry of the tragic was changed.   Wittgenstein (14) captures
this process (in mathematics) as follows:-

> . . . . One would like to say : the proof changes the
> grammer of our language, changes our concept.   It
> makes new connections and it creates the concepts for
> these connections.   (It does not establish that they
> are there; they do not exist until it makes them.)

As was pointed out (Ch.6), it is less misleading to talk,
not of our concepts changing, but of our <u>apprehension</u> or <u>grasp</u> of
them changing, although it is difficult to clearly draw such a
distinction.

To repeat an earlier example (from Ch.6), our apprehension
of the human body could be rendered more vivid by a consideration
of Picasso's 'new anatomy' (15).   Our model here might be the
showing of similarities and dissimilarities between what we can
call the 'perceptual' anatomy of Ingres (although there are also
problems and temptations here) and the anatomy of Picasso, based
on what we <u>know</u> to be there - profile and full face at one time,
to take an example which is clearly seen in "Girl Seated in a Red
Arm Chair" (1932).

As an aside perhaps we can suggest that this fact begins to
explain for us the difference between the sensitivity of the
artist and others.   The artist can see the insights offered in
these connections for himself, while we have to be shown them.
This too is in part a matter of degree, but the general idea is
clear and may be put crudely as follows: that the situation is
not like that of a craftsman, where we all might do what the
talented craftsman does but do it less well.   What the artist

---

(13) c.f. Weitz <u>Hamlet and the Philosophy of Literary Criticism</u>
Faber (1965) p.X.

(14) Wittgenstein <u>Remarks on the Foundations of Mathematics</u>
Blackwell (19 6) II § 31.

(15) This point was brought to my attention by the work of David
Chapman in some classes on (roughly) art-appreciation.
He would not necessarily agree with my use of these examples,
of course.

does, only he can do.   Or, as Schopenhauer (16), puts it:-

> Talent is like the marksman who hits a target which others
> cannot reach; genius is like the marksman who hits a
> target . . . . which others cannot even see.   (p.391)

Here we are emphasising the illuminating effects of the works of
great artists.

As in the case of criticism, the illumination does not depend
on the truth-conditions of what is said or shown.   We had
remarked of Mitchell 'critical' claim about the reason for our
reading novels that it was not <u>literally</u> true.   It was none the
less illuminating for that.   Consider also, to take an example
from the arts, the illumination offered by the poetry of Wallace
Stevens despite, as is arguably true (see Ch.9), its resting on
a decrepit idealist metaphysics.   In a rather similar way, the
value of the many insights into the natural world which Gerard
Manley Hopkins' poetry may offer seems independent of the truth
or falsity of his theory of inscape and instress (17), although
the insights are to be seen as based on this theory.   Indeed the
best 'argument' for the theory might easily be thought to be the
poems, and the illuminations they contain.   It is difficult to
see illuminations such as these as true or false, exactly.   What
is at stake here doesn't seem to be truth or falsity.   Perhaps
what is needed is a helpful-unhelpful scale (18).   And it may
well help me to understand the nature of 'reality' (to put it
tendentiously) if I am confronted with the kinds of picture of it
which Stevens offers in, for example, "Comedian as the letter C",
or Hopkins in "Pied Beauty".

---

(16) Schopenhauer <u>The World as Will and Representation</u> 3rd
     edition (1859) Dover ed. in two volumes. 1969. Vol. II.

(17) c.f. Gardner "Introduction" to <u>Gerard Manley Hopkins</u> :
     <u>poems and prose</u> Penguin (1953) pp. XX - XXI.

(18) Another example of a critical claim which might be better
     judged on a helpful-unhelpful rather than a true-false
     scale would be the remark of Terry Wogan on his BBC radio
     programme on Tuesday, 17 February, 1976.   Apropros of a
     new work acquired by the Tate gallery, a work by Carl
     André consisting of 60 fire-bricks spread out, Wogan
     commented:-

> It can't be a work of art.   The eyes don't follow
> you around the room.

(My thanks to Margaret-Mary Preece for bringing this example to
my notice.)

There are connections here with our discussion (in Ch.4) of 'twitting' with inconsistency as a means of 'resolving' disputes in this area. For I may be brought to see clearly in a work what you see as valuable in that work. It may be as if I saw it for the first time : and then my conception of what it is will be enriched. I won't necessarily agree with you, but at least I'll be some way towards understanding why you say whatever it is you say. Until Picasso made his bull's head from a bicycle saddle and handlebars, did we really know as much about either bull's heads or the bits of bikes? But the problem here is to say just what has been added to our understanding, for clearly something has. But what? To explain, we might draw out some of the comparisons which this work of Picasso's suggests : and another might draw out comparisons which lead him to believe that no new apprehension of bulls or bikes comes from this work. Here we would begin 'twitting' one another with inconsistency.

Again, when we are comparing cases and 'twitting' one another with inconsistency, it is hard to see how what either of us claims will be the true or false exactly. To go into this is a digression but may prove illuminating. In this case, the empirical examination will have sorted out a number of true/false questions and we might agree on many others, say the colours and the positions of lines and surfaces in a painting; and yet we disagree on its merits. And if I called your view "false", wouldn't I be rather over-reacting?

Two points are important here. The first, already made (Ch.6, Ch.7), is that not any interpretation of a work is a possible one. Hence it may be that I can show you that the interpretation you offer cannot be sustained. But often this won't be so, which brings us to the second point. For even when a critic's view is tenable, another critic may still accuse him of perpetrating falsehoods. Here he would produce evidence which establishes for him that, although taking such-and-such a line does not lead to inconsistency or nonsense, it is still not to be selected. He might, for instance, argue that, to use a pungent phrase of Anthony Flew's (19), it dies the "death of a thousand qualifications". That is to say, it avoids becoming nonsense at the price of extreme complexity, and so should not be preferred to simpler solutions. While this may not to us look like a situation where what one critic says is true and the other is false, the situation may seem entirely different to the critics. From where one of them stands, his opponent's view may look very false indeed.

---

(19) Flew. "Theology and Falsification" in Flew and MacIntyre ed. New Essays in Philosophical Theology Macmillan (1955) p.97

<u>That</u> interpretation of one critic's (or one author's) accusation that a rival's claims were false was a kind of digression, as noted. But it paves the way for discussion of another, perhaps more important, way in which a critic might accuse an opponent of falsehood : where one critic claims that another's interpretation is <u>morally</u> false. And this brings us to the heart of this section. As there are obvious connections between our discussion and discussion of the <u>kind</u> of truth(s) which it is appropriate to ascribe to fictions, it would be more convenient to discuss this topic in the wider context of the value of novels, indeed of art in general. However, this issue is far too complex to receive any more than a cursory treatment here, and that indirectly.

We are hoping to consider how literature could be see as true. This will amount to consideration of how literature could be seen as valuable. In part, it will allow us to ask how literature can connect with society. And one way, which draws out some connections with philosophy, is that literature (or art) be <u>morally</u> valuable, as suggested by Mitchell, in a way which does not involve us in seeing art as a social "tool", but only as art (20). That is, we are to look for <u>intrinsic</u>, rather than extrinsic, value (See Ch.7).

This gives us a chance to actually begin to compare some cases. For we can look for a certain amount of reflected light on the relationship between philosophy and literature, or between philosophy and the arts in general, from a consideration of pornography. Since it is, I think, by and large clearly not art, pornography may help us to understand the connections between art and life, those marked (Ch.5) in terms of "significance", because it will be <u>related</u> to similar concerns and connections.

What seems too obvious to require argument is that kinds of personal relationship we value are seen as devalued or debased in pornography. This is of importance because art can perhaps be seen as offering the possibility of new and relatively undistorting perspectives on personal interactions, on what have been called "life issues" (21). If we undestand pornography's connections with important issues in our lives, perhaps we will better understand how <u>art</u> connects with these issues. And remember now Mitchell's claim, quoted earlier, that the central concerns of at least <u>some</u> art were moral concerns.

---

(20) c.f. Beardsmore <u>Art and Morality</u> Macmillan (1971) passim.

(21) c.f. D. Best "The Aesthetic in Sport" <u>B.J.A.</u> 1974 p.212.

The debate over pornography is generally conducted in terms of pornography causing, or not causing, some future action. That is, in _extrinsic_ terms. Hence discussions of the possibility of there being a causal connection between, for example, erotica and sexual offices (22). And this debate mirrors discussions of the social good, or harm, that _art_ can do. Earlier (Ch.5, Ch.7) we began to argue that art was not to be viewed as a means to an otherwise specifiable end : that art was good _for itself_ in some sense (23). If we accept such an argument, and the parallel arguement in the case of pornography, we can begin to see _how_ and _where_ pornography might be thought depraving (24).

What counts as depraving, or for that matter enlightening, a human being is not really a matter for measurement. Hence sexual success is not to be measured, or at best to be inaccurately 'measured', in terms of, for example, intensity or extent of orgasm. If it were, it would be difficult to see why mastabation should not be the _very best_ way of guaranteeing such "success". No, sex is important as a part of our _lives_, our human **lives. In** our society deep and important _sexual_ relationships do not necessarily revolve around orgasm, for the significance of sex must be, to repeat, as a part of our whole lives. I enjoy lollipops, but they have no significance for me (c.f. Ch.5 for a discussion of the judgement/preference contrast). No doubt I could enjoy sex acts in a similar way : but that this could _in general_ be how sexual activity was seen seems an abomination. The _value_ we place on sex as a part of interpersonal relationship would be inexplicable in such a situation. The aim here is not a return to any pre-Freudian sexual taboos, but merely recognition that here and now certain things are seen as valuable and significant.

It must be acknowledged that moral choices and moral problems are choices and problems which bear on the lives of _us all_ in a way in which aesthetic ones do not (25). Nevertheless, we might

(22) c.f. Editorial "Pornography" The Human World No.3 (1971), which was the inspiration for much of the discussion here.

(23) Penetrating arguments for such a contention will be found throughout the works on aesthetics of Beardsmore; especially his Art and Morality Macmillan (1971)

(24) c.f. Jones Philosophy and the Novel OUP (1975) Ch.5 where parallel of learning from a novel and learning from personal relationships is explored.

(25) c.f. Beardsmore Art and Morality Macmillan (1971) pp.27-28.

say things about art similar to those said of the moral situation. It is fairly easy to imagine a society where art was not seen as of importance : but that would not be <u>our</u> society, nor any with close connections with ours.

To see the <u>value</u> of any comparison with pornography, we must see how art can enrich and enliven our understanding of the world, just as personal relationships can.   (Indeed how art can make us see personal relationships more clearly.) A person who knows, for example, all the suicide statistics of England may still feel that the 'nature' of suicide escapes him. Now reading Donne's <u>Biathanatos</u> and his "Nocturnall upon St. Lucy's Day" may give this kind of apprehension. Or it may not. But when it did, some aspect of the world, of 'how things are', became clearer. Of course, the kind of change here might not be very easily expressed. To say that you realise that potential suicides see the world as a black, pointless, unfriendly place may seem trite. But that might be the best you could do to get across your new apprehension of the situation. And, as such an example shows, you might now understand others around you. Here is art 'making sense' of a moral situation for you. And isn't this just the kind of "significance" (to use an expression from Ch.5) we expect from art? Isn't that possibility the kind of thing which marks it out as art?

It should be no less obvious that personal relationships can colour and enliven our perception or apprehension of the world. People in love might provide a clear example here, where what had seemed like very ordinary things and actions assume a huge importance.   But the way our relationships at school, say, or at work make vivid the world for us would provide equally clear examples.   And <u>one</u> kind of personal relationship which has this effect, the one under consideration here, is the sexual.   My apprehension of acts and events may be altered quite radically by seeing them in relation to, or as part of, a relationship with another person.   The point is too obvious to warrant exemplific- ation.   What is less obvious, perhaps, is that this apprehension will be altered if this relationship can no longer be seen as valuable.   If sexual activity is not seen as valuable, any 'reflected' values will be lost.   And it is here that pornography may be seen as debasing.   For pornography is seen as attempting to treat sex as without the kinds of importance it can have as part of our lives, and <u>only</u> have in this way.

Still someone might ask : "What is wrong with pornography"? Our reply might be roughly this : that to read and understand pornography is to understand, or 'take', sex in the way, in the 'language', of pornography. And this depraves by disconnecting sex from whatever significance it has in our lives.

It isn't that pornography <u>causes</u> depravity and corruption, but that it <u>is</u> depravity and corruption. For, to repeat a claim of Beardsmore (26) (from Ch.4.), it is by reference to such cases that we give terms like "corruption" meaning. And to say this is to claim that pornography is <u>intrinsically</u> corrupt. It is not that pornography may or may not lead to certain depravities. The evidence, I suspect, would suggest that it may even be <u>valuable</u>, viewed extrinsically. The point here is that our concern is with its intrinsic values, in just the way that our concern with art is with <u>its</u> intrinsic values.

I am trying to suggest that pornography depraves by showing personal relationships in a way which under-rates their value or importance <u>as</u> personal relationships; while art can enrich, by allowing us to see personal relationships or whatever more clearly or vividly. We might say that art offers truth about the relationships or whatever : but it does so <u>intrinsically</u>.

Yet someone might still ask : "Can pornography be art?" And a genuine answer would demand a comparison of cases, but it is clear that <u>some</u> pornography would call itself art. I do not mean the sensual drawings of Beardsley, or the nude scenes in Ken Russell's film "Women in Love", for these are clearly (parts of) works of art. But why are they not portographic, if indeed they are not? Or, to put that question more searchingly, why should we accept the claims of any pornography to be art? Picasso's later drawings are exclusively concerned with coupling; and yet it is easy to see their connections with what went on before in his art. They too are a sensitive study of an important human activity. To speak loosely, they 'uplift' the human relationships depicted. And they do this <u>intrinsically</u>. Any reasons which could be offered for the acceptance of what was thought pornography as art would, I suggest, be based on drawing just the kinds of connection between it and what had gone before in art discussed earlier (Ch.5). And this would involve us in seeing the work as of intrinsic significance. Yet to see it as of significance is precisely <u>not</u> to see it as pornography (27).

---

(26) Beardsmore "Consequences and Moral Worth" Analysis (1969)

(27) I am here ignoring works like those of De Sade which might, roughly, combine bits of pornography with bits of art (or of philosophy). Of these we should say (as per Ch.7) "there but for such-and-such goes a great work of art."

As Cavell (28) writes:-

Straight pornography is not a problem: a drug is not
a food.   (p.46)

Part of the insight in this comparison revolves around the
way that, for some addicts, drugs like heroin achieve the status
of a food, the importance of food.   And this affects the
addict's perception of food as well as of the drug.   We might be
tempted to say that the addict can no longer see things "as they
are", although this has a Realist sound to it.   Perhaps better
to say that his perception of 'reality' is distorted, and leave
unexplained how talk of "perception of 'reality'" is to be
explicated (29).

To recap, we got into this discussion in an attempt to
understand one kind of truth which the arts might have : and
looking at pornography's connections with society - where this
kind of truth was not apparent - may have helped us to focus on
the ways that the arts can change our apprehension of the world.
For one way in which this might occur, although by no means the
only way, was through the changing of some moral perspective.
To repeat a remark of Wittgenstein quoted earlier, the artist may
find himself saying:-

I have changed his way of looking at things.

We have seen the centrality of this idea for some literary art.
But such a recognition raises a whole host of other difficult
issues.   For now we are talking about how art can shed light on
reality.   Or, to put that more searchingly, how art can show us
facets of realities.   Yet we are back again to talk of
perception of 'reality', an expression we left unexplained.

However, such explanation might begin to be provided by an
example.   We are in effect considering the way writers can
produce or create realities, and what it means to say that they
can.   Many of the stores of Jorge Luis Borges illustrate this
tendency, and we can usefully mention two of them : "Tlon, Uqbar,
Orbis Tertius" and "A New Refutation of Time".   Both of these

---

(28) Cavell The World Viewed Viking (1971).   Much of the
     inspiration of this section comes from a desire to make
     sense of Cavell's ideas here.

(29) Some help on this issue might come from Winch Idea of a
     Social Science R.K.P. (1958) Ch.1; or from Hacker,
     Insight and Illusion O.U.P. (1972) especially the last
     chapter.

could be viewed as essays on, or reviews of, ideas encapsulated in other imaginary works. The way in which writers (and artists) create 'realities' can be exemplified by these works, in which the practice of such writers is made plain. These are, in effect, a kind of meta-literature. Borges aims to consider and evaluate such 'realities) as writers often create, and to do this by the creation of <u>another</u> kind of 'reality' : perhaps a critical 'reality'. Borges (30) explains as follows:-

> The composition of vast books is a labourious and impoverishing extravagance. To go on for five hundred pages developing an idea whose perfect oral exposition is possible in a few minutes! . . . . More reasonable, more inept, more indolent, I have preferred to write notes upon imaginary books. (p.13)

The stores themselves are mysterious. The first is a discussion of a new 'world', created along lines suggested by an Idealist philosophy such as Berkeley's by a number of (un-named) eminent thinkers. And the narrator in the story finds details of this 'world' in, naturally, a <u>book</u>. We are presented with facts about this world as though they were fictions, and fictions as though facts. For example, we are told (31) that in Tlon :

> Centuries and centuries of idealism have not failed to influence reality. In the most ancient regions of Tlon, the duplication of lost objects is not infrequent. Two persons look for a pencil; the first finds it and says nothing; the second finds a second pencil, no less real, but closer to his expectations. (Borges pp.37-8)

It seems natural to ask how this can be. Such occurrences do not make sense in our picture of what it is to understand the world. That such "duplication of lost objects" is a <u>possibility</u> given an Idealist philosophy (if it is) may well seem to us a powerful argument <u>against</u> such a philosophy. And Borges is not merely grasping the 'nettles' of such consequences. He is also illustrating the practice of the writer as creator and modifier of reality. By <u>discussing</u> this trait in others, Borges makes it explicit for us. And yet these 'others' are his own creations, parts of the 'reality' his literature erects.

---

(30) Borges <u>Fictions</u> Grove Press (1962)

(31) All quotations of the Stories from Borges <u>Labrynths</u> Penguin (1970), which contains both the pieces under consideration.

The situation is not so radically different in "A New Refutation of Time". Here we are presented with Idealist arguments against the reality of matter, space and the self, with quotations from Berkeley, Hume and Schopenhauer among others. And these arguments are then applied to time. Writers in both philosophy and literature have suggested that the reality of time is undeniable. If it were not so, they argue, we would be able to have the same moment over again (32). Every moment when such-and-such occurs would be indistinguishable from every other moment when such-and-such occurs. And this position is seen as untenable, absurd. It is seen, for example, as producing absurd consequences for numerical identity questions for persons. For now _who_ performed such-and-such an action? But Borges patiently _accepts_ such a view of time, and attempts to look at its consequences. Yet this is not exactly a story, as "Tlon, Uqbar, Orbis Terius" was. It is a kind of literary conceptual investigation, and hence a very appropriate example for our discussion. The form of the work is interesting. It consists of prologue and two essays on the same subject : and _we_ would say that these parts were written at different times (Borges dates the first essay 1944, and the second 1945); and yet the piece he attempts to 'refute' time. It attempts to move from Idealist arguements which identify the self with a series of 'chunks' of perceptual information to a denial of such an idea of succession. The arguments need not concern us, for they are important only in so far as they shed light on the practice of the writer in general. And for that we must turn to the conclusions.

One consequence of accepting the 'Refutation' has been noted: that the idea of succession disappears since the _same_ moment can occur at what we would call different times. And to say that they are the same moment denies this description. But another striking consequence is that simultaneity too can only amount to the _same_ moment recurring. It is no good, to take Borges own example (Borges p.258), to claim simultaneity for the actions of Captain Isidoro Suarez in deciding the victory of Junin and De Quincey in publishing a diatribe against Wilhem Meisters Lehrjahre, even if we acknowledge that both events could be dated in the first part of August 1824. As Borges says:-

. . . . the two men died - one in the city of Montevideo, the other in Edinburgh - without knowing anything about each other. (Borges p.258)

---

(32) But c.f. Moorcock The Time Dweller Mayflower (1969) where the hero is able to recycle and reuse the same moment.

But the two events become simultaneous, or at least contemporary, when I see them together. And it must be "I" and not "we" for, as Borges puts it:-

> . . . . if time is a mental process, how can thousands of men - or even two different men - share it?
> (Borges p.258)

To follow Borge's discussion is to enter a world which is not rendered intelligible in quite the way in which ours is. We accept his conjectures and understand them. And we accept them as real, although we know they are fictions. The Refutation of Time, Borges admits, is something

> . . . . in which I myself do not believe . . . .
> (Borges p.253)

The difficulty in believing such a line is obvious. And again an insight Borges offers is an insight into the business of writing novels as well as into the 'nature' of time, when he says:-

> All language is of a successive nature; (Borges p.260)

But the novelist will want, or need, to move in directions other than succession. Mitchell (33) discusses this point, referring to Borges, and listing a number of the sorts of time with which a novelist might be concerned. For time in novels can go backwards and forwards. It can even stand still, as in Tristram Shandy. And then who is to say what is and what is not contemporary? (Borges own story "Garden of the Forking Paths" might be seen as an illustration of this.) And "The New Refutation of Time" can be seen as a kind of meta-story on this theme (34).

What will be clearer from the discussion of Borges is the sense in which artists in general, and novelists in particular, can be concerned with the construction and investigation of 'reality'. That is, they can create situations which allow us

(33) Mitchell "Truth and Fiction" in Vesey ed. Royal Inst. of Philosophy Lectures Vol.6 1971-72 Philosophy and the Arts (1973) c.f. esp. pp.15-17.

(34) A similar reading, but in 'straight' philosophy, might be given to Bouwsma "The Mystery of Time", in his Philosophical Essays University of Nebraska Press (1965)

insight into human, and other, existence and human values (35).
And this surely reiterates the claim of Schopenhaur quoted
initially. For example, Proust A la recherche du temps perdu
or Borges "A New Refutation . . . ." can be seen as questioning
the nature of time, Tolstoi Father Sergius as questioning the
nature of religious belief and moral worth. And these topics
are the concerns of the philosopher as well as the author.

Here we are approaching questions about what we can tendentiously call the Nature of Reality. While this issue is far too
complex to be adequately considered here (36), some earlier
remarks may be recalled to be seen from a new perspective. When
discussing an apparently Realist claim of Wisdom's (Ch.3), we
argued that there is no list of properties of the world in
advance of our perception or knowledge of them. Although we did
not draw this moral there, that view has the consequence that the
truth or falsity of claims about 'how the world is' are no longer
seen as completely independent of any possible cognitions of 'how
the world is'. (This is the nexus of the marriage of logic and
epistemology referred to in Ch.1.) And that in turn makes it no
longer meaningful to alk of 'how the world is' divorced from a
particular conceptual structure : that is, divorced from a
particular view of it. To learn about the world, then, will be
to learn about world-views. The artist is eminently qualified
to provide examples or 'accounts' of such views and, in doing so,
he is investigating reality. Again we are acknowledging the
shared concerns of philosophy and art.

It must be recognised that it follows from this fact of
shared concerns that much of the work of the artist can be viewed
as epistemology. Not perhaps as formal epistemology, but
certainly as rooted in questions about how, and if, we can know
certain things. And this is particularly true in some cases.

---

(35) Perhaps this is one reason why the novel is widely used in
     modern moral philosophy. See, for example, Winch Ethics
     and Action R.K.P. (1972) and Phillips"Allegiance and
     Change in Morality" in Vesey ed. Royal Institute of
     Philosophy Lectures Vol.6 1971-2 Philosophy and the Arts
     Macmillan (1973).

(36) But C.F. Hacker Insight and Illusion O.U.P. (1972) p.302 ff.
     I have been talking in terms of 'reality' as though it were
     there, independently of language, to be understood. This
     is a clear way of putting certain points but, as
     Constructivism shows, it is misconceived. For a
     Constructivist the central philosophical problem is the
     relationship between language and the world.

For example (as argued Ch.9) concerns with the possibility of knowledge of the external world are central to the poetry of Wallace Stevens. Or, to take an even more extreme example, in Proust's novel the general question of the attainability of knowledge is under discussion. And a good critic might feel in a position to make some comment on this matter. So that Jones (37), for example, discusses and dismisses the view that the narrator in Proust's novel believes knowledge to be unattainable. Clearly such a discussion may shed quite a bit of reflected light on our understanding of the possibility of knowledge in general. Such a recognition might appear to make the position of the literary critic look a little strange. For if it is the philosopher who is concerned with the 'realities' of novels, where is the critic's proper domain?

Here we are stepping into the realm of Leavis. For if we ask how philosophy is related to literature, his seminal article "Literary Criticism and Philosophy" (38) should be ignored only at our peril, especially when some its positions have been supported by Bambrough (39). Leavis plainly states his belief that, despite possible interactions between philosophy and literary criticism,

> . . . . it is necessary to have a strict literary
> criticism somewhere and to vindicate literary
> criticism as a distinct and separate discipline.
> (Leavis p.212)

If, as I've been trying to suggest, the methods of literary critic have so much to offer philosophy we should perhaps fear philosophy's ceasing to be "a distinct and separate discipline".

What Bambrough (rightly) finds in Leavis is an appropriate attention to minutiae, and to the particular case : and a horror at the worst excesses of 'philosophising' literary critics. To give but one of Bambrough's examples, he says:-

> The definition of tragedy has by this time turned into
> the tragedy of definition . . . . (Bambrough p.278).

---

(37) Jones Philosophy and the Novel OUP (1975) Ch.4.

(38) Leavis "Literary Criticism and Philosophy" in his
The Common Pursuit Penguin (1952)

(39) Bambrough "Literature and Philosophy" in Bambrough ed.
Wisdom : 12 Essays Blackwell (1974)

Surely we can take his point. Generalisation and abstraction are often too tempting. They can offer us so much in some places that we assume they can do so across-the-board. And this results in the cramped notion of reasoning picked-out previously. But isn't Leavis's defensive claim to have a discipline of his own a sympton of something similar? (Bambrough hints as much p.278). Why is Leavis so worried about being 'taken over'? I don't lack his fears simply because I find practicioners of philosophy a fairly congenial lot, and think he might too. To be a happy captive is to be a captive none the less. No; for me there is plenty of room for an equitable overlap. Not all philosophy will look like criticism now looks, after all. Formal logic, for example, won't. (It will keep looking like mathematics.) And not all criticism will look like philosophy. Of course, it is relevant to ask about the kind of realities or the kind of manifolds appropriate to, or constructed in, certain works. And that is certainly very like, if not the same as, an epistemological question. But that is only one kind of question we can ask of a work of art. Among the other questions, many will not look like philosophy. For example, discussion of the 'how' of formal features of a work of art will be perhaps the most extreme cases of criticism which looks like criticism. (Or perhaps even this claim of mine betrays a cramped notion of how much manifolds work.)

To recap some of the discussion in this chapter, we have been trying to make sense of how both the artist, in particular the literary artist, and the philosopher attempt to understand the world, and to understand understanding. We considered the role of art in providing a certain kind of perspective, an intrinsically significant perspective, on moral affairs by comparing art and pornography. And this led us to question the connections between the changes of apprehension which art can provide and 'reality'. Here again we saw the work of the literary artist in providing us with insights, but now these took the form of insights into world-views. Our discussion of Borges is, in the last analysis, a brief consideration of some of these.

The effect of our examination, then, has been to point to ways in which philosophy resembles literature, while not ignoring those ways in which it differs from literature.

But more generally we have considered how aesthetic judgements are grounded in the direct comparison of cases, and how the reactions of certain persons may have the status of reasons for particular judgements. In a sense, this is the kind of

'justification' of literary-critical practice that is often
called for (40). And it paves the way for what might be called
(to follow Ch.1) "the aesthetician's choice". For if we accept
that all reasoning is rooted in the direct comparison of cases,
we accept that the real force of judgements about art is the
force of the particular. Then we can either turn our attention
to the particular, and become critics of the arts, or we can look
towards the philosophical core of what we are doing : that is,
towards epistemology and philosophical logic.

(40) c.f. Wellek and Warren A Theory of Literature 3rd edition
     Penguin (1963) esp. Ch.10 where some such 'justifications'
     are discussed.

CHAPTER 9   The savour and shimmer of words : a study of
                              Wallace Stevens (1).

> Here is a poet who was by nature a rhetorician, who saw
> language as ceremonious and dramatic gesture. He was a
> lover of the savour and simmer of words, passing them
> over his tongue like a taster of rare vintage.
>   (George Steiner (2)).

It might not be very clear, in spite of the earlier arguments (in Ch.6, Ch.8), just what a piece of literary criticism
is doing tacked on to the end of a work on aesthetics. Is it
some kind of appendix, or what? And my intention is not that it
be seen as a coda, but as an integral part of the text. Yet
that idea too can be misleading. For this is not a section
where the 'critical methods' outlined earlier are put into
practice : and it could not be, for two reasons. The first is
that no 'critical methods' were outlined previously. A critic
may explicitly employ the comparison of cases, but often he will
not. We are accepting his ability to draw such case-by-case
comparisons when we accept his credentials as a critic. And I
do not feel bound to make my comparisons any more explicit than
other critics. Hence no new style of criticism is at work here.

The second point was visible earlier, for when we considered
the case-by-case procedure, we emphasised that it could give rise
to both good and bad results. Since this is so, from the mere
fact that my interpretation of Stevens is an interesting one (if
it is) nothing follows. The ideas outlined in the previous
chapters do not stand or fall with my personal 'success' in this
chapter. On the other hand, an interpretation which does prove
interesting will be both a good example of practicing what one
preaches and a useful way of beginning to establish my credentials.

It may seem that the credentials of a writer on philosophy
should be established by philosophy. This is certainly true in
part. But if aesthetics really is as closely connected with the
arts and criticism of the arts as I have argued, the credentials

---

(1) This chapter was based on a dissertation submitted as part of
   final assessment for the B.A. University of Keele in July
   1973. It was written with the guidance of Dr. Andrew
   Crozier, now of University of Sussex, who made me see
   Stevens' verse as centrally important in the literary history
   of this century. For that, and for much else, I owe him my
   thanks. That the opinions here are not his responsibility
   goes without saying.

(2) Steiner "The Retreat from the Word" in his Language and
   Silence Penguin (1969) p.53

of any such writer might be questioned in the arts area too.
Thus I wish to echo Ruskin's (3) remark:-

> Whatever I have asserted throughout the work, I have
> endeavoured to ground together on demonstrations which
> must stand or fall by their own strength, and which
> ought to involve no more reference to authority or
> character than a demonstration in Euclid.   Yet it is
> proper for the public to know that the writer is no
> more theorist, but has been devoted from his youth to
> the laborious study of practical art.   (p ix)

There are one or two differences, of course.   I have not
the kind nor intensity of training that Ruskin had, nor should
pretend to it.   And that goes some way towards explaining why I
am happy that my interpretation of Stevens is not a particularly
original one.   Much of the impetus for it comes from Alvarez
(4), whose credentials as critic and author are certainly well
established.   The basis of this view of Stevens can be put (a
little baldly) as follows: that Stevens' poetry must be understood against the background of an Idealist metaphysics.   And
this itself is more or less inherited critical wisdom on
Stevens.

Just as it seems to me important to be clear that the
earlier chapters of this work do not stand or fall with this one,
it also seems important to be clear that the mode of discussion
of Steven's poetry here is not intended as a mere exemplific-
ation of what has been said before.   This discussion is theoretical because it seems to me that Stevens' verse warrants, and
indeed requires, theoretical discussion.   And perhaps because
that treatment is most likely to yield us insights into Stevens'
insights.

We can introduce our discussion by realising that many
critics, Rosemund Tuve for example, have expressed uneasiness
about critical judgements on poetry which do not consider
sympathetically the criteria by which the poetic diction was
evolved.   So that she prefaces her book Elizabethan and
Metaphysical Imagery (5) by a chapter significantly called

---

(3) Ruskin Modern Painters George Allen (1906) Vol.1 "Of
General Principles, and of Truth".   Preface to the 1st ed.
§ 4.

(4) Alvarez The Shaping Spirit Chatto and Windus (1958) esp.
Ch.VI "Platonic Poetry".   All references to Alvarez in
this chapter are to that work.

(5) Tuve Elizabethan and Metaphysical Imagery University of
Chicago (1947)

"The problem and what it involves", in which she claims that:-

> . . . . there is little hope of making valid critical
> remarks about . . . . images unless we use all the tools
> we have to find out what they are in the poem _for_ : I
> shall therefore begin boldly at the theoretical end.
> (p.22)

This is what is intended here. In Stevens' case in
particular criticism will find it difficult to get underway until
the preconceptions of his verse are elucidated, since what we can
call Stevens' meta-poetic intentions (what his images are in the
poem _for_) seem to me to be strictly metaphysical in the tradition
of the great Idealist metaphysicians of the seventeenth and
eighteenth centuries. Just as certain concepts in the writings
of such thinkers must be understood by reference to a total world-
picture in order to be understood at all, so it seems to me that
any judgement of Stevens' verse must at least begin from an understanding of the ground-rules of Stevens' thinking - what we might
call his world. This is of particular importance when considering Stevens, for with a world will go what we might characterise as
a philosophy of language, a view of the relationship between
language and 'reality'. And Stevens' poetry is centrally
interested in the relations between language and objects, in how
words mean, and the like. Surely it is no accident that Stevens
too thought of his poetry in terms of a world, his "mundo" (6).

My aim, therefore, is to display, with as few judgements as
possible, Stevens' conceptual structure and world-view, as
displayed in his poetry. And in doing so I hope to be providing
a little more than just a reiteration of the inherited opinion.
Moreover, I hope that a better understanding in Stevens' "world",
his view of 'reality', may provide illumination for our views of
'reality'. Or, to put the point a little less tendentiously,
that such an investigation may light on, and affect, the geometry
of some of our concepts (7). Stevens' training was essentially
linguistic : Greek and Latin at Reading High, then English,
French and German at Harvard. (This makes an interesting
contrast with Eliot, whose training was in philosophy.) This
did not turn Stevens, as Eliot's rigorous training of himself had
done, into a voracious reader of the works of others. Of course,
he had read French Symbolist poetry, and much that was current in
in the poetry of his day, especially Eliot. But he read for

---

(6) c.f. Stevens "Figure of the Youth as Virile Poet" in his
    The Necessary Angel : Essays on Reality and the Imagination
    Faber (1951) p.58 hereafter cited as N.A.

(7) c.f. Bambrough Reason, Truth and God Methuen (1969) p.61 on
    this point.

"simple pleasure" - the very same simple pleasure he hoped others
would get from his verse - and not for instruction.   As he said
(8):-

> My state of mind about poetry makes me very susceptible
> and that is a danger in the sense that it would be so
> easy for me to pick up something unconsciously.   In
> order not to run that danger I don't read other people's
> poetry at all.

Stevens' preoccupation with the relationships between ideas,
words and the things themselves might be seen as a consequence of
his training with language.   Now such a concern might easily be
viewed as philosophical : and this feeling is strengthened when we
recognise the <u>direction</u> it took in Stevens.   If we ask how
language is 'attached' to reality, we are likely to find that the
tie is one which cannot be exactly specified.   (Arguments in
Ch.8 should suggest that this is because the question is misconceived.)   We can bring out this difficulty by consideration of
a standard answer to questions about perceptual knowledge, one
which identifies being red with (roughly) looking red in normal
lighting conditions to the normal sighted.   That is, one which
answers the question about how things <u>are</u> in terms of how they
<u>look</u>.   But the look of things changes.   And what are normal
lighting conditions or normal sight?   If the look of things
changes, how can we hope to adequately describe what we see?

Stevens' concerns range around here.   He is continually
baffled by the impossibility of describing anything at all with
finality.   This gives rise to, for example, "Sea Surface Full of
Clouds" (Stevens p.98) (9) with its function of variation on a
fixed structure.   Each time the verse-shell reappears the
qualifying words have changed.   The "gilt umbrellas" become,
almost as we watch them, "sham", "pied" and "frail".   And the
chocolate begins "rosy" and becomes "chop-house", "porcelain",
"musky" and finally "Chinese".

Here we have the poetry of irritation, to use a phrase of
Alvarez (Alvarez p.129), in just this sense : that observation
will be impossibly endless.   The conscientious manner in which
Stevens varies his rhetoric and pace in poems such as "Sea
Surface . . . .", and throughout his work, is an attempt to
develop an instrument flexible enough to cope with this subject.

---

(8) Letter to J.R.Feo (22 January, 1948), quoted in Ehrenpreis
    ed. <u>Wallace Stevens</u> Penguin (1972) p.158.
(9) <u>Collected Peoms of Wallace Stevens</u> Faber (1955).
    All references to "Stevens" are to this volume.

But more than this, it is from here that Stevens' analytic movement started, the movement which we can characterise as away from
detail to the related ideas.

Unlike a usual method in poetry, which starts from the fullness of experience and searches for hidden motivations, Stevens
is content to deal primarily in what such a method ignores,
namely abstractions.   Stevens (10) says:-

> . . . . his own measure as a poet . . . . is the
> measure of his power to abstract himself, and to
> withdraw with him, into his abstraction, the reality
> on which the lovers of truth insist.   He must be
> able to abstract himself, and also to abstract
> reality, which he does by placing it in his
> imagination.   (pp. 23-4)

Acceptance of the limitation of finality of description is
only the beginning for Stevens.   He works strenuously for something more positive.   If 'things as they are' are at best a
little frustrating, there is one moment when they are truly
alive : the moment when they are caught, in all their flexible
subtlety, by the imagination.

Stevens' poems are more than exercises of the imagination,
of course, for they are (often) about these very themes : about
the imagination, about the validity of metaphor, etc.   But we
must consider just what problem Stevens sees for description and
how the imagination can help solve it.   Once we have acknowledged
the impossibility of any description being satisfactory, because
of the changing conditions of both objects and perceivers, we are
left looking for some common or essential element which will allow
the best our descriptions can be to have some relevance.   We are
looking for what is behind what we are seeing.   To put that
another way, we are looking for Reality behind the world of
Appearance : we are trying to look through the "veil of
perception" (11).   Stevens clearly emphasises his belief that
there is such a veil in poems like "Sea Surface . . . .", and his
solution too is apparent in that poem : and perhaps most clearly
in poems such as "The Idea of Order at Key West" (Stevens p.128),
which we will consider later.   The 'order' which can be found in
the world is, for Stevens, the order which the mind makes of it,
through the imagination.   Here again the doctrine is best

---

(10) Stevens "The Noble Rider and the Sound of Words" N.A.

(11) A phrase of Bennett's, from his "Substance, Reality and
Primary Qualities" reprinted in Martin and Armstrong ed.
Locke and Berkeley Macmillan p.90.

explained in terms of the works of philosophers. Those who urged that object could be viewed as, or were, 'logical construct-ions' out of sense-data (12) were, to put it crudely, claiming that our minds organised the perceptual information which they received to give us the picture of objects in the world. Stevens accepts that there is more to the world, to the Reality of the world, than a succession of such 'pictures'. But how can we know it? How can we reach Reality through the "veil of perception"? Stevens' answer is twofold. Firstly he claims that the faculty of the imagination can provide the answer, because through the action of the imagination it is possible to come into contact with Reality. But, secondly, not just any imaginative projection will do. (perhaps "meditative" is a more appropriate word, in some contexts, for what Stevens means. He probably would not have distinguished between them.) As Stevens (13) himself puts it:-

> If I am right the essence of art is insight of a
> special kind into reality. (p.238)

Now this "special kind" of insight relates art and Reality in a way not so very different from one interpretation of the Schopenhaurer quotation given earlier (at the beginning of Ch.8). It explains why the justification of the possibility of poetry was a chief poetic aim of Stevens. For if poetry is possible, if metaphor is valid, then this "special kind" of insight can reach from poetry (from art) to Reality. The investigation of this possibility, which can easily be viewed as an epistemological possibility, is centrally important in Stevens' work, for it explains the relationship between the poetic imagination and Reality.

We will need to attempt to spell-out this relationship through a consideration of Stevens' poetry, and in particular through coming to some sort of understanding of his notion of "the supreme fiction". Thus far I have been trying to suggest what we might find in Stevens' work. Now it is up to me to show that it is there.

So let us begin, by way of illustration, with some of what is going on in one of the finer short poems : "Of Heaven considered as a Tomb" (Stevens p.56). The place to begin is with the title. This not only presents us with certain comic expectations, since it is funny or paradoxical, but also suggests that formal sub-headings of a text book of, say, grammar. That is to say, it is

---

(12) See, for example, Russell Problems of Philosophy OUP (1912) p.26.

(13) Stevens "On Poetic Truth" in his Opus Posthumous Knopf (1957), hereafter cited as OP.

assertoric. And it picks out a metaphor which governs the poem :
that of death. The poem itself begins by invoking those who
describe and discuss the after-life. Immediately we realise
that the poet's concerns are linguistic.

What <u>word</u> have you, <u>interpreters</u> . . . .

Here it is explanations that are required of the reader. Words
must be present to provide the descriptions which alone can
solve the difficulties of "knowledge", of reaching beyond the
veil of perception.

The controlling image of the poem is the night sky with its
stars. There is a pun on "heaven" in its cosmological and
religious senses at work here. The souls do literally
".... walked by night ...." with their ".... lanterns borne
aloft ...." if they are seen as stars. In this poem death is
imagistically associated with the sky, through such devices.
The body of the poem answers two questions. These are, first,
as to how the dead regard themselves : and, second, whether death
can really lead beyond change to where Reality exists as an
absolute. (Here is the influence of certain Platonic ideas from
Stevens' tutor, Santayana : a view of the dead soul as having
direct knowledge of what is ultimate Reality.)

We follow the progress of the lanterns in the sky until they
cease ".... to creep across the dark ....", and we can follow no
longer. The poet then instructs the "interpreters" to call for
an answer they cannot possibly obtain; and all they hear in
reply is an echo of their own voices.

To describe the night sky, "heaven" in this sense, as
".... gusty cold ...." is the beginning of Stevens' attempt to
satirize vulgar images of afterlife. He attempts to turn
spurious death into real death : for it is the phoney and
dishonest conscience which projects or contains this kind of
ambiguous, 'worldly' image of heaven. Only those whose life has
had a happy ending, ".... our old comedy ...." as Stevens calls
it, are allowed lanterns and, freed by death, allowed to seek for
whatever it is. But for Stevens this cannot be an account of
death. It is all together too much like life. We can imagine
Stevens echoing Wittgenstein's (14) remarks:-

Death is not an event in life.

---

(14) Wittgenstein <u>Tractatus Logico-Philosophicus</u> RKP trans.
Pears and McGuiness (1961) 6.4311

The "experience" that differentiates the dead from the living has
disappeared.   The search of those souls would be endless ("about
and still about") and pointless.   Stevens emphasises this when he
refers to "... what ever it is they seek ..." instead of specify-
ing an object for thier search, for their search has no object.
They are in the same difficulties as us.   And this is not an
accurate picture.   It will not do to have souls in the night sky,
for that is to make them like us, with out epistemological
problems.   In Stevens' own picture, they must, as we do not, have
access to Reality.

The second question arises from Stevens' tentative but
prescriptive answer to the first.   The dead must regard themselves as dead, as different.   This is how the afterlife should
be viewed.   Here Stevens' language is apocalyptic and biblical
("spiritous", "Foretell", "abysmal", "host") for this is the end
of the world as we know it.   The night is "abysmal" in just this
sense: that it is absolute, and beyond time.

There is no point in Stevens' injunction to the "interpreters" to call after the "dark comedians".   The idea of asking
them anything is absurd, for they are beyond the constructed
'reality' of the world of Appearances.   Stevens stresses his
point to the language.   All that remains of their shouts will be
echoes : just so, "hue" and "Halloo", and "icy Elysee", provide
echoic effects for this emphasis.

Much of the poem, then, rests on an Idealist metaphysics.
It remains difficult to explain how Stevens stresses such an idea.
In other poems, for example "Ploughing on Sunday" (Stevens p.20),
Stevens enacts a contrast between the 'poetic' (Idealist) and the
empirical through his vocabulary: extreme artifice and precosity
on one hand, the bare blunt vernacular on the othere.   (Another
such poem might be "Comedian as the letter C" Stevens p.25)
In "Of Heaven ..." however the diction remains uniformly mannered.

What gives the clue that this poem is incompatible with a
Realist metaphysics is the apparently reasoned way in which the
antinomic is presented.   The two suggestions put forward are in
fact not completely incompatible, as in rhetoric they should be.
A middle position is not excluded.   It is possible to be beyond
time ("... into nothingness ...") and still "... range the
gusty cold ..." with the provisos first that death is not
personal dissolution, which must be so for any "afterlife"
account, and secondly, that afterlife is enough like life to
share many of the same properties, with similar sorts of rating
for importance.   For an Idealist this second condition would not
be fulfilled.   For death would allow knowledge beyond what can
be known while alive, by parting the veil between us and Reality,
the "veil of perception".   The antinomy only exists, therefore,

for an Idealist. (This represents a slight simplification, but suggests the direction of the argument.)

Metrically the poem contains little innovation. The rhythm is as steady and consistent as the syntax is usual and complete. This should come as no surprise. We could view the ancestry of this poem in Milton's "L'allegro", where an element in the natural, here the night sky, is developed by the rhetoric as a metaphor. Such poems might, in Milton's day, have been set-pieces which undergraduates prepared for competitions in declamation and argument. Stevens' employment of this form, which goes some way towards explaining the formal titling and the mannered diction, and his use of the rhetorical device of antimony has the effect of leaving any declaration of his position rather unspecified. There is no stated commitment either way, for the points for and against are framed as mere suggestions. ("Do they....?" "Or does ....?"). The whole form of the poem is assertoric, but with formal qualifications. But analysis of the metaphysics of the poem does, as we have seen, provided a picture of Stevens' own views, one part of his world.

However, we are no nearer Stevens' account of the imagination and its role in his world-view. The place for us to begin any discussion of Stevens' account of the imagination is with a poem. If we consider the movement of the imagery in even a poem such as this, where the role of the imagination is submerged, we can gain some inkling. For the images are all abstractions : we have moved a way from the 'reality' of Appearances. But how?

If we genuinely are **beyond** the world of Appearances, we are not employing **perception,** for that is our mode of apprehension of Appearances. Hence it seems only natural to claim that imagination is at work. But Stevens is not happy with such an account. He acknowledges that if poetry at its best is to be possible, it must reach beyond Appearance : but this is not to deny the central importance of 'facts'. To employ the imagination is not to divorce oneself from the world of 'facts'. Stevens (15) makes this view explicit when he says:-

To be at the end of fact is not to be at the beginning
of imagination, but it is to be at the end of both.
(p.175)

(15) Stevens "Adagia" in O.P.

The reason is clear. We must not think of any 'fact' as complete in itself. Every contact with the "reality" of the world of Appearances, and more so with Reailty, is a contact through the mind. Hence Stevens' picture is not so very different from that of Coleridge (16):-

> The primary Imagination I hold to be the living power
> and prime agent of all human perception . . . . (p.167)

Coleridge goes on to compare the creative powers of the imagination with those of God, in creating the world. The process at work in imagination, and also in perception since the imagination is seen as a requirement for perception, echoes the creative process underlying the universe. But for Coleridge this was a situation which only affected the poet in any special way because of his greater sensitivity. For Stevens the poet is in a distinctly better position, for the poet can hope to reach the Real. When Stevens' (17) claims:-

> The accuracy of letters is accuracy with respect to
> reality, (p.71)

he is affirming his belief that "letters", poetry, can make contact with Reality. But how can this be? To answer is to recognise how the creative imagination functions, in Stevens' world, to 'inject' the aesthetic element into the poet's work. For works are the works of an artist in so far as they represent the interplay of the creative imagination and the World of Appearances. Aesthetic value is, for Stevens, a kind of eternal value : and this is incompatible with his picture of the "chargability" of the world around us. Hence there must be some faculty which is not bounded by the World of Appearances. Since Appearance is spatio-temporal, this will necessarily be a mental (that is, non-spatio-temporal) faculty, if it exists at all. And since it has to do with aesthetic value, the mental faculty must be, or be connected with, the poetic imagination.

But more can be made plain. Since the world of Appearance could not be described, and yet some description is (a part of) the poet's task, the poet must distance himself from the world of Appearances, for only by 'standing back' can he achieve a kind of apprehension different from the customary one. And how can such 'standing back' take place? Stevens' answer is that the poet must meditate. (Now we are near the heart of Stevens' world.

---

(16) Coleridge Biographia Literaria (1817) Dent (1975)

(17) Stevens "Three Academic Pieces" in N.A.

And the fact that the arguments for its 'construction' might be refuted - as I believe they can - is not material here. For our interest lies in investigating this terrain.)

So how are we to understand the term "meditation", a term mentioned earlier?   As the essential exercise which, if constantly practiced by the poet, brings the scope of the poetic imagination into play : and this proves to be important.   For it is not enough to describe Appearances, for such descriptions will lack that imaginative 'element' which is also the appreciative or aesthetic element for Stevens.   So, in "Idea of Order at Key West" (Stevens p.128) the sea is meaningless, where this means undescribable, except as it is related to the girl and her singing. It is the singing and the sound of her words that we can understand:-

it was she and not the sea we heard   (Stevens.129)

The imagination's task in all this is, roughly, to create the harmony out of the elements given to it.   Thus the "Blessed rage for order . . . ."   (Sevens p.130) does not imply that order can be achieved.   In fact quite the reverse.   Instead the poem trusts in the only practical assistance in achieving order, the imagination.

When Stevens (18) calls some of W.C.Williams' poems "sentimentalization" if seems to me this is just because Williams produces details which are not in essence attempts at descriptions of an object or a state of affairs, but portraits of personalities.   Such images come from, or through, a personal appreciation of the object.   This Stevens will not allow, for such accounts would rely on perceptions, not on the imagination.   In "Idea of Order at Key West", the listener's mind is what creates the control.   It is not merely that some 'mental' landscape is provided.   There is more than that.

More even than her voice, and ours. (Stevens p.129)

We are working from what is perceived, and what is 'described', to the Reality behind these descriptions.   The "more" here is what is essential in this scene.   And that is not to be explained in terms of the particulars, the 'things', but in terms of abstractions and ideas.   We might characterise the procedure by saying that the course of any poem is this : some perceptual elements are introduced onto the mental stage, the self ponders these given situations and then resolves them using the imagination.   (Or at least attempts to.)

---

(18) Stevens "Williams" in O.P. p.255

In this poem, however, we might say that there is also an intellectual analysis of the problem as well as a meditative one. The overblown rhetoric of:-

> The lights in the fishing boats at anchor there,
> As the night descended tilting in the air,
> Mastered the night and portioned out the sea,
> Fixing emblazoned zones and fiery poles,
> Arranging, deepening, enchanting night,   (Stevens p.130)

belongs to the former, while the casting about for both sense and syntax earlier in the poem reflect, or perhaps are, the meditative ponderings of the poetic mind.

Stevens called a whole book Ideas of Order. This in itself should tell us something, for the idea of order in this poem is to be found in that unique conjunction of landscape, singer and listener. The ideas in this poem are interpretative of images, not rigid or separate generalisations. The scene described, if scene it be, is merely the starting point for a voyage of abstraction. We are not told about the woman at all. We are not even given her ontological status, real or ghostly; for the poem is not about her, nor about the sea. It is, as most of Stevens' poems are, concerned with our modes of perception of the sea.

Another poet, Hart Crane, for example, might write the following (ostensibly about Melville as it turns out) (19):

> Often beneath the wave, wide from this ledge
> The dice of drowned men's bones he saw bequeath
> An embassy. Their numbers as he watched,
> Beat on the dusty shore and we obscured.

This is definitely a poem about the poet and the sea. It works on in an obscure way, rather as if Crane were telling you some facts about himself. With "Idea of Order at Key West" my impression is much more of a statement of the only possible way to view the sea. That is, it is about perception of the sea. There is no way of moving from here to the sea in one direction or the post in the other.

> The sea is not a mask. No more was she,
> The song and water were not medleyed sound
> Even if what she sang was what she heard, (Stevens p.128)

---

(19) This comparison and its discussion are drawn from Alvarez
     when writing about Auden. See Alvarez p.104. The poem is
     "At Melville's tomb" Collected Poems and Selected Letters
     and Prose of Hart Crane Liveright Publishing Corp., New York
     (1933, 1958, 1966) p.100.

These are assertions of how the situation must, conceptually, be considered. In order to explain (where this means something like "describe") the sea and its relation to the song, we can begin with these facts as Stevens states them : That the sea is only understandable in terms of the song, the word; and the word only has sense because it is organised by the Singer's imaginative faculty.

> Since what she sang was uttered word by word.
> (Stevens p.128)

The manner in which this discussion has been presented might suggest the conclusion that the order is, in some way, a projection of either the poet's self or the singer's self. But it is neither. The intention is not simply to realise the inadequacy of description, and then lapse into subjectivism. Instead there is a tense process of moving from the apparent purity of description to the Reality behind what is 'described', a Reality of logical abstraction.

> . . . . It was her voice that made
> The sky acutest at its vanishing
> She measured to the hour its solitude. (Stevens p.129)

Certainly she "measured", but she did not create. For an Idealist such as Stevens, nature can only be a logical construction from the particulars of sensory experience. If there is to be Reality, as Stevens assumes, it must lie beyond the bounds of ordinary experience. And to reach it, we must imaginatively abstract from our experiences.

Here is the point at issue with Ramon Fernandez (20) who holds that:

> . . . the known depends greatly on the act of knowing . . .
> (p.43)

The mind is elevated by Fernandez until it seems to provide, in the act of knowing, knowledge. What remains inexplicable is that the referential framework for this knowledge is provided by the boats. For Stevens, on the other hand, what has been called the "open texture"(21) of Reality is admitted to be beyond the

---

(20) Fernandez Messages : Literary Essay Kennikat Press (1967)

(21) c.f. Waismann "Verifiability" reprinted in Parkinson ed. The Theory of Meaning OUP (1968). It must be acknowledge that, for a Constructivist, Waismann's account must be regarded, as at best, a first approximation.

range of complete description.   But our imaginative abstractions
will be guided in various ways.   Just as the words are not the
water's noise, the night remains unaltered by the moving of the
fishing boats.   Of course, our perceptions are another matter.
Language forms <u>one</u> fine mesh with which we catalogue experience,
an a-temporal one; and, in the case of the boats, perception
forms another, which does change with time.

We might say that language and the movement of the boats
provide alternative frameworks for the ordering of perception.
(Recall the importance of the imagination in perception.)
This ordering is the basis for the constructed 'reality' of the
world of Appearances, and also will ground the poet's efforts
to reach the Real;

> , . . . that there never was a world for her
> Except the one she sang and, singing, made.
>   (Stevens p.130)

The 'commotion' inside the girl does not provide the world,
although she "made" it.   Neither does the ruffling of the
surface of Reality, reflected in the boats moving.   It is something which sparks between them like electricity : the essential
imaginative life.   For this imagination is able to reach from
the poet to Reality.

Certain passages can be seen as offering persuasive definitions of the notion of imagination.   Thus when we encounter such
an explanation of this 'doctrine' of the power of the imagination
we may consider how it is used.

> The world, a turnip once so readily plucked,
> Sacked up and carried overseas, daubed out
> Of its ancient purple, pruned to the fertile main,
> And sown again by the stiffest realist,
> Came reproduced in purple, family front,
> The same insoluable lump . . . .
>   ("Comedian as the Letter C" Stevens p.45)

The image of the world as turnip is a simple one to follow.
The active imagination of man can cut it up and parcel it out —
or so it seems.   But this finally proves impossible.   And an
alternative is found.

> . . . . The fatalist
> Stepped in and dropped the chuckling down his craw,
> Without grace or grumble . . . . (Stevens p.45)

The world <u>must</u> be digested whole or it cannot be digested at
all. Neither of these options allows us to <u>know</u> the world. To
suppose it may simply be absorbed whole is absurd. No fatalist
could have so large a craw; and no knowledge is gained if no
description is fitted. Any attempt to <u>describe</u> the world, therefore, is bound to be piecemeal. And, as such, doomed to dismal
failure. This conclusion is a reflection deep into the heart
of the poet too, for it invalidates everything (or almost everything) that he is trying to do. Metaphor is then useless,
simile is worse. It is a situation which cannot go unresolved
if poetry is to be possible. Stevens (22), the poet, resolves
it in linguistic terms:-

> Poetry is almost incredibly one of the effects of analogy.
> This statement involves much more than the analogies of
> figures of speech since otherwise poetry would be little
> more than a trick. But it is almost incredibly the
> outcome of figures of speech or, what is the same thing,
> the outcome of the operation of one imagination on
> another, through the instrumentality of the figure.
> To identify poetry and metaphor or metamorphosis is
> merely to abbreviate the last remark.

In practical terms this means that we can consider poems such as
"Comedian as the Letter C" in terms of two strands : one is the
abstract subject - man in Reality, man as the subject of fate -
and the other the concrete subject - the experiential confusion
of such a man. Stevens is arguing from the florid images of
the world to abstractions, to claims about all men and the human
condition. Yet the Reality behind those images is itself an
abstraction.

What has seemed missing from the portrait of the world as
presented in, for example, "Idea of Order of Key West" or
"Comedian as the Letter C" is a consideration of the more general
implications of man viewed as caught between his imagination and
the 'reality' of Appearances. Consider, for example, this from
a much later poem:-

> Our sense of these things changes and they change,
> Not as in metaphor, but in our sense
> Of them. So sense exceeds all metaphor.
>
> It exceeds the heavy changes of light.

> (from "Bouquet of Roses in Sunlight" Stevens p.431)

---

(22) Stevens "Effects of Analogy" in <u>N.A.</u>

Here we are presented with the problem of description in all its vividness, with its implications for the artist made plain. How can poetry go forward if its material is _less_ effective than even our inadequate senses?

It turns out to be all a matter of belief. We cannot choose what to believe in, for we are trapped between our fragmentary and transitory experience and our artistic desire to grasp its essentials. Lodged in this situation, we have no tenable alternatives. As Stevens lists them:-

> One might in turn become less diffident
> Out of such mildew plucking neater mould
> And sprouting new orations of the cold.
> One might. One might. But time will not relent.
>
> ("The Man whose Pharynx was Bad" Stevens p.96)

Stevens' solution is still more startling than his formulation of the problem. He declares (23):-

> The final belief is to believe in a fiction, which you know to be a fiction, there being nothing else. The exquisite truth is to know that it is a fiction and that you believe in it willingly. (p.163)

Perhaps this is all very well in itself, but exactly what fiction one chooses to believe in is important, surely? Is it to be nothing more than an arbitrary decision? And with that question goes one about just what he can _mean_ by the term "fiction" in this context.

Luckily for his thesis, Stevens had found both an answer and a motto in an earlier poem.

> Poetry is the supreme fiction, madame.
>
> ("A High-toned Old Christian Woman" Stevens p.59)

We find we must believe in poetry, in its possibility and its value. Poetry can extend the range of knowledge simply because it rests on belief (in the validity of metaphor, the relation between words and things and so on.) But what else can be said of poetry, and hence of the supreme fiction, taking Stevens' own as an example?

---

(23) Stevens "Adagia" in O.P.

If I wished to abbreviate my remarks on Stevens' view of poetry so
far I might well choose the subtitles of Stevens' masterpiece,
"Notes towards a Supreme Fiction" (Stevens p.380):-

> It must be abstract
> It must change
> It must give pleasure.

"Notes . . . . " is a long and complex poem, with poetry and its
difficulties as the subject.   The continuity depends on the
obsessions of the imagination to come to terms with, that is, to
describe, Reality.   This process can only be achieved by meditation and the work of the imagination.

It took me some time to realise just how long a poem it is.
Its 662 lines represent an enormous achievement of both scale and
quality.   As Kermode (24) said of Stevens use of the long poem:

> . . . . it yielded him more favours than any other
> poet of the century.   (p.10)

Even if we cannot go all the way with this, it clearly contains a
grain of Truth.   In order to have room for the breadth of his
ideas, Stevens did need to employ a longer verse form.   It is my
opinion, not based on much information, that as long before he
wrote the "Notes . . . . " (published 1942) as 1922, when he was
revising "Comedian as the Letter C", Stevens was thinking into the
possibilities of writing longer poems.

> Thought tends to collect in pools.

Stevens (25) had written.   Until this time the pools had been
slowly forming, in different isolated places.   One of the places
they agglomerated was "Owl's Clover" - a very long poem which
Stevens rejected from his Collected Poems.

Finally, the pools seem to have flowed over, to form
"Notes . . . . ".   In doing so, some of the ideas have crystal-
ised, becoming clearer and more confident.   Now Stevens begins
explicitly by asserting that the aesthetic experience itself is
what unites the poetry and the propositions, for it provides the
means of understanding both.   (Here, as detailed before,
Stevens considers that there is a special modality of experience
at work, which makes the aesthetic experience "aesthetic" rather
than anything else.)   The imagination is, of course, the main
spring of this account.

---

(24) Kermode Wallace Stevens Oliver & Boyd (1960)

(25) Stevens "Adagia" in O.P. p.170.

In the uncertain light of single, certain truth,
Equal in living changingness to the light
In which I meet you, in which we sit at rest,
For a moment in the central of our being,
The vivid transparence that you bring is peace.
                        (Stevens p.380)

The epigraphal poem to the "Notes . . . " asserts the
conjuction of the "vivid transparence" of Reality with the
"living changingness" which is the stuff of Appearance in that
"moment in the central of our being," the actual aesthetic
experience. (This notion too is Idealist, of course. For, as
argued Ch.5, it will tend to strike us as counter-intuitive that
there should be one or even a range of uniquely aesthetic
experiences.)

No systematic, or even unsystematic, account of the "Notes
towards a Supreme Fiction" will do justice to the poem. But
some comments are pertinent. There is no metaphysical theme
which we have not already covered, but the old Appearance/Reality
difficulty is considered with a new sureness. The tone of the
poem is confident and didactic. (Notice he tells us what the
supreme fiction must be rather than what it is.) It is "the
vast repetitions final in/themselves . . ." which make for the
supreme fiction. This is a mirror for our modes of perceiving
the world.

It must be abstract, or better a fabrication, because the
world we see is a fabrication or construction from the elements
of our experience. The poet, the aesthetic experiencer, therefore makes or abstracts his fiction from the conceptual bed rock
of understanding through imagination. And it is these construct-
ions which allow the poet to relate the world of experience, or
of Appearance, to the underlying Reality.

The poem itself forces home this point. It begins by
admonishing the quester after fiction to see the sun as it is,
without the evasion of a metaphor. Yet the sun is a metaphor,
a figure. And our contact with it is only at a figurative
level. Metaphor must be valid, for it is the primary mode of
perception in Stevens' world.

There is a project for the sun. The sun
Must bear no name, gold flourisher, but be
In the difficulty of what it is to be. (Stevens p.381)

Only a fabrication could have the logical coherence necessary to
relate to Reality while still being anchored in the goings-on in
this world. But this world does not stand still. We cannot
describe exactly how the world is, for what we see changes what

there is. The supreme fiction must, therefore, change in order
to express the infinite function of variation. The satisfaction
of the imagination comes from affirming what it makes true. But
in a world shifting its aspects, the imagination too must be
flexible. It must change.

> Violets, doves, girls, bees and hyacinths
> Are inconstant objects of inconstant cause
> In a universe of inconstancy. This means
>
> Night-blue is an inconstant thing . . . (Stevens pp.389-
> 390)

In a world where only belief is actualised, we must manifest that
belief positvely into the world, so that it may affect our lives.
But how? Certainly not through religious celebration, which
Stevens dismisses as

> . . . a facile exercise . . . (Stevens p.398)

No, we must take each moment as it is caught by the imagination,
alive in all its subtlty, for only then do the moments take on
meanings. And here the meaning or significance would be
aesthetic significance. We must snatch our belief from the
flux of Appearance, as a changing construction : and this will
allow us the pleasure of entering the world of Reality. This
pleasure is a requirement here, for it is the aesthetic pleasure
of the creator. But "pleasure" is too cold a word. We are
able to take joy from abstracted and particularised things as
manifestations of the Real, the joy of loving informed Reality.
It is useless to impose an alien order on the Real   (This is
Canon Aspirin's mistake.)

> . . . to impose is not/to discover . . . (Stevens p.403)

That would simply be to love the abstract for itself. The
supreme fiction will give pleasure, indeed must give pleasure,
simply because it provides a doorway into Reality.

Anyone asserting, as I have been, that it is his account of
the imaginative life which gives Stevens' world its coherence
cannot afford to ignore a poem which boldly states:

> The world imagined is the ultimate good.
> ("Final Soliloquy of the Interior Paramour"
> Stevens p.524)

This line is not uncertain, does not trouble itself with the
Protean 'reality' of Appearance. Instead it asserts: but an
assertion of what? More, surely, than the basic claim that only

those fabrications of the imagination are coherent.   He continues:

> This is, therefore, the intensest rendezvous.

It is the intensest rendezvous simply because the 'logical construction' that is our 'reality' (that is, Appearance) and real Reality are nearest together when the creative imagination has allowed sensory elements to recede from a central position in the mind's eye.

> It is in that thought that we collect ourselves,
> Out of all the indifference, into one thing :

That is why the impossible indefiniteness of descriptions is not stressed here.   We have the image of a blurred object.   It would confuse the picture further to suggest that the image itself might be blurred.

The conclusion of the poem, however, takes up another, quite different, point : that this world's coherence allows our relationship with what is 'given' in perception a wide scope:

> In which being there together is enough.

This scope must exist because the particulars provide referential links for our words with the world, and hence with the supreme fiction.   And it does not exist simply because background details of the sense-given can then be supplied, but as a requirement of the 'logic' of this world.

Stevens stresses the certainty of his final position through the language.   In these later poems the assertions are no longer qualified by the tentative.   In linguistic terms, this poem is without the proliferation of modal auxiliaries – may, might, must, could – which had characterised the resolution of many earlier poems.   For example, "Comedian as the Letter C:"

> so _may_ the relation of each man be clipped.
> (Stevens p.46)

Now something has been resolved.   This is the "Final Soliloquy . . ." because no vital questions remain.   Meditation and the supreme fiction will allow us to assert that "God and the imagination are one" (Stevens p.524) as creators of the artist's world – which amounts to the artist's world-view.

We can now go on to consider the connection between the actual words and these ideas.   It would not be so very far from the truth to entitle this discussion: Notes towards a supreme diction.   For Stevens' position as a master-craftsman of

language is indisputable. It would be trite to say that Stevens'
poetry has a constant concern with the possibilities and limits
of language, including the contradiction inherent in language as
a medium of poetry, for this would be true of many great poets.
Stevens' concerns, however, seem much more linguistically biased.
His poems range around the possibilities of poetry, the validity
of metaphor and so on.

His style is an obstruction to easy understanding, for it is
encrusted with those rhetorical turns of phrase which remain
wholly mysterious to persons trained in, say, the prose of
Hemingway. He beats, then, against the present tide. However,
Stevens' style becomes a delight when you immerse yourself in the
element in which he moves, his world. Without doubt, Stevens'
metaphysical intentions were grand. To sustain them he <u>needed</u>
a grand language. Just as on the philosophical front he was
fighting a rear-guard action, so in linguistic terms he struggled
to prevent the 'thinning' of poetic vocabulary, which took the
ideal of Flaubert (and Pound) - le mot juste - and reduced it to
the scale of basic language, a diminuation of linguistic
possibilities.

As Steiner (26) once put it, without intending the remark to
apply to Stevens:-

> The writer is the guardian and shaper of speech, but he
> cannot do the job alone.

In standing in the old tradition of fullness, Stevens is attempting to allow language once again to achieve the same scale as the
manifold experiences of the world. This attempt entailed
excesses in Stevens - in "Owl's Clover" for example - but not so
very many.

Much of the critical acclaim for Stevens was directed at
his earliest book <u>Harmonium</u> (1923). This seems sad, for the
book contains a peculiar linguistic uncertainty. The language
is full, but does not seem wholly Stevens' own. This is not to
suggest that the worlds are inappropriate in any way. A comment
of R.P.Blackmur (27) comes to mind here, one which later criticism
tends to take for granted. Blackmur says:

---

(26) Steiner "The Retreat from the Word" in <u>Language and Silence</u>
     Penguin (1969) pp.54-55.

(27) Blackmur "Examples of Wallace Stevens", reprinted in
     Ehrenpreis <u>ed.</u> <u>Wallace Stevens</u> Penguin (1972)

An air of preciousness bathes the mind of the casual reader
when he finds such words as fubbed, girandoles, curlcues,
catarrhs, gobbet, diaphanes, clopping, minuscule, pipping,
pannicles, carked, ructive, rapey, cantilens, buffo, fiscs,
phylactery, princox, and funest . . . Not a word listed
about is used preciously; not one was chosen as an
elegant substitute for a plain term; each, in its context,
was a word definitely meant.   (p.60)

I have sought to justify these exotic words by reference to
the additional vitality that such increments bring to language
and, in the context of the poem, by agreeing with Blackmur that
they are the right word for that context.   But "that context" is
also determined by Stevens' world picture.   The precise word is
required.   And these "precise" words in turn determine that
Stevens' world has, as I have claimed, an Idealist epistemology.

I have chosen to write as though Stevens' rhetoric was a
product of his epistemology.   In a sense (that he probably had
the epistemology first) this may be the case.   His diction was
certainly refined until it expressed those questions which
concerned him.   But there is another equally acceptable explanation : that Stevens' ontological and epistemological problems
found solution in the rhetoric itself.   As these are poems
about the possibility of poetry we may conclude that, in so far
as these are poems, poetry is possible.   And this fact justifies
our concern with Stevens' world.

However, my analysis of that world ignored certain key
elements.   The comic has not been mentioned, for example.   But
perhaps this reflects my preoccupations.   I can do no better
than award the last word on worlds (as the last world on words)
to Stevens himself (28).

It is true that I have never been to Europe.   On the
other hand, I have been almost everywhere in Florida.

But, of course, this is not the final word.   For this account of
Stevens' work   offers no positive evaluation of his world.   And
yet, after a fashion it does.   Stevens' concerns with the
possibilities of poetry, and with the possibilities of language,
can inform and illuminate our understanding of poetry or of
language.   It does not matter that his metaphysics differ from
mine, or that I think decisive objections to his view can be

---

(28) Stevens.   Letter to B. Heringman September 1953 reprinted
     in Ehrenpreis ed. Wallace Stevens Penguin (1972) p.211.

produced.   For while acceptance of the view may be a pre-
requisite of entering into every facet of Stevens' world, it is
not required in order that we learn from or appreciate that world.
There is one Realist sound to talk of ". . . every facet . . .",
so it is perhaps more accurate to say that we can 'find in ourselves' many of Stevens' concerns without sharing his world-
picture.   For to do that is to understand Stevens' work, at
least partially.

        Recognition of this fact ties the critical discussion more
closely in with what has gone before.   The connection may be
summarised in the following way.   An attempt to produce a
coherent picture of philosophical aesthetics had involved recognition of the central place of the case-by-case procedure.   This
in turn entailed that any general claims made in philosopical
aesthetics, or any distinctions drawn, would ultimately rest on
the direct comparison of cases.   We saw how understanding was to
be cashed in terms of 'finding such-and-such in yourself' : and
that this would amount to seeing certain comparisons as
important.   This realisation allowed the focusing of our attention on the process of 'twitting' with inconsistency;   and
recognising that such a process required that the insights or
'perceptions' of those involved in such discussion, at least in
so far as the discussion concerned the arts, would often have
the status of reasons for the judgements that were made.   This
fact allowed us to characterise the critic, whose reactions
will usually count as reasons for his judgements; and, it also
shed some illumination on the 'objectivity' of aesthetic
judgements, or evaluations of the arts in general.   But it
served to make philosophical aesthetics more and more closely
resemble art-criticism, or art-appreciation, as practiced by
informed critics.   For the process of 'finding in oneself' the
concerns of some work, or of coming to see certain similarities,
or to offer certain illuminations, is the process of both
philosophy and literature, as well as literary criticism.   The
aim of this chapter has been to facilitate 'finding in oneself'
the concerns in the poetry of Wallace Stevens.

Two notes in conclusion

No formal conclusions for this work could be suggested because it is hoped that its primary drive will, in effect, be methodological. The arguments for the case-by-case procedure's centrality, and to explode various 'cramps' in our notion of reasoning are its heart. None of its substantive conclusions have much claim to outstanding originality. The discussion of the critic, for example, rests centrally on coming to see his <u>reactions</u> as reasons for his judgement : and this in turn rests on an acknowledgement of the valuableness of the direct comparison of cases as a method of justification or proof, and its position as the nexus of any logical-model of reasoning. However, two notes may pick-up interesting issues:-

<u>A note</u>: One point stands in need of reiteration. We can put it as follows. The case-by-case procedure is not a method. It does not allow us to say : "Well, do this first, that next, and you'll see or you'll understand or you'll have the answer." This is so for two reasons. First, that there can be <u>bad</u> case-by-case procedures as well as good ones (as already mentioned): and there can be ones which go nowhere at all. And second, that following a method or recipe which prescribes the direct comparison of cases gives no help as to <u>which</u> cases are selected. That is, the case-by-case procedure may free us from cramped notions of proof <u>in order</u> that we reflect, consider and investigate the cases in question, but it does not deal with, or process, those cases for us. We still have to <u>see</u> and <u>recognise</u> similarities and differences, affinities and disaffinities, <u>for</u> ourselves.

Hence advocating adoption of case-by-case models for reasoning, or of the case-by-case procedure, should not been seen as a panacea for ills of philosophy, but rather as a kind of pre-operative consideration. So the case-by-case procedure is not a method. But if it <u>were</u> a method, there is a sense in which it would be an infallible one, one which could not make mistakes. (See second note.)

<u>Another note</u>: It seems inevitable that many people will find the thesis of this work wholly unconvincing. One needs only to consider the number of books which have struck one as unconvincing to be certain of this. It should seem unfortunate to such people that, as suggested in Ch.2, what they will do to attack the thesis of this work will be to suggest counter-examples to my claims, or use such examples either to point to differences I have failed to mark, or to the absence of differences I have claimed. For, given this history of this subject, only a fool would claim to have done the work of comparison <u>perfectly</u>.

Should anyone claim I've botched the job of arguing for a
particular kind of aesthetics, or of philosophy, they will, I
am confident, be themselves employing a case-by-case procedure.
And since the claim throughout this work has been that the
case-by-case procedure is crucial, there is a clear sense in
which this work cannot (except in details) be overthrown by
any case-by-case procedure.

The following bibliography contains a complete list of all
philosophical works referred to. Usual references to journals
etc. have been employed throughout. It does not include novels,
poems etc. But full citations for these appear in the text,
where they are relevant. Nor does it include reference to papers
of mine, although some relevant ones of these are included in the
following collection:

McFee   Chelsea Papers in Human Movement Studies
         (Philosophy and Movement : Collected lectures by
         Graham McFee) 1977.

Bibliography (of philosophical works referred to.)

1. Armstrong - see Martin and . . .

2. Austin   Philosophical Papers   O.U.P. (1961)

3. Ayer   The Origins Of Pragmatism   Macmillan (1968)

4. Baker   "Criteria : a new foundation
                      for semantics"   Ratio 1975

5. Bambrough   Conflict and the Scope of   Univ. of Hull
                   Reason   (1974)

6. Bambrough   "Literature and Philosophy" in Bambrough ed.

7. Bambrough   Reason, Truth and God   Methuen (1969)

8. Bambrough   "To reason is to generalise" Listener 1973

9. Bambrough ed.   Wisdom : Twelve Essays   Blackwell (1974)

10. Barrett   "Are Bad Works of Art 'Works
                      of Art'?" in Vesey ed.

11. Barrett ed.   Collected Papers on   Blackwell (1965)
                   Aesthetics

12. Beardsley   Aesthetics : problems in   Harcourt-Brace
                   the philosophy of criticism   (1958)

13. Beardsley   - see Wimsatt and . . .

14. Beardsmore   Art and Morality   Macmillan (1971)

15. Beardsmore   "Consequences and Moral   Analysis 1969
                   Worth"

16. Beardsmore   <u>Moral Reasoning</u>   RKP (1969)

17. Beardsmore   "Two Trends in Contemporary
               Aesthetics"   BJA 1973.

18. Bennett   <u>Kant's Analytic</u>   Cambridge (1966)

19. Bennett   "Substance, Reality and
               Primary Qualities" in   Martin & Armstrong
                                                  <u>ed</u>.

20. Berlin <u>ed</u>.   <u>Essays on J.L.Austin</u>   OUP (1973)

21. Best   "The Aesthetic in Sport"   BJA 1974

22. Best   <u>Expression in Movement and</u>   Lepus (1974)
               <u>the Arts</u>

23. Blizek   "An Institutional Theory
               of Art"   BJA 1973

24. Bouwsma   <u>Philosophical Essays</u>   Univ. of Nebraska
                                                   (1965)

25. Casey   <u>The Language of Criticism</u>   Methuen (1966)

26. Cavell   <u>Must We Mean What We Say?</u>   Scribners (1969)

27. Cavell   <u>Senses of Walden</u>   Viking (1972)

28. Cavell   <u>The World Viewed</u>   Viking (1971)

29. Curl   "Aesthetic Judgements in
               Dance" in <u>Collected Conference Papers on</u>
               <u>Dance</u>   A.T.C.D.E. (1974)

30. Danto   "The Art-World"   JP 1964

31. Dickie   <u>Art and the Aesthetic</u>   Cornell UP (1974)

32. Diffey   "Essentialism and the
               definition of 'art'"   BJA 1973

33. Diffey   "The Republic of Art"   BJA 1969

34. Dilman   <u>Induction and Deduction</u>   Blackwell (1973)

35. Dilman   "Paradoxes and Discoveries" in Bambrough <u>ed</u>.

36. Elton <u>ed</u>.   <u>Aesthetics and Language</u>   Blackwell (1954)

37. Fann ed.   Symposium on J.L.Austin   RKP (1969)

38. Flew   "On the Interpretation of
                     Hume" in Hudson ed.

39. Flew   "The Jensen Uproar"   Philosophy 1973

40. Flew   "Theology and Falsification in Flew and
                                                  MacIntyre ed.

41. Flew and MacIntyre ed. New Essays in   Macmillan (1955)
                     Philosophical Theology

42. Gardiner   Schopenhauer   Penguin (1967)

43. Gombrich   Art and Illusion   Phaidon (1960)

44. Hacker   Insight and Illusion   OUP (1972)

45. Hare   Freedom and Reason   OUP (1963)

46. Hudson ed.   The Is/Ought Question   Macmillan (1969)

47. Johnson   "Aesthetic Objectivity and
                     the Analogy with Ethics" in Vesey ed.

48. Jones,P.   Philosophy and the Novel   OUP (1975)

49. Jones,S.   "The evaluation of art : a
                     dialogue" in Chelsea College of Physical
                                     Education Yearbook 1976

50. Joyce   Principles of Logic   Longmans
                                                  3rd ed. (1920)

51. Kennick   "Does traditional aesthetics
                     rest on a mistake?" in Barrett ed.

52. Lake   "The Irrefutability of Two
                     Aesthetic Theories" in Elton ed.

53. MacIntyre   -   see Flew and . . .

54. Malcolm   Knowledge and Certainty   Prentice-Hall
                                                  (1963)

55. Malcolm   Ludwig Wittgenstein : a   OUP (1958)
                     memoir
56. Margolis ed.   Philosophy Looks at the Arts Scribners (1962)

57. Martin and Armstrong ed. Locke and Berkeley Macmillan

58. Mitchell   "Truth and Fiction" in Vesey ed.
59. Mill   System of Logic   (1843)
60. Mounce   —   see Phillips and . . .

61. Newell   The Concept of Philosophy Methuen 1967

62. Osborne ed.   Aesthetics   OUP (1972)

63. Parkinson ed.   The Theory of Meaning   OUP (1968)

64. Passmore   "The Dreariness of Aesthetics" in Elton ed.

65. Peirce   Collected Papers of   Harvard U P
                    C.S.Peirce   (1933)

66. Phillips   "Allegiance and Change in
                    Morality" in Vesey ed.

67. Phillips and   Moral Practices   RKP (1969)
    Mounce

68. Pitcher   "Austin : a memoir" in Berlin ed.

69. Pitkin   Wittgenstein and Justice Univ. of
                                              California
                                              (1972)

70. Quine   From a Logical Point of   Harper Row
                    View   (1953)

71. Quine   Word and Object   M I T (1960)

72. Rhees   Discussions of Wittgenstein RKP (1970)

73. Rhees   Without Answers   RKP (1969)

74. Russell   Problems of Philosophy   OUP (1912)

75. Schopenhauer   The World as Will and Representation
                              Dover ed. in two vols. (1969)

76. Sclafani   "'Art and Artifactuality" Southwestern
                              Jn. of Philosophy 1970

77. Shiner   "Wittgenstein on the Beautiful,
                    the Good and the Tremendous" BJA 1974

78. Stebbing   <u>Thinking to Some Purpose</u> Penguin (1939)

79. Strawson   <u>The Bounds of Sense</u> Methuen (1966)

80. Strawson   <u>Freedom and Reason and</u>
        <u>Other Essays</u>   Methuen (1974)

81. Toulmin   <u>Human Understanding</u> OUP Vol.I (1972)

82. Toulmin   <u>The Uses of Argument</u> Cambridge (1958)

83. Urmson   "What makes a situation
        aesthetic?" in Margolis <u>ed.</u>

84. Vesey <u>ed.</u>   <u>Philosophy and the Arts</u> Royal Institute
        of Philosophy Lectures Vol.6. 1971-2
                  Macmillan (1973)

85. Waismann   "Verifiability" in Parkinson <u>ed.</u>

86. Warnock   "John Langshaw Austin, a biographical
              sketch" in Fann <u>ed.</u>

87. Warnock   "Saturday mornings" in Berlin <u>ed.</u>

88. Weitz   <u>Hamlet and the Philosophy</u>
        <u>of Literary Criticism</u> Faber (1965)

89. Weitz   "The Role of Theory in
        Aesthetics" in Margolis <u>ed.</u>

90. Wimsatt and "The Intentional Fallacy" in Margolis <u>ed.</u>
   Beardsley

91. Winch   <u>Ethics and Action</u>   RKP (1972)

92. Winch   <u>The Idea of a Social Science</u> RKP (1958)

93. Wisdom   <u>Paradox and Discovery</u> Blackwell (1965)

94. Wisdom   <u>Philosophy and Psycho-</u> Blackwell (1953)
        <u>Analysis</u>

95. Wisdom   "Proof and Explanation" unpublished lectures
        delivered in 1957 at the Univ, of Virginia.
                   (<u>V.L</u>)

96. Wittgenstein <u>The Blue and Brown Books</u> Blackwell (1958)

97. Wittgenstein <u>On Certainty</u>   Blackwell (1969)
            trans. Anscombe and Paul.

98. Wittgenstein   Lectures and Conversations
                       on Aesthetics, Psychology and Religious
                       Belief   Blackwell (1970)

99. Wittgenstein   Philosophical Grammar   Blackwell (1974)
                                           Trans. Kenny

100. Wittgenstein   Philosophical Investigations
                          Trans. Anscombe   Blackwell (1953)

101. Wittgenstein   Philosophical Remarks   Blackwell (1975)
                          Trans. White and Hargreaves

102. Wittgenstein   Remarks on the Foundations
                           of Mathematics   Blackwell (1956)
                          Trans. Anscombe

103. Wittgenstein   Tractatus-Logico Philosophicus
                          Trans. Pears and McGuiness   RKP (1961)

104. Wittgenstein   Zettel   Blackwell (1967)
                          Trans. Anscombe

105. Wollheim   Art and Its Objects   Penguin (1968)

106. Wollheim   On Art and the Mind   Allen Lane (1973)

107. Yalden-Thomson   "The Virginia Lectures" in Bambrough ed.

About the Author.

Born in London, Graham McFee received a B.A. in English and Philosophy at the University of Keele, and remained there to research in the philosophy of personal identity for a masters degree, awarded in 1975.

At present he is a lecturer in philosophy at East Sussex College of Higher Education, Eastbourne, a position he has held since 1974.

His interests range over all the arts, and his poetry has appeared in a number of small magazines. Living on the south coast of England occasionally enables him to indulge hobbies such as sailing and sub-aqua, as well as his passion for bridge.

He is married to a professional dancer.

Counting himself a disciple of Wittgenstein, his major current projects are an account of the arts based on Wittgenstein's later semantics (Constructivism), and a book on the aesthetics of film.